Biblical

Hermeneutics

of Liberation

The Bible & Liberation

An Orbis Series in Biblical Studies

Norman K. Gottwald and Richard A. Horsley,
General Editors

The Bible & Liberation Series focuses on the emerging range of political, social, and contextual hermeneutics that are changing the face of biblical interpretation today. It brings to light the social struggles behind the biblical texts. At the same time it explores the ways that a "liberated Bible" may offer resources in the contemporary struggle for a more human world.

Already published:

The Bible & Liberation Series

Biblical Hermeneutics of Liberation

Modes of Reading the Bible in the South African Context

Second, revised edition

Gerald O. West

Cluster Publications
Pietermaritzburg

Orbis Books
Maryknoll, New York

BS
476
.W46
1995

The Catholic Foreign Missionary Society of America (Maryknoll) recruits and trains people for overseas missionary service. Through Orbis Books Maryknoll aims to foster the international dialogue that is essential to mission. The books published, however, represent the opinions of their authors and are not meant to represent the official position of the Society.

First published in 1991 in South Africa by Cluster Publications. This second, revised edition (1995) is published in South Africa by Cluster Publications, P. O. Box 2400, Pietermaritzburg, 3200, and in the United States by Orbis Books, Maryknoll, N.Y. 10545.

© Copyright Gerald Oakley West 1991
Second, revised edition 1995.

ISBN   0-9583807-9-1(Cluster Publications)
ISBN   1-57075-020-3(Orbis Books)

Printed by The Natal Witness Printing and Publishing Company (Pty) Ltd.

Library of Congress Cataloging-in-Publication Data

West, Gerald O.
       Biblical hermeneutics of liberation: modes of reading the Bible in the
    South African context / by Gerald O. West.
       p.   cm. (The Bible and liberation series)
    Originally published: Hilton, Republic of South Africa: Cluster Publications,
    c1991.
       Includes bibliographical references and index.
       ISBN 1-57075-020-3 (pbk.)
       1. Bible Hermeneutics. 2. Liberation theology. 3. Black theology. 4.
    Theology, Doctrinal South Africa. I. Title. II. Series: Bible & liberation series.
    BS476.W46 1995
    220.6'01 dc20

                                                                              94 43953
                                                                                   CIP

Contents

Preface

One of the risks of working contextually is that contexts change, and in South Africa this is clearly so. Yet I offer this study because I believe that it may be useful in the ongoing process of transformation in South Africa. One of the joys of working contextually is the people you work with, creative people who care. This study emerges from relationships with such people.

There are many outside of South Africa who stand in solidarity with our struggle for liberation and who have encouraged and guided me in this work. In particular I want to thank John Rogerson, Stephen Fowl, and Mark Brett for their encouragement, guidance, and friendship. I also want to thank Christopher Rowland and Haddon Willmer for their encouragement and suggestions. I gratefully acknowledge the financial support and encouragement I received from Trevor Huddleston, the Africa Educational Trust, the South Yorkshire Charity Information Service Trust, The Whitefield Institute, the Radley Charitable Trust, The Sir Richard Stapley Educational Trust, The William Temple Foundation, the All Saints Education Trust, the United Society for the Propagation of the Gospel, and Christ Church Fulwood, St Thomas' Crookes, and Central United Reformed Church in Sheffield.

This study owes most to those in South Africa with whom I have worked. In particular I want to thank Jim Cochrane, Gunther Wittenberg, Jonathan Draper, Sid Luckett, Klaus Nürnberger, Frank Chikane, Tim Long, Itumeleng Mosala, Chris Langefeld, Graham Philpott, and Tony Balcomb for their encouragement, guidance, and friendship. I also want to thank the many students with whom I have worked and from whom I have learned a great deal. In particular I want to thank Bernadino Mandlate, James Hlongwa, Ashley

Mkhonza, Holger Szesnat, Margarete Ruf, Megan Walker, Victor Makhetha, Meshack Mabuza, Gertrud Wittenberg, Kirsten Peachey, and Linda Noonan. I gratefully acknowledge the financial support and encouragement I received from Desmond Tutu, the South African Council of Churches, John Suggit, Grahamstown Cathedral, and my family.

I dedicate this study to ordinary readers, who will probably not read it but who will, I hope, teach me how to serve them with it.

Preface to the Second Revised Edition

We celebrate a remarkable election. Nelson Mandela has become our president! If anyone had asked me if this would happen when I was writing the first edition of this book I would have laughed, and then cried. Miracles do still happen, and we have seen the presence of the God of life in so much. The forces of the idols of death are still at work and apartheid has damaged us deeply, but our hope is brighter and there is much to celebrate. And yet we remember the too many who did not live to cast their vote or see their liberation. Our ancestors in the struggle celebrate with us and continue to struggle with us for full liberation and life for all.

I did not expect the first edition to be read as widely as it has been, and it is a great joy to hear from a diverse readership that the book has been of some use, particularly in South Africa. I have learned much from those who have talked to me about aspects of the book that they found useful, difficult, or problematic. My own work has been profoundly shaped by their contributions. And it is their ongoing interest in the book that has prompted this revision.

So much has happened since I wrote the first edition, and yet as I read and reread it, trying to understand how best to revise it, I realized how many of the questions and concerns are still with us. While our socio-political crisis has abated, the interpretive crisis has, I would argue, deepened. We are in danger of forgetting what we have learned through the struggle for liberation. And the struggle for full liberation and life is not complete.

I wish to extend my gratitude to Cluster Publications for making this book available, accessible, and affordable in South Africa and to Orbis Books for sharing this vision.

Once again, I dedicate this revision to ordinary readers among the poor and marginalized who now play a greater part in the book, because they are teaching me how to serve them. I also dedicate this revision to Bev Haddad, who is *that companion.*

Foreword to the Revised edition

Since its publication in 1991, this book has become justly well-known in South Africa. Owing to limited distribution abroad, however, it has only begun to achieve recognition in other countries where its focus on biblical hermeneutics shaped by local contexts is a lively ongoing topic. The present co-publication with Orbis Books will help West's contribution to enter more fully into hermeneutical discourse and practice in other lands. I can personally attest that the assignment of this book in a Doctor of Ministry program at New York Theological Seminary - followed by a visit in person from the author - elicited a warm response and a spirited discussion in our seminar.

Historically, West succeeds in showing the twists and turns that biblical hermeneutics have undergone over the past two centuries, both world-wide and in South Africa. In this regard his rich bibliographic resources on South African biblical hermeneutics will both surprise and instruct many readers.

Comparatively, West argues cogently that the several forms of liberation hermeneutics (e.g. Latin American liberation theology, Afro-American theology, and feminist criticism) share common methods and perceptions but have some distinct "angles of vision" that are instructive to all practitioners of liberation hermeneutics.

Theoretically, West makes a strong case for the liberative possibilities in three forms of biblical criticism that are often regarded as out-and-out incompatibles: reading *behind* the text for social setting (e.g. Gottwald, Mosala, Fiorenza), reading *in* or *on* the text for literary and theological discernment (e.g. Trible, Boesak), and reading *in front of* the text for new possibilities of perception and practice (e.g. Croatto). At this point, West is helpful in clarifying what many of us are discovering in practice: there simply is no single method that assures or exhausts the liberative functions of Scripture.

To my mind the richest harvest of this book is what may be called loosely its "practical contribution", which is in fact the focused application of the above historical, comparative and theoretical perspectives. West uses his extensive experience in Bible study outside the academy, especially through the Institute for the Study of the Bible - a South African project broadly analogous to the base communities in Latin America - to focus on a critical issue that has nowhere else been so directly and carefully addressed.

That issue is the challenge of joining academically trained and untrained readers in joint Bible study. West employs the helpful distinction between "trained" and "ordinary" readers. He describes the assets and liabilities of both kinds of readers and the special problem of "balance of power" which is upset whenever the Bible study becomes excessively "academic", on the one side, or drifts into pious clichés, on the other side. In neither case does the group truly encounter one another around the text. At this point, West draws on his experience to suggest ways in which this impasse of diversely prepared readers can be broken through to the benefit of all in the group.

This reality of the sometimes shocking interface between trained and ordinary readers was borne home to me with special force when in 1992 I attended a three-hour African Independent Church service in Transkei. Arriving as barely announced visitors, my wife and I were invited - without preparation or forewarning - to speak in dialogue with three other "sermons". It seemed to me that amongst the five of us speaking in that service a new biblical interpretive fabric was being woven on the spot. I found myself saying things that a "trained" Bible scholar would not normally say, as I also said things that an "ordinary" reader would find strange - yet I was listened to with respect, as I also listened to others with respect for the improvisational project we had embarked on. West's book helps us to understand situations in which we do biblical interpretation but are not in sole control of the process, either through circumstances or, more deliberately, through our decision to relinquish control.

For an in-depth introduction to biblical hermeneutics, for a grasp of what is happening in South African biblical hermeneutical theory and practice, and for insightful guidance on doing truly liberative interpretation in groups of mixed readers in any context, this is a work of uncommon insight and practical instruction.

Norman K. Gottwald
December 1994

Introduction

"At times, interpretations matter. On the whole, such times are times of cultural crisis. The older ways of understanding and practice, even experience itself, no longer seem to work. We can find ourselves distanced from all earlier ways. Then we need to reflect on what it means to interpret".[1] This is the purpose of this study, to reflect on what it means to interpret the Bible in a context of cultural crisis, a context where interpretations matter.

The particular context of crisis of this study is the South African situation of struggle. The struggle against apartheid has been won. We have celebrated "the new South Africa" in democractic elections. But there are those who struggled with us who died before they could participate in our election, and there are those who have voted but for whom much has still to change. So the struggle is not yet complete. The struggle for full liberation and life continues. The forces of death are still with us, but our stuggle with the God of life for liberation and life continues.[2] In this study I use the term "struggle" to mean the struggle of the poor and the marginalized in South Africa for liberation *from* the legacy of apartheid and *for* life.[3] In the South African context this struggle is largely the struggle of the black community,[4] but as Albert Nolan notes, "In the townships what people are concerned about is not your ancestry or the colour of your skin but whether you are on the side of the system or on the side of the struggle".[5] In other words, the specific purpose of this study is to reflect on what it means to interpret the Bible from the side of the South African context of struggle for liberation and life.

This particular context of struggle is, however, situated within the wider context of biblical interpretation in theologies of liberation.[6] So although the primary focus of the study is biblical interpretation within the South African context of liberation, there is a continual dialogue with biblical interpretation in other contexts of liberation. These other contexts of liberation include, in particular, Latin American liberation theology, North American black theology, and feminist theology.

There is also a wider context still within which this study is situated, the context of biblical hermeneutics and biblical studies. Indeed, this wider context also includes literary and philosophical hermeneutics.[7]

These concentric, yet connecting contexts reflect my own background, interests, and commitments.[8] My primary commitment, however, is to the South African context of struggle and this emphasis dominates the study.

In the light of these commitments the purpose of this study is threefold. The primary purpose of the study is to analyze and clarify the interpretive questions which have arisen among those who interpret the Bible within the South African context of struggle. The main argument for this focus on analysis and clarification is my concern to facilitate dialogue among those committed to the South African context of struggle.

A secondary purpose, closely related to the primary purpose, is to respond to some of the analysis and clarification by suggesting possible ways forward. All of the possibilities emerge from ongoing dialogue in the South African community of struggle and so are potential rather than prescriptive.

Another secondary purpose of the study is to challenge the wider discipline of biblical studies. The established methodology of First World biblical interpretation, often regarded as a universally valid norm, has recently been challenged. The challenge comes from different quarters of Africa, Asia, and Latin America, but it also comes from certain groups within the First World, for example, from Christians within feminist and labour movements.[9]

Another reason, therefore, for focusing this study on analysis and clarification is my concern to portray the internal logic of biblical interpretation in contexts of liberation. The problems of understanding between biblical interpretation in contexts of liberation and traditional biblical studies are so compounded that it useful and justifiable to devote a study to an analysis of the "new paradigm" with the hope of promoting its better understanding and so its challenge.

The analyses of this study are based on texts, most of which are texts written by academically trained people. Such an approach obviously excludes the majority of ordinary readers of the Bible whose interpretations are expressed in sermons, prayers, songs, proverbs, poems, and newspapers. This study, therefore, is also based on such sources, although to a limited extent. Throughout these analyses I have attempted as far as possible to quote and summarize rather than paraphrase in order to allow the poor and marginalized to speak for themselves.

The setting for this study is Old Testament biblical studies. So although the study is primarily methodological, the methodological discussion arises out of particular readings of particular texts.

The study begins with a sketch of the current interpretive context, particularly as it affects biblical interpretation. In sketching this context, a context of crisis, chapter one attempts to hear a variety of voices from a variety of disciplines. What these voices have in common is that they question any mode of inquiry that tries to deny its own hermeneutic character and mask its own historicity so that it might claim ahistorical certainty. Futher, they affirm the historicality of all understanding, inquiry, and interpretation. My choice of the African-American philosopher and theologian Cornel West as the guiding voice in this chapter is consistent with my commitment to a context of struggle for liberation and life.

The theoretical dimensions of the hermeneutic debate of chapter one lead into a theoretical and historical analysis of the interpretive crisis in South Africa. Chapter two argues that although there is a measure of socio-political liberation in South Africa, there is still a profound interpretive crisis, an interpretive crisis with historical and methodological dimensions. This chapter begins with a brief historical perspective on biblical interpretation in South Africa which is followed by a brief examination of the present state of South

African biblical studies. The bulk of the chapter then examines in some detail the methodological crisis within black biblical hermeneutics in South Africa.

These two chapters, then, serve as a framework for a detailed discussion of two modes of reading a biblical text, the Cain and Abel story, in the South African context in chapter three. One mode of reading has its focus on the text while the other mode of reading has its focus behind the text. These two readings of the Cain and Abel story, one literary and the other sociological, arise from the work of two black South African interpreters. The concern of this chapter is not to ask which reading methodology is right, but rather to analyze what is going on methodologically in a particular mode of reading, and then to analyze the relationship between a particular mode of reading and the struggle for liberation and life in South Africa. It is out of this analysis that crucial questions emerge, some of which are taken up in subsequent chapters.

The analysis in this chapter, therefore, sets the scene for the remainder of the study, and in each of the subsequent chapters the modes of reading of Alan Boesak and Itumeleng Mosala, the two black interpreters discussed here, form a unifying thread.

Chapter four examines the question of the relationship between the reader and the community. The nature of this relationship is seen as a critical characteristic of liberation hermeneutics. While the primary interlocutors of Western theology and biblical studies are the educated and powerful, the primary interlocutors of liberation theologies are the poor and marginalized. This difference is arguably the defining characteristic of liberation hermeneutics.[10] This relationship of accountability to and solidarity with the poor and oppressed, which is crucial to theologies of liberation and which challenges the dominant epistemology, is explored here with particular reference to the South African context of struggle.

Having considered the reader's embeddedness in a community, chapter five analyzes the situatedness of the text. The central question here is the status of the biblical tradition and text in liberation hermeneutics. This question arises from the growing recognition of the ideological nature of the biblical text, and has been raised particularly forcefully by feminist interpreters, whose work is used here to facilitate my analysis. In this and the following chapter the literary and sociological modes of reading discussed in chapter three are examined in more detail.

Chapter six returns to the question of the relationship between a particular mode of reading and the context of liberation, particularly to the controversial question of whether any particular mode of reading is more appropriate than others in a context of liberation. This chapter is constructed around a dialogue between the "behind the text" mode of reading of Mosala, Norman Gottwald, and Schüssler Fiorenza, the "on the text" mode of reading of Phyllis Trible and Boesak, and the "in front of the text" mode of reading of J. Severino Croatto and Boesak. All of these biblical interpreters are committed to a context of struggle, but they adopt differing methodological approaches to the biblical text. Throughout this discussion the arguments of chapter four continue to emerge and finally to pose the question of whether the issue of reading methodology is as important as it is made out to be.

From the more theoretical discussions of biblical scholars in chapter six, the study moves in chapter seven into a rather different key. The focus of this chapter is the ordinary reader, who is present, but offstage, in the preceding chapters. In South Africa, as elsewhere, the majority of interpreters of the Bible are not trained or semi-trained readers, but ordinary readers. More importantly in South Africa, most of these ordinary readers are from "the base",[11] from the poor and oppressed. This chapter analyzes empirical data from a variety of case studies of ordinary readers reading the Bible. This analysis is then related to the analysis of the preceding chapters as I attempt to locate the ordinary reader within liberation hermeneutics.

In chapter eight, the concluding chapter, the challenge to the discipline of biblical studies, implicit in all of the above, is articulated.[12] The crucial question of the relationship between trained and untrained (particulary the poor and oppressed) readers of the Bible forms the core of the challenge.

In an Afterword I respond to the challenge of chapter eight by giving a brief account of a recent initiative in South Africa with which I am involved, the Institute for the Study of the Bible. Arising out of the need for the Bible to speak into the lives of the poor and oppressed in the South African context, the Institute for the Study of the Bible offers some insights into the complex but important interface of biblical scholarship and grassroots readings of the Bible.

It is true that the point, and, indeed, the cry in South Africa, is not to interpret the world but to change it. "But, we will change too little, and that probably too late, if we do not at the same time change our understanding of what we mean when we so easily claim to interpret the world".[13]

Chapter One

The Interpretive Crisis: The Text and the Reader

Introduction

The purpose of this chapter is to give a shape to the interpretive crisis in which we find ourselves, and in so doing serves to provide a broader framework in which to discuss the interpretive crisis in South Africa. The terrain we need to consider in order to plot the shape of the broader interpretive crisis is vast. The areas I have chosen to survey are therefore selective and are related to my own interests in biblical, literary, and philosophical hermeneutics. Those who are eager to get to the South African context, and who consider this chapter's scope rather too broad, should not feel constrained to read the whole of this chapter. A reading of the conclusion should be sufficient to provide a sense of the shape of the broader interpretive crisis. Those who will read this chapter carefully are reminded that the primary focus here is not on the detail but on the shape of the interpretive crisis in biblical, literary, and philosophical hermeneutics.

In sketching the current hermeneutic context, particularly as it affects biblical interpretation, both John Barton and Edgar McKnight draw on the schema proposed by M.H. Abrams in *The Mirror and the Lamp*.[1] The history and practice of literary criticism are outlined by Abrams in terms of the dominance of one of four elements: the work, the artist, the universe imitated in the work, and the audience. Barton retains the shape of Abram's diagram but adjusts the terms to reflect the specific interests of biblical critics.[2]

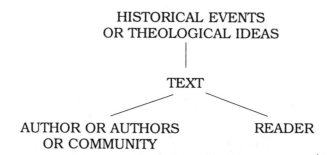

HISTORICAL EVENTS
OR THEOLOGICAL IDEAS

TEXT

AUTHOR OR AUTHORS   READER
OR COMMUNITY

Bernard Lategan proposes a similar schema,[3] but bases his schema on a simple communication model consisting of three elements: source, message and receptor. "The first element (source) has mainly to do with origins and text production, the second with text preservation and mediation, the third with reception and interpretation". He adds that although "the basic model does not necessarily reflect a chronological sequence, it is possible to relate major shifts in the history of interpretation to various sectors of the model".[4]

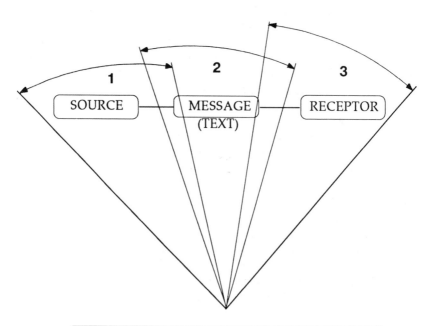

B. Lategan's schema of the phases of Biblical interpreation

Barton, with respect to Old Testament criticism, and Lategan, with respect to New Testament criticism, offer similar accounts of the nature and the chronological ordering of these shifts. Both agree that biblical criticism begins with a shift away from an ahistorical approach to an emphasis on questions of origin: sources, authorship, *autographa*, historical reconstruction.[5] From these historical interests developed the various historical-critical approaches: textual criticism, source criticism, form criticism, tradition criticism and redaction criticism. The central concern of all these critical approaches is the relationship between the text and the author or source.

A shift then occurred with the advent and subsequent influence of structuralism which was reflected in a move from an interest in the origins of a text to an interest in the text itself. The text itself became the focus. The predominant interest of this shift was the synchronic analysis of the text on its own terms without recourse to external factors. In other words, there was a move away from both the "genetic fallacy", explanation in terms of origins, and the "referential fallacy", explanation in terms of extratextual reality.[6] From these interests in the text itself developed structuralist, literary, and, Barton argues, canonical approaches.[7]

The dominant feature of recent developments in the field of hermeneutics is a shift away from "the text itself" towards an interest in the relationship between the text and the reader.[8] The reader is no longer seen as merely a passive acceptor of the text but as an active, even creative, contributor in the interpretive process. "In a certain sense it was inevitable that reception would sooner or later become the object of methodological reflection. The cycle of understanding remains incomplete until communication reaches its 'destination', what Ricoeur . . . calls 'the culmination of reading in a concrete reader'".[9]

While Ricoeur comments on the aptness of this shift, and McKnight demonstrates this shift, David Tracy recognizes the instability generated by this shift.

> In recent years we have come a long way from the now old New Criticism's belief in the stability of an autonomous text. We are in the midst of a deconstructive drive designed to expose the radical instability of all texts and the inevitable intertextuality of all seem-

ingly autonomous texts. The once stable author has been replaced
by the unstable reader. Written texts seem, commonsensically, stable enough. But when we reflect on any effort to understand them
by interpreting them, they begin to seem far more puzzling and
unstable than we first might have imagined.[10]

As the above quotation suggests, there is something of a
crisis in biblical and literary hermeneutics. I will analyse
aspects of this crisis in more detail below. Here I want to
make the point that this crisis is part of a wider hermeneutic
crisis in the natural sciences, philosophy, historiography,
the social sciences, and theology. In other words, the instability of both text and reader in biblical interpretation is only
one expression of a more widespread instability in Western
hermeneutics, making it useful to place the more specific
issues in this larger context.[11]

The Enlightenment scientific paradigm

Since the Enlightenment, science has provided the dominant model for talking about the world and, indeed, texts.[12]
Like many other disciplines biblical studies too embraced
this model. "Following this paradigm, biblical scholars constructed a model for interpreting texts which paralleled the
way scientists were interpreting the world. They assumed
that texts were like the world, stable and objective realities
whose details, if examined with appropriate methods, would
reveal their meaning to the unbiased observer".[13] The historical-critical method emerged and with it the first shift
mentioned above.

It must be made clear here that the purpose of this brief
sketch is not to caricature either the Enlightenment scientific method or the historical-critical method. Its purpose is
to highlight some of the issues which are important for my
discussion of biblical interpretation in theologies of liberation. In particular, I want to highlight two assumptions which
often underlie these approaches: the presence of an "objective observer" and an "objective object".

The bulk of this chapter, then, will be an attempt to hear
a variety of voices: voices within the natural sciences,

historiography, philosophy, literary theory, theology, and biblical interpretation; voices which have been raised rejecting
"scientism" with its "pretensions to a mode of inquiry that
tries to deny its own hermeneutic character and mask its
own historicity so that it might claim ahistorical certainty";[14]
voices affirming the hermeneutic character of all understanding, inquiry, and interpretation. In amongst these voices we
will also hear, if we listen carefully, the voices of the poor
and oppressed.

From stability to instability

The critique of the Enlightenment scientific paradigm begins, ironically, within the natural sciences themselves.

> The examples are by now familiar: quantum theory, the discovery
> of such uncannily Joycean phenomena as quarks, the acknowl-
> edgement of the role of the scientific interpreter in all experiment,
> the realization that all data are theory-laden. More recently, less
> familiar examples have also been observed: the role of imagination,
> metaphor, and metonymy in scientific inquiry itself; the insistence
> among the postpositivist philosophers of science on the historical
> context of all scientific paradigms (Kuhn) and the topical, and
> thereby historical, character of all scientific arguments (Toulmin).
> In all these developments, former scientistic claims to ahistorical
> certainty and nonhermeneutical insights have collapsed. Science
> has become again both historical and hermeneutical.[15]

More specifically, and obvious from the above, is the demise of the "objective observer". The philospher of science,
Thomas Kuhn questions a number of the assumptions underlying the Enlightenment paradigm but especially that of
the objective observer. Commenting on Kuhn's work Herzog
concludes,

> The observer is not objective but 'paradigmative'. All searchers and
> researchers work with points of view and vested interests which
> influence what they see and affect what they discover. To put the
> issue in the language of the classical model, theory *precedes* ob-
> servation, indeed, is an indispensable precondition of observation
> rather than being the considered outcome of neutral and unbiased
> investigation.[16]

Karl Popper, a historian of science, makes a similar point
when he writes, "The belief that science proceeds from ob-

servation to theory is still so widely and firmly held that my
denial is often met with incredulity . . . But in fact the belief
that we can start with pure observation alone, without anything in the nature of a theory, is absurd".[17] In an earlier
work Popper argues that neither history nor science is a
matter of dredging up facts by the bucketful. A better image,
he suggests, is that of a searchlight playing upon areas of
reality; the point about the searchlight being, of course, that
it is inevitably directed from a point of view and that what it
illuminates is determined as much by this as by what is
there for it to shine upon.[18]

As is apparent from the above, it is not only the objective
observer which is unstable, the "objective object" too is unstable. "Reality is no longer viewed as an objective and static
world, operating by immutable laws and awaiting discovery.
Nor is it conceived as constructed out of blocks of matter
arranged in various combinations but rather as a continuum
of matter-energy ever evolving and dynamically changing".
Herzog is here describing the paradigm shift from a Newtonian
cosmos to an Einsteinian universe. He continues, "Even to
explore such a world is to change it, as Heisenberg noted.
Indeed, to discover the world is to create it, since the paradigm that renders discovery possible is a human creation".[19]

Demythologizing the scientific paradigm: from the modern to the postmodern

Given this brief introduction to the questioning of the Enlightenment scientific paradigm, I will now turn to a more
detailed analysis. The guiding voice in this analysis will be
that of Cornel West, a black African-American philosopher
and theologian. The choice of this voice "from below" is significant; it is significant because it represents a perspective
from among the poor and marginalized and this is the perspective from which I have chosen to give shape to the interpretive crisis.

Perhaps the most radical critique of the Enlightenment
scientific paradigm and its influence in other disciplines is
to be found within American neo-pragmatism. Cornel West

charts the emergence of American neo-pragmatism against a background of Viennese-style logical positivism, Oxford-inspired linguistic analysis, Continental phenomenology and existentialism, and homespun naturalism.[20] He argues that by the late fifties the basic presuppositions of the predominant paradigm of Anglo-American philosophy, loosely dubbed "logical positivism", were beginning to be questioned from within by Willard Van Orman Quine, Nelson Goodman, and Wilfred Sellars.

> To put it crudely, logical positivism rested upon three basic assumptions. First, it assumed a form of *sentential atomism* which correlates isolated sentences with either possible empirical confirmation, logical necessity, or emotion. Second, it emerged with a kind of *phenomenalist reductionism* which translates sentences about physical objects into sentences about actual and possible sensations. Third, it presupposes a version of *analytical empiricism* which holds observational evidence to be the criterion for cognitively meaningful sentences and hence the final court of appeal in determining valid theories about the world. These independent yet interrelated doctrines—held at various times by Rudolf Carnap, Carl Hempel, and other logical positivists—were guided by distinctions between the analytical and the synthetic, the linguistic and the empirical, theory and observation.[21]

West then goes on to show how each of these basic assumptions is threatened by the conclusions reached by Quine, Goodman, and Sellars.

Quine's work, which was by far the most influential, emphasized three aspects: an "*epistemological holism* which shifted the basic units of empirical significance from isolated sentences to systems of sentences or theories; a *methodological monism* that abandoned the analytic-synthetic distinction; and a *naturalism* which rejected a first philosophy prior to science".[22] Goodman's work also focused on three aspects: "a *logical conventionalism* which replaced accurate pictorial depiction with acceptable verbal description as the end and aim of constructing versions of the world; a *postempiricist antireductionism* that highlighted the theory-laden character of observation; and an *ontological pluralism* which relegated the notion of truth to that of fitness and encouraged diverse, even conflicting, true versions of the world instead of a fixed world and unique truth".[23] Sellars' work concentrated on two aspects: "an *anti-foundationalism* in epistemology which undermined attempts to invoke self-justifying, intrinsically credible, theory-neutral or noninferential elements in experience which provide foundations for other knowledge-claims and serve as the final terminating points for chains of epistemic justification"; and a "*psychological nominalism*" which "held that knowledge begins with the ability to justify—the capacity to use words—and since language is public and intersubjective, all 'given' elements which purportedly ground knowledge are matters of social practice".[24]

A distinctive feature of the related although sometimes conflicting philosophical positions of Quine, Goodman and Sellars is their affinities with the viewpoints of the early American pragmatists, Charles Peirce, William James, and John Dewey.[25] However, what West refers to as neo-pragmatism only emerges with the contributions of Thomas Kuhn's *The Structure of Scientific Revolutions* and Richard Rorty's *Philosophy and the Mirror of Nature.* First, for Kuhn and Rorty, epistemological holism led to a "distrust of the whole epistemological enterprise".[26] As West notes, Quine quickly quipped that such scrapping of his underdetermined yet minimally foundational "observation sentences" results in "epistemological nihilism" which he unequivocally rejects.[27] Second, "methodological monism yielded a rapacious antirealism in ontology against which Sellars revolted and of which Quine recanted". And third, "monocosmic naturalism blossomed into polycosmic pluralism—dethroning the authority of science as the monopoly on truth and knowledge—which radically called into question Quine's ontological allegiance to physics and Sellar's neo-Tractarian defense of the correspondence theory of truth".[28] In other words, if Quine, Goodman, and Sellars are the patriarchs of postmodern American philosophy, then Rorty and Kuhn are the renegade stepchildren who have followed through most thoroughly on their anti-realist, historicist and conventionalist implications.[29]

In summary, West detects three major moves or shifts which characterize the postmodern American philosophy of Quine, Goodman, Sellars, Kuhn, and Rorty. The first move is towards anti-realism or conventionalism in ontology, a move that

leaves no room for a correspondence theory of truth (of any importance) in that it undermines the very distinctions upon which such
a theory rests: the distinctions between ideas and objects, words
and things, language and the world, propositions and states of
affairs, theories and facts. The result is not a form of idealism
because the claim is not that ideas create objects, words create
things, language creates the world, and so forth. Nor is the result a
form of Kantianism because the claim is not that ideas constitute
objects, words constitute things, language constitutes the world,
and so on. Rather the result is a form of pragmatism because the
claim is that evolving descriptions and ever-changing versions of
objects, things, and the world issue forth from various communities as responses to certain problematics, as attempts to overcome
specific situations and as means to satisfy particular needs and
interests. To put it crudely, ideas, words, and language are not
mirrors which copy the 'real' or 'objective' world but rather tools
with which we cope with 'our' world.[30]

In the language of Rorty's essay "The World Well Lost", the
theory-laden character of observations relativizes talk about
the world such that appeals to "the world" as a final court of
appeal to determine what is true can only be viciously circu-
lar.[31] "We cannot", West contends "isolate 'the world' from
theories of the world, then compare these theories of the
world with a theory-free world. We cannot compare theories
with anything that is not a product of another theory. So any
talk about 'the world' is relative to the theories available".[32]

The second move is towards the demythologization of "the
Myth of the Given", or anti-foundationalism in epistemology,
and takes the form of an attack on prelinguistic awareness
and various notions of intuition. Knowledge "is not a matter
of grasping fixed forms, static essences or permanent sub-
stances and structures".[33] In other words, what is rejected is
that there is a self-justifying, intrinsically credible, theory-
neutral, noninferential element in experience which provides
the foundations for other knowledge-claims and serves as
the final terminating points for chains of epistemic justification.[34] "All such models view ahistorical, terminal confrontation—rather than historical, fluid conversation—as the de-
terminant of human belief".[35] "Rather", West argues, "knowledge is a matter of perceiving phenomena under description,
within a theory or in light of a version in order to, to use a
Wittgenstinian phrase, 'help us get about'".[36]

The last major move of postmodern American philosophy is towards detranscendalizing the transcendental subject or dismissing the mind as a sphere of inquiry.[37] Subject-talk, particularly for Sellars and Rorty, is mere convention, a matter of social practice rooted in our needs, interests, and purposes. Or, as West goes on to argue, in the words of Nietzsche, who prefigures this and other developments in postmodern American philosophy, "subject-talk is a linguistic social practice derived from our grammar, namely, the subject-predicate structure of our judgments".[38]

William Dean, who draws on the work of West, comes to similar conclusions in his analysis of what he calls the "new historicists", Rorty, Goodman, Hilary Putnam, Richard Bernstein, and Frank Lentricchia.[39] The new historicists, Dean suggests, can be seen to share a number of points. They have argued that "there is not a deeper truth behind or beneath the events of social history, despite the long tradition that says there is. Further, and more explicitly historicist, they have argued that actual truths are entirely historical creatures, conceived within history, directed at history, and grown in a historical chain, as interpretation refers to interpretation refers to interpretation throughout history".[40]

> The new historicist denial of universal truths or extrahistorical realities amounts to a denial of the standard forms of foundationalism, of realism, and of the transcendentalized subject. One experiences history, (1) not foundations beyond history; (2) not realities that can be known as correlatives, without the perspectives and prejudices of historical knowers; (3) not universal characteristics inherent in the subject, regardless of the subject's historical conditions. Further, the new historicism abandons, as a legacy of Cartesian foundationalism, the assurance that the world is divided into mind and body, spirit and matter, and replaces it with a belief in mind/body/affectional wholes. In epistemology this has specific consequences; an epistemological dualism is replaced by an epistemological monism.[41]

In Rorty's words "it's words all the way down", meaning not that reality is simply linguistic but that it is composed of interpretations heaped upon interpretations.[42]

Dean's main contribution to this discussion is an analysis which extends beyond philosophy into literary theory. He argues that while Rorty and Goodman were developing the new historicism within philosophy, Frank Lentricchia was reaching similar conclusions within literary criticism. Lentricchia's new historicism emerges from his rejection of both structuralism and a poststructuralist formalism. Lentricchia argues, says Dean, that poststructuralists like J. Hillis Miller, Geoffrey Hartmann, and Paul de Man "were correct in rejecting the structuralists, who sought to explain literature by reference to a logical code lying beneath the text". They were also correct "in affirming, with Jacques Derrida, that literature was never to be seen as a form of 'speaking,' where 'speaking' is the act of giving voice to the presence of being as it shows through the text or the reader". Also, they correctly "followed Derrida in affirming that literature was a form of 'writing,' where 'writing' is the interpretation of earlier 'writings,' which are interpretations of still earlier 'writings'". Lentricchia applauded these "newly fashionable Yale Derrideans for their acceptance of Derrida's picture of reality as 'a chain of texts' an image squaring almost perfectly with Rorty's 'words all the way down'".[43]

Lentricchia objects, however, to what he regards as their formalism and their consequent flight from history. He rejects this "formalism" because the text and the play with texts are made to be sufficient unto themselves, to have no significant connection to history. And in this respect, just as this irrelevance to history made the earlier New Critics unacceptable, so too the Yale Critics offer no important advance on just those critics they had hoped to supersede.[44] Lentricchia also argues that the Yale Critics are ahistorical in a second way. Not only are they formalist but they are also subjectivists in that they give "all power to the reader's solitary act of interpretation" and so fail to recognize how the reader, as well as the text, is contextual.[45]

Lentricchia's own position, Dean argues, emphasizes the historicism rather than the formalism of Derrida. Derrida's task, says Lentricchia, is to follow "the ineffaceable historicity of discourse", the "trace-structure" of the chain of texts (where "texts" are understood to include social artifacts as well as literary artifacts), showing how texts reinterpret earlier texts that reinterpret still earlier texts.[46] The point of Derrida's deconstruction of the ontological presence of being is to reconstruct the historicity of texts. "The starkness of this position becomes apparent when it is realized that there is nothing to consult beyond the history of texts and the history of those who interpret texts, and who in interpreting, 'write' new texts".[47]

Having had a brief and selective look at the changing shape of interpretation, it is important to consider some of the implications of the above discussion. Once again we will follow the shape of West's argument.

Beyond objectivism

Both West and Dean recognize that certain crucial consequences flow from these historicist positions. West outlines two. First,

> the distinction between the 'soft' human sciences and the 'hard' natural sciences collapses. The basic difference between the *Geisteswissenschaften* and the *Naturwissenschaften* is neither the self-defining character of the former nor the context-free facts of the latter. Rather the difference is between the relative stability of normal vocabularies in the natural sciences and the relative instability of normal vocabularies in the human sciences.

West goes on to emphasize that "this rudimentary demythologizing of the natural sciences is of immense importance for literary critics, artists, and religious thinkers who have been in retreat and on the defensive since the Enlightenment".[48] The second consequence is that "the conception of philosophy is no longer that of a tribunal of pure reason which defends or debunks claims to knowledge made by science, morality, art, or religion. Rather the voice of the philosopher is but one voice".[49]

Dean agrees with West, but uses different language in outlining the two consequences which he sees arising from these historicist positions. "When the new historicists accept history and historical experience, they accept (1) a pluralism that is unlimited" and "(2) an empiricism that is radical". He goes on to elaborate.

> The pluralism is unlimited because, so long as foundational realities are not experienced, there is no cause to seek something be-

yond the plurality of particulars that are experienced. Admittedly, generalizations must be made, but they must be treated as just that—as generalizations, mere abstractions attempting to describe characteristics of the particulars of the world and never as something in their own right. The empiricism is radical in the way suggested by William James. That is, so long as a realism that is positivistic is denied, then there is no particular reason for restricting experience to reports of the five senses or to quantitative observations. If history is to be experienced, then all experience of history, the valuational as well as the factual, must be included, and all the faculties, the affective as well as the five-sensory, must be used.[50]

Beyond nihilism

In discerning the shape of the interpretive crisis it is important to recongnize that both West and Dean are aware that there are also negative consequences emerging from these historicist positions. West argues that if Nietzsche prefigures certain important developments in postmodern American philosophy, and West demonstrates quite clearly that this is the case, then it is appropriate to note that Nietzsche believed such developments ultimately lead to a paralyzing nihilism and ironic skepticism unless they are supplemented with a new world view, a new "countermovement", to overcome such nihilism and skepticism.[51] And so while "The crucial moves made by postmodern American philosophers are highly significant in that these moves disclose the unwarranted philosophical assumptions and antiquated theoretical distinctions upon which rests much of modern analytic philosophy",

> Yet—and in this regard they resemble their counterparts in postmodern literary criticism—postmodern American philosophers have failed to project a new world view, a countermovement, 'a new gospel of the future'. Quine's and Sellars' updated versions of scientism not only reflect their positivist heritage, but, more importantly, reveal their homage to an outmoded cultural mode of thought. Goodman's attempt to infuse the idea of style with new life is intriguing yet ultimately resorts to an old aristocratic preoccupation. Kuhn's unequivocal promotion of the proliferation of learned societies (or groups) engaged in puzzle-solving under converging paradigms amounts to an unimaginative ideology of pro-

fessionalism. And Rorty's ingenious conception of philosophy as cultured conversation rests upon a nostalgic appeal to the world of men (and women) of letters of decades past. These viewpoints do not constitute visions, world views or, to use Gilles Deleuze's phrase, 'discourses as counter-philosophies' to the nihilism to which their positions seem to lead. Instead their viewpoints leave postmodern American philosophy hanging in limbo, as a philosophically critical yet culturally lifeless rhetoric mirroring a culture (or civilization) permeated by the scientific ethos, regulated by racist, patriarchal, capitalist norms, and pervaded by debris of decay.[52]

Further, while West accepts that "Rorty's neo-pragmatism ingeniously echoes the strident antihumanist critiques such as those of Martin Heidegger, Jacques Derrida, and Michel Foucault of a moribund bourgeois humanism", he asks, "Does Rorty's neo-pragmatism only kick the philosophical props from under bourgeois capitalist societies and require no change in our cultural and political practices?"[53] West's central argument here is that "it is impossible to historicize philosophy without partly politicizing (in contrast to vulgarly ideologizing) it". He recognizes that the relation of philosophy to history and politics is complex, yet he argues that "embarking on a historicist project which demystifies philosophy entails dragging-in the complexities of politics and culture".[54] In other words, "Rorty leads philosophy to the complex world of politics and culture, but does not permit it to get its hands dirty".[55]

> To undermine the privileged notions of objectivity, universality, and transcendentality without acknowledging and accenting the oppressive deeds done under the aegis of these notions is to write a thin, i.e., intellectual and homogeneous, history—a history which fervently attacks epistemological privilege but remains relatively silent about political, economic, racial, and sexual privilege. Such a history which surreptitiously suppresses certain histories even raises the sinister possibility that the antiepistemological radicalism of neo-pragmatism—much like the antimetaphysical radicalism of poststructuralism—may be an emerging form of ideology in late capitalist societies which endorses the existing order while undergirding sophisticated antiepistemological and antimeta-physical tastes of postmodern avant-gardists.[56]

In his analysis of Frederic Jameson's Marxist hermeneutics, West offers a similar penetrating critique, this time of deconstructionism. West recognizes that Jameson's battle against modern Anglo-American thought is aided by poststructuralism in that deconstructions disclose the "*philosophical* bankruptcy of this bourgeois humanist tradition". "Yet", West argues, "such deconstructions say little about the *political* bankruptcy of this tradition; further, and more seriously, deconstructions conceal the political impotency of their [own] projects".[57] Later he argues that if one takes history seriously, as do the post-1844 Marx, John Dewey, and Rorty, "then metaphysics, epistemology, and ethics are not formidable foes against which to fight nor are the Ali-like shuffles of the deconstructions which 'destroy' them impressive performances". In other words, "our history has not posed metaphysical, epistemological, and ethical problems that need to be solved or 'gone beyond'; rather, it has left us these problems as imaginative ideological responses to once pertinent but now defunct problematics". "On this view", he continues later, "deconstructionists become critically ingenious yet politically deluded ideologues who rightly attack bourgeois humanism, yet who also become the ideological adornments of late monopoly capitalist academies".[58]

West's analysis is clear: "To resurrect the dead, as bourgeois humanists try to do, is impossible. To attack the dead, as deconstructionists do, is redundant and, ironically, to valorize death".[59] West's claim here is not simply that these attacks "valorize textuality at the expense of power, but more importantly, that they are symbiotic with their very object of criticism: that is, they remain alive only as long as they give life to their enemy. In short, deconstructionist assaults must breathe life into metaphysical, epistemological, and ethical discourses if their critiques are to render these discourses lifeless".[60] West stands with Nietzsche when he argues that unlike the deconstructionists, Nietzsche's aim is to debunk and demystify in order to build anew, to project a new world view, a "countermovement", a "new gospel of the future".[61]

The shape of West's argument is now becoming clear. West recognizes that forms of neo-pragmatism like Rorty's

> can serve as a useful springboard for a more engaged, even subversive, philosophical perspective. This is so primarily because it encourages the cultivation of critical attitudes toward all philosophical traditions. This crucial shift in the subject matter of phi-

losophers from the grounding of beliefs to the scrutiny of ground-
less traditions—from epistemology to ethics, truth to practices, foundations to consequences—can lend itself to emancipatory ends in
that it proposes the tenuous self-images and provisional vocabularies that undergird past and present social orders as central objects of criticism.[62]

And, West continues, this shift is particularly significant
for "those on the underside of history" because "oppressed
people have more at stake than others in focusing on the
tenuous and provisional vocabularies which have had and
do have hegemonic status in past and present societies".[63]

But critique is not sufficient; Rorty's critical advice to
Michel Foucault applies equally to himself when he writes,
"His obviously sincere attempt to make philosophical thinking be of some use, do some good, help people, is not going to
get anywhere until he condescends to do a bit of dreaming
about the future, rather than stopping dead after
genealogising the present".[64]

West is prepared to do some dreaming; but before I come
to this let us briefly consider Dean's response to the relativism that he too sees hovering over the new historicism. Dean's
discussion is particularly helpful in that he draws attention
to the work of those new historicists who move beyond nihilism and skepticism, and in so doing he foreshadows elements of West's "dreaming".

Dean points out that there are those within the new historicism who are concerned to save it from the dangers of
relativism. They do this, he says, by means of a pragmatism
that arbitrates, that enters as an answer to the problems
created by unlimited pluralism and radical empiricism. Pragmatism, Dean argues, arbitrates disputes by concentrating
on the historical consequences of ideas and by asking which
ideas contribute more to history.[65] For example, like Hilary
Putnam,[66] Richard Bernstein contends that we no longer need
to think that if something is not established objectivistically,
then it is merely relativistic and so meaningless.[67] Our period, the period beyond the period dominated by what he
calls "the Cartesian anxiety", is characterized by "a position
beyond objectivism and relativism, where objectivism and
relativism are being replaced by *phronesis*, where discourse

seeks only to contribute to the practice of the community" [68] Bernstein describes how the Continental hermeneutics of Hans-Georg Gadamer and Jürgen Habermas, the philosophy of science of Kuhn, Paul Feyerabend, Imre Lakatos, and Peter Winch, the political philosophy of Hannah Arendt, and the neopragmatism of Rorty form a new "cable" of philosophic opinion in which objectivism and relativism are being replaced by the acceptance of a practical and communal knowledge which tests the truth of a position by asking whether and how it might apply to the practice, that is, the history, of the community.[69]

For example, Lentricchia, like West, extends the political dimensions of community in ways that he believes are atypical of the genteel world of the philosophers and literary critics. He seeks to extend the community from that of the polite, leisured conversation of the university intellectual to the practical conversation of society at large as it struggles to build a viable life.[70] In his *Criticism and Social Change* which was, he says, "triggered" by Hayden White, but which is largely an exposition of the historicism of the literary critic Kenneth Burke, Lentricchia argues for adding to the value-free programs of pragmatism and deconstructionism the social values of Antonio Gramsci, who has provided a noncoercive and cultural version of Marxism.[71] Lentricchia is concerned to extend interpretation beyond the intellectual interpretation of the past to include the social interpretation of the past, "a social interpretation accomplished in order to contribute to the social change of the future".[72] Lentricchia offers a similar critique to West of Rorty when he contrasts the metaphors of conversation used by Rorty and Burke, arguing that Rorty's use of conversation "reflects the bourgeois individualism of the culture in which it is gaining acceptance", whereas when Burke uses conversation he does so "in terms of political and economic consequences in addition to the more personal satisfactions it might render".[73]

In summary, Dean argues that while modernism has been skeptical of our knowledge of the external world, the new historicism typically has not been. "The modernist skepticism is evident in Descartes's rationalism, in David Hume's empiricism, in Kant's struggle with solipsism, in problems faced by German idealism, in Husserl's phenomenology, in existentialism, and in the more frantic, vainglorious, and non-historicist side of deconstructionism".

However, according to the new historicism, we do know the world, but we know it not by looking beyond the contingencies of history but only by looking at the contingencies of history. The new historicism "has rejected an imprisonment in the subjective ego and a flight from history" and has "accepted an unalloyed dependence on history". These two epistemological features of the new historicism set it apart from modernism and align it with postmodern ways of speaking.[74]

Dean recognizes that the consequent uncertainty "would lead an old historicist like Paul Tillich to find in it a counsel of despair, an abandonment of thought to relativity and to meaninglessness". "But", he argues, "the new historicists would see this criticism as resulting from an improperly forced option between absolute truths independent of the contingencies of history and a meaningless relativity". They would strive for a third position, "beyond objectivism and relativism", which permits meaningful reflection on an aspect of history from a historical standpoint.[75]

Each of the people we have discussed, Dean maintains, holds open that hope. Even Rorty calls on us to "combine private fulfillment, self-realization with public morality, a concern with justice".[76] Putnam concludes with the assertion that "we are not trapped in individual solipsistic hells, but invited to engage in a truly human dialogue; one which combines collectivity with individual responsibility".[77] Goodman maintains that the highest truth is one that fits into a community's practice.[78]

However, such hope is still too vague, located as it is in some universal notion of society. Cornel West's dreams and hopes are located far more specifically in particular communities, which is a crucial factor to recognize in discerning the shape of the interpretive crisis from the perspective of the poor and oppressed.

A particular community:
the African-American community

As I mentioned earlier, Cornel West is prepared to "dream", to propose "a new gospel of the future", to be a part of a "countermovement". So while he accepts the negative hermeneutic potential of the relativist, even nihilist, implications of neo-pragmatism, "Yet after the smoke clears, the crucial task is to pursue thick, i.e., social and heterogeneous, historical accounts of the emergence, development, sustenance, and decline of vocabularies and practices in the natural and human sciences against the background of dynamic changes in specific (and often coexisting) modes of production, political conflicts, cultural configurations, and personal turmoil".[79] In other words, "It should be clear that Rorty's thin historicism needs Marx, Durkheim, Weber, de Beauvoir, and Du Bois; that is, his narrative needs a more subtle historical and sociological perspective".[80] Implicit in the social locations of the last two names is the need to root the positive hermeneutic moment, the dreaming, in particular communities. As Ernst Troeltsch and Dewey suggested years ago, "a wholesale historicism leads to at least four possible responses: a paralyzing skepticism, a 'might makes right' cynicism, an unacknowledged intuitionism, or a critical self-situating contextualism".[81]

In *Prophesy Deliverance!: An Afro-American Revolutionary Christianity* West critically situates himself in the African-American context from within which he develops a thick history of African-American Christianity.[82] West's broad aim is "to launch the prospect of an African-American religious philosophy with a deep sense of cultural and political engagement", the primary objective of which is to offer "a demystifying hermeneutic of the Afro-American experience which enhances the cause of human freedom".[83] He sees such a religious philosophy arising out of three main sources: American pragmatism, prophetic African-American Christian thought, and progressive Marxism.

Here he focuses on three aspects of pragmatism: (1) Dewey's recognition that philosophy is inextricably bound to culture, society, and history; (2) a rejection of knowledge as

private, foundational, and theory-free, but rather a product
of the social practices of a community of inquirers; (3) the
dethronement of epistemology as the highest priority of modern thought in favour of ethics, by which he means "the
search for desirable and realizable historical possibilities in
the present". However, he also recognizes the limitations of
pragmatism, "its relative neglect of the self, its refusal to
take class struggle seriously, and its veneration of scientific
method and the practices of the scientific community"[84]. In
other words, unlike American pragmatism, West is concerned
to emphasize the political dimensions of knowledge. But it is
still important to recognize that pragmatism does play a crucial role for West in initiating the "urgent task" of "exposing
the reactionary and conservative consequences of bourgeois
humanism, the critical yet barren posture of poststructuralist
skepticism and deconstructionist ironic criticism, and the
utopian and ultimately escapist character of the . . . gnosti-
cism of Bloom and the . . . pragmatism of Rorty".[85]

West's positive hermeneutic also proposes dialogue between prophetic African-American Christian thought and progressive Marxism, "a serious dialogue between black theologians and Marxist thinkers", a dialogue based in part on their
common focus "on the plight of the exploited, oppressed, and
degraded peoples of the world, their relative powerlessness
and possible empowerment".[86] So for West a systematic treatment of a black Christian position would include "the philosophical methodology of dialectical historicism, the theological world view of prophetic Christianity, the cultural outlook
of Afro-American humanism, and the social theory and political praxis of progressive Marxism".[87] He concludes,

> Revolutionary Christian perspective and praxis must remain an-
> chored in the prophetic Christian tradition in the Afro-American
> experience which provides the norms of individuality and democ-
> racy; guided by the cultural outlook of the Afro-American human-
> ist tradition which promotes the vitality and vigor of black life; and
> informed by the social theory and political praxis of progressive
> Marxism which proposes to approximate as close as is humanly
> possible the precious values of individuality and democracy as soon
> as God's will be done.[88]

West applies these objectives to the specific historical community of African-Americans and does so with the intention

of changing that group's social history.[89] West is "not concerned with 'foundations' or transcendental 'grounds'", but is, rather, concerned with "a genre of writing, a textuality, a mode of discourse that interprets, describes, and evaluates Afro-American life in order comprehensively to understand and effectively to transform it".[90] West moves beyond objectivism by means of a postmodern perspective, but while acknowledging and using postmodern ways of speaking, he moves beyond the lure of skepticism and nihilism by means of a prophetic vision rooted in a specific community, a community of the poor and marginalized.

The shape of West's analysis of the interpretive crisis is now clear. The remaining task of this chapter is to consider whether we can detect a similar shape in the crisis in biblical interpretation.

Plurality and ambiguity in biblical interpretation

Against such a background, sketched with broad strokes, it is hardly surprising that there is something of a crisis in biblical interpretation. And, as Tracy points out, "A crisis of interpretation within any tradition eventually becomes a demand to interpret this very process of interpretation",[91] a task which Tracy does not shy away from. In this final section of the chapter we will briefly consider the impact of this wider hermeneutic crisis on the work of a "mainstream" biblical interpreter, David Tracy, whose recent work reflects many of the elements already discussed. Once again, it is the shape of Tracy's arguments rather than the detail that is foregrounded.

As has been indicated, Tracy recognizes the hermeneutic crisis: "We find ourselves historically distanced from the classics of our traditions. We find ourselves culturally distanced from those 'others' we have chosen both to ignore and oppress. We find ourselves distanced even from ourselves, suspicious of all our former ways of understanding, interpreting, and acting".[92]

Tracy also recognizes that one of the major "interruptions" of interpretation is the radical plurality of language. He charts the history of this linguistic turn through Wittgenstein, Heidegger, and de Saussure. He sees three major alternatives in post-Saussurean hermeneutics, each highlighting a particular aspect of de Saussure's kernel formulation: "In the linguistic system, there are only differences". First, there are the structuralists and semioticians who attempt to uncover the basic units of various sign systems (e.g. Lévi-Strauss). They highlight "system" in de Saussure's formulation. These approaches, argues Tracy, challenge amongst other humanistic concepts "their grounding of all reality in the human".[93] Second are the deconstructionists, who emphasize "difference" in de Saussure's formulation . "Deconstructionists challenge all claims to uncovering the fully systemic character of any language by insisting upon the implications of the fact that no system can adequately account for its own ineradicably differential nature".[94]

> In sum, for poststructuralists, meaning functions among the whole chain of signifiers. We never in fact reach a unitary meaning purely present to itself as a sign freed from all the differences needed to produce the meaning. No sign, on Saussure's own analysis, is free from the traces of other officially absent signifiers. The traces of those absent signifiers must operate through the whole differential system ad infinitum for any sign to have meaning at all.[95]

In addition, and "Above all, Derrida joins Lévi-Strauss and all structuralists in exposing the illusory character of the self portrayed as a self-present user of language as instrument, the self as a reality-founding ego".[96] In other words, Tracy's argument is that "Our knowledge of reality is irrevocably linked to our use of language. Our use of language is possible because of the differential relations that constitute the words of the particular language. Any claims to full presence, especially claims to full self-presence in conscious thought, are illusions that cannot survive a study of language as a system of differential relations".[97]

But, Tracy asks, and here he feels the pull of nihilism and skepticism, if all is difference, can any genuine interpretation occur?[98] Like West and Dean, Tracy wants to affirm that interpretation is still possible, albeit carefully reconsidered. He uses two arguments to return to his notion of interpretation as conversation. First, that deconstructive analyses are not put forward to ground a situation but rather they are meant to function as linguistic therapy. And second, that Derrida's "typical strategy, and his contribution, seems less directed at texts than at individual words".[99] And this brings him to the third option, language as neither system alone nor use alone but as discourse. "To discover discourse is to explore language as a reality beyond individual words in the dictionary, beyond both synchronic codes (*langue*) and individual use of words (*parole*); it is to rediscover society and history". He elaborates on this when he says, "To acknowledge that language is discourse is to admit the need for ethical and political criticism of the hidden, even repressed, social and historical ideologies in all texts, in all languages as discourse, and, above all, in all interpretations".[100]

However, like Dean, Tracy wants to insist that to lose any belief in pure self-knowledge is not to deny the possibility of knowledge itself. "What we know, we know with relative adequacy, and we know it is bounded by the realities of language, society, and history".[101] In other words, "If we are not to retreat from what the early stages of the linguistic turn taught us—the inevitability of the realities of history and society in all language—then we must, at some point, turn from an interpretation of language-as-object back to an interpretation of language-as-use. We must turn from the deconstruction of words to a chastened interpretation of texts".[102]

Tracy also recognizes that another major "interruption" of interpretation is the radical ambiguity of history. He argues that no text comes to us without "the plural and ambiguous history of effects of its own production and its former receptions". But, he continues,

> To see how ambiguous our history has been, however, is not simply to retire into that more subtle mode of complacency, universal and ineffectual guilt. Rather as Abraham Joshua Heschel insisted: 'Not all are guilty but all are responsible.' Responsible here means capable of responding: capable of facing the interruptions in our history; capable of discarding any scenarios of innocent triumph written, as always, by the victors; capable of not forgetting the subversive memories of individuals and whole peoples whose names we do not even know. If we attempt such responses, we are making a

beginning—and only a beginning—in assuming historical responsibility.[103]

For Tracy, then, this responsibility involves two strategies: first, "to face the actuality of the ideologies in ourselves
and even in our most beloved classics";[104] and second, to
"learn to listen to the narratives of others, especially those
'others' who have had to suffer our otherness imposed upon
their interpretations of their own history and classics".[105] And
of course, these two strategies are linked: "To hear the readings of the oppressed means that the rest of us need to acknowledge the ambiguity of the relationships of power and
knowledge in our own discourse". But of course, he continues, and the parallels with West are clear, "that imperative
to listen cannot be the final word. If criticism and suspicion
stop there, what really has been accomplished? Something,
perhaps: a correct religious sense of our guilt and our need
for repentance but not a critical response or an active solidarity".[106] He specifically rejects a pluralism that masks "a
genial confusion in which one tries to enjoy the pleasures of
difference without ever committing oneself to any particular
vision of resistance and hope".[107]

Tracy's understanding of the shape of the interpretive crisis is similar to that of West's. Having briefly outlined the
radical plurality of language and the radical ambiguity of history Tracy argues that such postmodern positions on language and history intensify "the central insight that has
guided us throughout these reflections: all experience and
all understanding is hermeneutical".[108] Consequently, to interpret must now mean that we attend to and use the
hermeneutics of both retrieval and suspicion, and often retrieval through suspicion.[109] Tracy is here advocating, for the
believer, both a "hermeneutics of trust" and a "hermeneutics
of suspicion", recognizing, however, that we can only trust
ourselves to a conversation with significant texts if we admit
that everything, ourselves, our texts, and the conversation
itself, is deeply affected by the ambiguity and plurality that
touch all. "There is no innocent interpretation, no innocent
interpreter, no innocent text".[110] Retrieval now demands both
critique and suspicion. Indeed, the retrieval process must
incorporate both critique and suspicion.[111] Moreover, and

crucially, like West, Tracy locates such retrieval within a particular vision of resistance and hope which includes solidarity with the poor and oppressed.

> All the victims of our discourses and our history have begun to discover their own discourses in ways that our discourse finds difficult to hear, much less listen to. Their voices can seem strident and uncivil—in a word, other. And they are. We have all just begun to sense the terror of that otherness. But only by beginning to listen to those other voices may we also begin to hear the otherness within our own discourse and within ourselves. What we might then begin to hear, above our own chatter, are possibilities we have never dared to dream.[112]

Conclusion

The stable text and reader will never be the same again. In the preceding discussion both have come under a diverse but always penetrating scrutiny. The situatedness of both the text and the reader is clear. In West's and Tracy's accounts the shape of the interpretive crisis is similar: both place the observer (reader) and the object (text) under careful scrutiny. Both recognize the powerful negative hermeneutic potential of moving beyond objectivism. However, and in this respect they differ from many of their postmodern contemporaries, both West and Tracy also argue for a positive hermeneutic which goes beyond skepticism, nihilism, and play. Their positive hermeneutic consists of a prophetic vision of resistance and hope that roots their interpreting within an active and transformative solidarity with a particular community, the community of the poor and oppressed.[113]

Both West and Tracy recognize the interpretive crisis in biblical, literary, and philosophical hermeneutics. However, they refuse to allow their recognition of the demise of objectivity to lead them into either the play of pluralism or the despair of nihilism. Instead they advocate doing their interpreting from within an active and transformative solidarity with the poor and oppressed.

The influence of theologies of liberation, particularly their biblical hermeneutics, is evident in our discussion of West and Tracy. So although West and Tracy are responding to the broader interpretive crisis they are also responding to the interpretive crisis posed by contexts of liberation. To such contexts we now turn, focusing throughout on the South African context of liberation.

Chapter Two

The Interpretive Crisis: Reading the Bible in South Africa

Introduction

"The time has come. The moment of truth has arrived. South Africa has been plunged into a crisis that is shaking the foundations and there is every indication that the crisis has only just begun and that it will deepen and become even more threatening in the months to come. It is the KAIROS or moment of truth not only for apartheid but also for the Church".[1] Thus begins *The Kairos Document*'s challenge to the Church in South Africa, a challenge which, The Kairos Theologians go on to argue, "impels us *to return to the Bible* and to search the Word of God for a message that is relevant to what we are experiencing in South Africa today".[2]

Recently South Africa has emerged from this crisis. However, a significant feature of the second edition of *The Kairos Document* is the statement that the socio-political crisis "impels us *to return to the Bible* and to search the Word of God for a message that is relevant to what we are experiencing in South Africa today". Implicit in this call to "return to the Bible" is the recognition that a crucial part of the South African crisis is an *interpretive* crisis—and this crisis is still with us. Indeed, our emergence from the socio-political crisis has, I would argue, deepened the interpretive crisis. We are in danger of forgetting what we have learned from the struggle against apartheid, and we were only just beginning to learn what this might mean for our reading of the Bible and our doing of theology. The struggle against apartheid was a vital resource for our return to and our rereading of the Bible. The struggle for justice, democracy, reconstruction and development must now become another resource for our rereading. The temptation is "to go back to being the church",[3] to forget what we have learned from "the struggle" and forget that we are still engaged in a struggle between the forces of death and the God of life. There is now some space for reflection on the experience of struggle and its consequences for our rereading of the Bible, so this is precisely the time to engage the interpretive crisis. And as I have argued in the previous chapter, a crisis of interpretation within any context eventually becomes a demand to interpret the very process of interpretation.

The purpose of this chapter is to outline the biblical interpretive crisis in South Africa. In subsequent chapters various elements of this interpretive crisis will be analyzed in more detail. In this chapter I will briefly consider the interpretive crisis within the predominantly white academy in South Africa before devoting a more detailed analysis to the interpretive crisis within black liberation hermeneutics. As with the first chapter, the perspective of this chapter is "from below"; the biblical interpretive crisis in South Africa is discussed from the perspective of those committed to the liberation struggle.

The Bible in the academy

In two articles Dirk Smit offers an incisive analysis of biblical scholarship in South Africa.[4] Smit's analysis focuses on Afrikaner Reformed biblical scholarship, the dominant form of biblical scholarship in South Africa, and suggests a useful framework for understanding the Bible in the academy. He distinguishes, broadly speaking, three important stages.

> In a first stage, prominent scholars played an important role in legitimating apartheid and opponents were ostracized from the South African scholarly scene.[5] In a second stage, the socio-politi-

cal interpretation of the Bible has been strongly rejected, in the name of the ethos of scientific research. At present, in a third stage, the debate between scientific, historical scholarship and committed, socio-politically involved reading, is urgent but diffuse, since it is being argued at so many different fronts.[6]

In elaborating on these stages, Smit argues that looking at the past decades "one can perhaps say that the stage where Afrikaner Reformed biblical scholarship served the *apartheid* ideology, was replaced by one in which a scientific ethos dominated, in which the scholars tried to carry on as if nothing was happening in society".[7] Specifically, "New Testament scholarship was going through a period in which the ethos and practices of institutionalized scientific scholarship were freely accepted, safeguarding the practitioners from the aberrations and conflicts of both the socio-political and ecclesial-dogmatic struggles".[8]

Interestingly enough, Smit adds, the scholars from the Afrikaner Reformed circles, with the exception of a few working within non-ecclesial academic contexts "could not rid themselves completely from the powerful controls and the inherent constraints of the institutionalized ecclesial and doctrinal spheres, with the one important result that they never took the *historical-critical* paradigm fully seriously".[9] So their search for a "neutral", "objective", and respectable scientific method found its focus elsewhere. It came as no surprise Smit argues, "that these scholars found the literary-aesthetic paradigm . . . so suitable to their interests and ethos. It allowed them the opportunity to operate within the scientific ethos, and to steer free of both socio-political and ecclesial-dogmatic conflicts, and yet not find themselves in the difficulties brought about by the historical-critical paradigm".[10]

The situation is only a little different among English speaking biblical scholars.[11] While English speaking biblical scholars have not legitimated apartheid to the same extent, and while they have been trained in the historical-critical approaches, they too have failed to complete the hermeneutic circle and address the question of what the text means for South Africa today.[12] As Walter Wink and William Herzog argue, there was a time when the historical-critical method could effect a kind of conversion. It could liberate the person captive to orthodox and other stereotypes. But in South Africa, as in other contexts, it has lost much of its power in personal and social transformation. By detaching the text from life biblical criticism has become trapped in "the abyss of an objectified past", where the "ideology of objectivism" has made the researcher accountable primarily to the guild of biblical scholars. So many of the questions asked of the biblical text are not those being asked by ordinary people. The dilemma facing historical-critical scholarship, according to Wink and Herzog, is largely due to the lack of a real life context that would function as a galvanizing orientation point of the research effort. As a consequence, for many biblical scholars today "the most urgent question has become that of finding a context in which their interpretations of the Bible might have significance - or, stated more fundamentally, a context which would give that interpretation significance".[13] In South Africa, however, where the context cries out for significant interpretations, the historical-critical method "appears in the mantle of science deriving its justification from the critique of tradition, *'thereby keeping actual power relations inaccessible to analysis and to public consciousness'*".[14]

This bracketing-off of the day-to-day socio-political crisis in South Africa, whether within the Afrikaner tradition or the English tradition, has not only made biblical scholarship largely irrelevant to the South African context, it has also had the effect of distancing the reading of the Bible, entrenching the notion that the Bible is the property of the academy.[15]

Furthermore, the awareness within the academy of the plurality and ambiguity of all interpretation, more prevalent in the Afrikaans speaking institutions, has led to the proliferation of "interesting", detached readings, rather than "interested", committed readings.[16] "Interesting readings", the dominant tendency in academic readings of the Bible in South Africa, not only recognize the plurality of interpretive interests but go on to embrace and encourage the maintenance of a plurality of interests.[17]

While a plurality of interests can play a useful critical role in subverting dominant interests, as I have argued in the

previous chapter, such a position does raise ethical and political questions.[18] Terry Eagleton puts the question cogently
when he argues that although his discussion has considered a number of problems of literary theory "the most important question of all has as yet gone unanswered. What is
the *point* of literary theory? Why bother with it in the first
place? Are there not issues in the world more weighty than
codes, signifiers and reading subjects?".[19] The point Eagleton
is making here is that most literary critics would not regard
literary theory as relevant to such matters as Western capitalism, and this, he asserts, is exactly their problem. "The
story of modern literary theory, paradoxically, is the narrative of a flight from . . . real history."[20] But, and this is his
main argument, "There is, in fact, no need to drag politics
into literary theory: as with South African sport, it has been
there from the beginning". In other words, "literary theories
are not to be upbraided for being political, but for being on
the whole covertly or unconsciously so".[21] Such is certainly
the case in the South African context.

Even though there are signs of a more engaged biblical
scholarship "they are still very reserved in their conclusions
and very much aware of the ethos of institutionalized scientific scholarship".[22] However, in the South African context
the pursuit of "neutral", "scientific", or "interesting" readings means fiddling while South Africa burns.[23] Or, as
Jonathan Draper puts it, "'Interesting readings' abound in
the New Testament Society of South Africa . . . but outside
the gates stand the angry [black] youth asking why they
should read the Bible at all!"[24]

Having briefly examined white biblical scholarship we now
turn to the angry and urgent questions still being asked in
the black community.

The Bible in the black community

The Bible is and has been one of the basic sources of African and black theology.[25] However, we are still impelled, as
The Kairos Document proclaims, to re-read the Bible. The cry
of the poor and oppressed to return to the Bible, to re-read

the Bible, arises out of their recognition of the Bible as both a problem and a solution, as both an oppressor and a liberator.

Takatso Mofokeng begins his essay on "Black Christians, the Bible and Liberation", one of the few works which discusses the history of the Bible in the South African context from a black perspective, with the following provocative paragraph.

> No statement in the history of political science as well as that of Christian missions expresses the dilemma that confronts black South Africans in their relationships with the Bible with greater precision and has whipped up more emotions than the following: 'When the white man came to our country he had the Bible and we had the land. The white man said to us 'let us pray'. After the prayer, the white man had the land and we had the bible'. With this statement which is known by young and old in South Africa, black people of South Africa point to three dialectically related realities. They show the central position which the Bible occupies in the ongoing process of colonization, national oppression and exploitation. They also confess the incomprehensible paradox of being colonized by a Christian people and yet being converted to their religion and accepting the Bible, their ideological instrument of colonization, oppression and exploitation. Thirdly, they express a historic commitment that is accepted solemnly by one generation and passed on to another—a commitment to terminate exploitation of humans by other humans.[26]

This story and Mofokeng's interpretation of it indicate two related interpretive crises. The first can be called a historical crisis. Here the focus is on the role of the Bible in South African history as both an instrument of social control and an instrument of social struggle. The second, the central concern of this chapter, can be called a methodological crisis. Here the focus is on biblical interpretation and the Bible itself as both a problem and a solution.

The historical crisis

Briefly, it is generally accepted that the Bible first reached South Africa through the sometimes uncomfortable but nonetheless successful partnership between colonialism and the Christian missionary enterprise.[27] Some African historians have argued that the missionary enterprise used colonialism as an effective and readily available vehicle to reach the religious heart of the so-called "dark continent".[28] Other African historians, however, have argued persuasively that it was colonialism that used the missionary enterprise to soften the hearts and minds of the black people.[29] According to Gwinyai Muzorewa, "What is indisputable is the fact that the colonists tended to use the missionaries to make their task easier . . . consequently, there is a thin line between the missionary intention and the intent of the colonizer".[30]

While such a summary would be true for the majority of missionary activity which was linked to British colonialism, it does not necessarily fairly reflect the practice of all missionary work. Many missions were not related to the local colonial powers, for example, Norwegian, Swedish, and Moravian missions; and much early penetration of missions was prior to anything that can meaningfully be called "colonialism". Indeed, in some regions, traders and missionaries operated before imperial interests grew, and there are many cases of these people acting against organized colonial interests.[31] Even Dutch and later Afrikaner "colonialism" was more properly a form of "tribal" conquest than colonialism.[32]

Generally, even when speaking of missionaries and missions at their best, the overwhelming impression on black South Africans is that the Bible that first came to South Africa with the Dutch conquerors and then British colonialism was a Bible that justified and legitimized colonialism, imperialism, domination and European superiority.[33]

Although the role of the Bible in this history is not clear and requires further research, in many cases "the missionaries have given us not the Bible but the *Summa theologica*" or its equivalent.[34] "They came with all their divided traditions, denominations and mission societies, but the fundamental division they left us was the division between a white Church and a black Church".[35] This was and is still a political division that cuts right through the church in South Africa, a division which has had a profound effect on the interpretation of the Bible.

Within this divided church, however, runs a prophetic reading of the Bible. At one level this is embodied in certain prophetic figures, missionaries like van der Kemp, John Philip, Bishop Colenso and Trevor Huddleston, and church leaders like Beyers Naudé, Allan Boesak, and Desmond Tutu.

At another level the voice of a prophetic reading has been associated with groups like the Southern African Catholic Bishops' Conference (SACBC), the Christian Institute, the South African Council of Churches (SACC), and the Institute for Contextual Theology (ICT).[36] In addition, there have been a number of prophetic statements and declarations like the 1957 Catholic Bishops' statement that apartheid is intrinsically evil, the 1968 *Message to the People of South Africa* which rejected apartheid as a pseudo-gospel, the 1982 *Belhar Confession* which denounced apartheid as a sin, a heresy, and a mockery of the gospel, the 1985 *Kairos Document* which challenged the churches to side with the struggle for liberation, the 1986 *Evangelical Witness in South Africa* which called evangelicals to repentance for not having preached a prophetic and radical gospel, the 1988 *Relevant Pentecostal Witness* which calls for the return to Pentecostalism's roots among the poor and oppressed, and the 1989 *Road To Damascus* which calls for conversion on the part of those who have consciously or unconsciously taken sides with the oppressor.[37]

More important for the purposes of this study are the readings of the Bible which have been a part of the life of the ordinary, "grassroots", oppressed black community over a period of nearly a hundred years. This is particularly evident in the large group of churches known as the African Independent Churches (AIC) which represent about thirty percent of the black population.[38]

In the late nineteenth century the AIC began to break away from the missionary churches, partly because of the white domination, racism, and paternalism in those churches, and also partly because African Christians were unwilling to abandon their African culture.[39] Independence for these churches meant among other things new ways of interpreting the Bible, which included trying to interpret the Bible in terms of African culture, and in terms of the black experience of suffering, insecurity, and oppression.[40]

The readings of the Bible arising from these churches have not, however, been consistently prophetic. "In fact they represent a bewildering complexity of interpretations and practices".[41] Some of their readings are very traditional, in the sense that they are dependent on the teaching and practice of the missionary churches. Others have much in common with charismatic and pentecostal traditions. "Only a few could be described as preaching a 'social gospel' in the usual meaning of the term".[42]

However, we must be careful not to base our analysis of these churches on the available "public transcript". A more careful analysis which takes into account "the hidden transcript", that which is done behind the back of the dominant and which is deliberately hidden from the public view, might indicate that the roots of black theology in South Africa are to be found in these churches. What is clear, as John de Gruchy argues, is that "in an important sense black theology in South Africa began with the revolt of black Christians at the turn of the century, a revolt which found institutional expression in the African independent churches".[43] Other roots of black theology can be found in black Christian leadership in the mission churches, particular in leaders like D.D.T. Jabavu, Z.K. Matthews, and Albert J. Luthuli.[44] The picture is even more complex when we recognize, as leaders of the AIC constantly claim, that many of those who belong to the mission churches by day, also belong to the AIC by night! So long before the term "black theology" was used, there were resources for prophetic readings of the Bible.

"Black theology" under this term emerged in the context of the Black Consciousness Movement in the late 1960's and the early 1970's, in particular out of the 1971 black theological project of the University Christian Movement (UCM).[45]

> It came into being as a cultural tool of struggle propounded by young black South Africans who were influenced by the philosophy of black consciousness. The immediate target of black theology was the Christian church and especially Christian theology. The point of contention was the perceived acquiescence of the christian church and theology in the oppression and exploitation of black people. Black theologians argued, justifiably, that not only was the church relatively silent on the question of oppression, but that the thoroughly Western and white outlook of its theology helped to reproduce the basic inequalities of an apartheid society. Consequently, black Christian activists emphasized the need for a black theology of liberation.[46]

The tasks of this theology were to be measured against the broad goal of the liberation of black people. Therefore black theologians included among their tasks two primary tasks. Because the question of cultural dependency was regarded as being, among others, at the base of oppression and exploitation, "one of the critical tasks of black theology would be to work towards the cultural autonomy of black people", by "exposing the imposition of the cultural forms of the dominant classes on the oppressed". The creation and development of black theology itself would also be part of the wider task of "creating autonomous weapons of social and cultural struggle".[47]

The churches and particularly the theological seminaries were to be the starting point for this activity and reflection on black theology. "The wider black community, however— and especially the most oppressed sections of it—was to be the real base from which and in which black theology would take root and develop". The crucial point here is that there was never any doubt in the emergence of black theology that it "was to be developed as an instrument of struggle for the liberation of oppressed and exploited black people in South Africa".[48]

However, and this is the crux of the historical crisis, notwithstanding the vigorous and various work within black theology over the last fifteen to twenty years, "black theology has not yet properly emerged as an autonomous weapon of struggle". Itumeleng Mosala finds evidence of this in "its inability to become a useful weapon in the hands of the oppressed and exploited black people themselves".[49] Instead it has remained the monopoly of educated, middle-class, black Christians. It has not been able to develop organic links with the popular struggles of especially the black working class people who are the most exploited section of the black community.[50]

> In the meantime the oppressed black masses relentlessly continue their struggle against apartheid and capitalism—with or without the leadership and cultural equipment of black theology. As one might expect, however, many forms of resistance that the oppressed create for themselves remain open to co-optation and undermining by the dominant classes. The latter are able to co-opt and undermine the discourses of the oppressed on the grounds of intellectual and theoretical superiority. Needless to say, the oppressed are very often unable to contest this claimed intellectual and theoretical

superiority. In the realm of religious practice, this state of affairs underscores the absolute necessity of a theoretically well-grounded and culturally autonomous black theology of liberation.[51]

The central argument of Mosala's critique of black theology is that "the reason for black theology's failure among the oppressed has to do with its class and ideological commitments, *especially with respect to its biblical hermeneutics*".[52] Unless, Mosala contends, "black theologians break ideologically and theoretically with bourgeois biblical-hermeneneutical assumptions, black theology cannot become an effective weapon of struggle for its oppressed people". In other words, implicit in the historical crisis is a methodological crisis.

The methodological crisis

The central question of this methodological crisis is, then, "What is the most appropriate hermeneutical approach to be followed so that Black Theology may become a truly liberating force in the black community?"[53] Or, reflecting Mosala's emphasis, what will a *theoretically well-grounded* biblical hermeneutics of liberation look like?[54]

According to Mosala there are two main issues which need to considered here. First, "there is the question of the historical-cultural foundations and links of black theology and how these affect black theology's biblical-hermeneutical assumptions".[55] This issue is particularly important in an attempt to develop a biblical hermeneutics of liberation because it arises from "an understanding that people's reading of the Bible is framed by their history and culture".[56] In other words, in order to become a weapon of struggle for the oppressed black people, "black theology needs to relocate itself within the historical and cultural struggles of these people".[57]

Second, and this is the crux of the methodological crisis within liberation hermeneutics, "black theology must openly declare where it stands ideologically and theoretically. It is not enough to be on the opposition side in societal struggles. The very fact that a specifically black theology of liberation is needed, in spite of the existence of opposition theologies in traditional Christian circles, underscores this point". In other words, "Existential commitments to the liberation struggles of the oppressed are inadequate because those who are committed in this way are often still ideologically and theoretically enslaved to the dominant discourses in the society". In the case of black theology, and specifically in respect of the biblical hermeneutical aspect being dealt with here, "this means that the liberating power of this theological discourse becomes limited. Even more serious, the ideological and theoretical enslavement of black theology to the biblical hermeneutics of dominant theologies leads to a promotion of those theologies rather than black theologies". In sum, "a clear ideological and theoretical break with the dominant practices and discourses is necessary if a biblical hermeneutics of black liberation is to emerge".[58]

Conclusion

In this chapter I have argued that the Bible has been perceived as both an oppressor and a liberator within the black community, whether from a historical or a methodological perspective. Although the historical dimension is a part of the present interpretive crisis in South Africa, the major part of this crisis is methodological. That this is the case can be seen by returning to *The Kairos Document.*

The methodological concerns of Mosala are echoed in the *The Kairos Document* with which we began. The following paragraph which introduces a proposal towards a prophetic theology is an important example.

> To be truly prophetic, our response would have to be, in the first place, solidly grounded in the Bible. Our KAIROS impels us *to return to the Bible* and to search the Word of God for a message that is relevant to what we are experiencing in South Africa today. This will be no mere academic exercise. Prophetic theology differs from academic theology because, whereas academic theology deals with all biblical themes in a systematic manner and formulates general Christian principles and doctrines, prophetic theology concentrates on those aspects of the Word of God that have an immediate bearing upon the critical situation in which we find ourselves. The theology of the prophets does not pretend to be comprehensive and complete, it speaks to the particular circumstances of a particular time and place—the KAIROS.[59]

The use of the word "concerns" above is particularly apt here. This paragraph, like the rest of *The Kairos Document* and other works of black theology, contains elements that "concern" Mosala in both senses of the word. On the one hand, the paragraph contains elements of his two main tasks which need to be considered in *a theoretically well-grounded* biblical hermeneutics of liberation. In particular, there is a concern for commitment to the community of the poor and the oppressed, and there is a recognition that *The Kairos Document*'s biblical hermeneutics involves a break with dominant biblical hermeneutics.[60] On the other hand, the paragraph contains elements which worry Mosala in that they do not contribute to *a theoretically well-grounded* biblical hermeneutics of liberation. In particular, there is no clear ideological and theoretical understanding of the break with dominant biblical hermeneutics, which may mean in fact that *The Kairos Document* is still ideologically and theoretically enslaved to the dominant discourses in biblical hermeneutics.[61]

This chapter, then, has presented in outline the methodological concerns which I will elaborate and analyze in the following chapters.

Chapter Three

Modes of Reading the Bible in the South African Context of Liberation

Introduction

In chapter one I sketched the shape of a crisis in all interpretive activity. In chapter two I outlined an interpretive crisis in biblical hermeneutics in South Africa. These two chapters provide a theoretical framework for the discussion of this chapter. Chapter three, then, analyzes two modes of reading a biblical text, the Cain and Abel story, in the South African context of liberation. One mode of reading has its focus on the text while the other mode of reading has its focus behind the text. These two readings of the Cain and Abel story, one literary and the other sociological, arise from the work of two black South African interpreters.

As the first chapter suggests, there are a variety of factors, both theoretical and pragmatic, involved in the shift towards the reader. In biblical interpretation in particular, a number of related theoretical and pragmatic factors have turned the focus onto the relationship between the text and the reader. It is appropriate to briefly discuss some of these factors before my discussion of the two modes of reading the Cain and Abel story.

Liberative trends in biblical studies

In the context of this study one of the most important of these factors is a recovery of a form of pragmatism "which is more interested in the *effects* of communication than in its mechanics, and which flows from a growing dissatisfaction with 'standardized' or 'prescribed' readings that do not fit the specific circumstances of the contemporary reader".[1]

Such concerns have a long history in biblical interpretation. The whole notion of "hermeneutics" has undergone revision and expansion. As Anthony C. Thiselton points out,

> Traditionally hermeneutics entailed the formulation of rules for the understanding of an ancient text, especially in linguistic and historical terms. The interpreter was urged to begin with the language of the text, including its grammar, vocabulary, and style. He [sic] examined its linguistic, literary, and historical context. In other words, traditional hermeneutics began with the recognition that a text was conditioned by a given historical context. However, hermeneutics in the more recent sense of the term begins with the recognition that historical conditioning is two-sided: *the modern interpreter, no less than the text, stands in a given historical context and tradition.*[2]

As we have seen in the previous chapter, this recognition has led Wink and others to critique what Wink calls "the ideology of objectivism" in the historical-critical approach.[3]

Wink's reservations about historical-critical methods are twofold. First, he argues that they do not complete the whole hermeneutical process. Second, he argues that while the questions posed by the historical-critical method are admittedly necessary,[4] they are not always the questions which best allow the text to "speak" to people today. The texts of the Bible, he insists, speak to practical issues about life, especially life within communities. These are not always the same as the questions which interest the scholarly guild.[5]

Lategan too notes that there is growing dissatisfaction with the exegetical results achieved by means of the historical-critical method. This dissatisfaction, Lategan adds, is not simply a naive rejection of critical thought.[6] In the case of the Indian Jesuit, George Soares-Prabhu, this dissatisfaction comes from someone who is trained in using the tools of modern historical criticism and who admits that historical

criticism cannot be by-passed; he simply doubts its suffi-
ciency.[7] His experiences in teaching and pastoral work in
India have led him to describe the historical-critical method
as "ineffective, irrelevant, and ideologically loaded" and to
propose a more contextual approach to biblical interpretation.[8]

Two aspects of the above discussion should be hightlighted
here. First, there is growing insistence, particularly in the
Third World, that interpretation should produce "practical",
relevant results. Second, there can be no doubt that the situation of the reader functions as a co-determinant in the communication process. Lategan elaborates on this second point
when he says,

> In fact, the movement towards 'contextual theology' is another
> manifestation of this trend. Seen from a hermeneutical perspec-
> tive, the different 'interest' theologies, like black theology and lib-
> eration theology can be interpreted as a further development along
> this line. The situation of the reader or the receiving community is
> accorded normative status, which not only determines the the-
> matic approach to biblical material, but also becomes a lever to
> dislodge established exegetical procedures.[9]

Two broad "modes" of reading have emerged in response
to such reader oriented critiques of the historical-critical
method, one literary and the other sociological.[10]

Literary approaches

As the work of Hans Frei indicates, interest in the narrative aspects of biblical texts goes back a long way in the history of interpretation.[11] In both New Testament and Old Testament this dimension has always received attention.[12] But
there can be no doubt that in recent years there has been a
rediscovery of narrative and story in both biblical studies
and theology. Gabriel Fackre argues, significantly, that the
renewed interest in narrative is part of a wider cultural movement.

> The reclaiming of imagination in countercultural and other move-
> ments of the sixties and seventies is inextricable from the growing
> interest in story. Disenchantment with things abstract, rationalis-
> tic, cerebral, didactic, intellectualist, structured, prosaic, scientistic,
> technocratic, and the appeal of the concrete, affective, intuitive,
> spontaneous, poetic contributed to the story focus. The challenge
> of right brain to left brain and the preference of 'first order lan-

guage' to second and third order communication prepared the narrative soil.[13]

Lategan sees a connection between these developments and "the remarkable growth of Bible study groups on grassroots level", which, he suggests, are "not so much stimulated by a desire for a more simplistic approach . . . as it is part of a protest against the separation of expert and layman, theological faculties and church members, theory and *praxis*, theology and experience".[14]

Sociological approaches

From quite another angle comes the return of the historical question, but on a different level and in a different form. It reappears in a renewed "sociological" interest in the setting of the text and the reader,[15] in which "social scientific criticism completes the task of historical criticism by providing more or less detailed social referential readings of the biblical texts".[16] Once again, this is an area in biblical studies and theology in which there is a resurgence of interest. This is perhaps most evident in "materialistic" exegesis, which, significantly, Lategan argues is the "most extreme form of reception-oriented hermeneutics".[17]

Here it is important to note, as Lategan does, that although the focus in materialist readings is on the situation or context of production of the text, "this is done from a reader's perspective". What is at stake, he continues, is the *application of these texts in a contemporary situation. In conjunction with this, claims made on the basis of traditional interpretations are critiqued by revealing the biases which they harbour. "The reaction of materialistic exegesis against ruling conventions of exegesis is in fact a reaction against what is perceived as the ruling class".[18]

In summary, the shift toward the reader, whether via literary or sociological modes of reading, is also a shift towards pragmatism and contextual interpretation. "By accident or design, this development churned up in its wake issues that were supposed to be dead and buried and forced hermeneutics to reconsider some of its most prized positions".[19] And reconsider we must, particularly in the South African context of struggle. A detailed analysis of two readings of a specific biblical text will form the basis of this review in this chapter.

Two modes of reading the Cain and Abel story

We come now to two modes of reading the Cain and Abel story in the South African context. One mode of reading has its focus on the text while the other has its focus behind the text. It is not my concern to ask which method is "right", but rather to analyze what is going on methodologically in a particular mode of reading and how this relates to the context of struggle for liberation and life in South Africa. In the South African situation these are not merely "interesting" questions, they are questions that matter.

The focus here is on those who are committed to reading the Bible from within and for the community of struggle, the community of those who are victims of and those who are opposed to the apartheid system. Specifically, I will concentrate on the work of two black South African writers, Alan A. Boesak and Itumeleng J. Mosala, especially on their readings of the Cain and Abel story. I will include a detailed outline of their respective readings of the Cain and Abel story and an analysis of their respective modes of reading. This discussion will lead into an analysis of the relationship between a particular mode of reading and the liberation situation. Finally, I will sketch why it is that such analysis matters, particularly in the South African context, but also within biblical studies generally.

This chapter is, then, the fulcrum of the study. The analysis and discussion of these two readings raise the questions which will be dealt with in the remaining chapters of the study.

Reading the text

Boesak's reading of the story itself begins with a brief discussion of the possible significance of the names "Abel" (perhaps derived from the Hebrew *hebel*) and "Cain" (Hebrew *kayin*), suggesting that "In this story, then, there is a younger brother, a smaller and weaker brother; and a stronger brother, the ruler, the creator".[20]

He then draws attention to what he sees to be the narrative emphasis on "brother". "The author time after time underlines the fact that Cain and Abel were brothers. We are not to forget that they were brothers". Boesak then elaborates what it means to be a brother.

> This responsibility involves being human in community with one another in God's world. It means to seek together for true humanity; to attempt together to make something of God's objectives visibly operative in the world; to let something of God's own heart become visible in fraternal relationships; and, in corporate relationship to history, to humanize the world and keep it humanized. This is what it means to be a brother.

But "Cain rejects this human responsibility in the most abominable manner: he murders his brother". "The story does not focus merely on a crime, but on the most heinous crime. Cain did not kill some anonymous person; he murdered his own brother". In other words, "this story concerns the core of humanity".[21]

Boesak detects sarcasm and humour in Cain's response to God's question "Where is your brother Abel?". "Cain asks God, 'Am I the herdsman of the herdsman?' But God does not share Cain's humour, for the matter at hand is very serious. It involves life and death".[22]

God's punishment of Cain is then discussed in some detail. Boesak underlines Cain's fear, even though Cain is not punished with death. "Why do you do this to me? My punishment is too heavy to bear". Boesak argues that "Cain knows, however, what it means that he no longer fits in with the land". As a farmer the "whole of his life and all his hope is bound up with the land". "Now Cain must leave all this. He no longer possesses the land. He must go and live in the land of Nod". And, Boesak continues, "Nod is 'east of Eden' - that is, away from the land that God designated as the place where Cain and Abel were to live human lives, where they were to be men, brothers, real people. Eden was the place, the garden, where true humanity was born; where God brought people together; where God said, 'Here, together, in community, we begin human history.'"[23] Boesak concludes his discussion of the first curse by developing the image of "the earth". "The earth can no longer be fruitful for him. It is after all the same earth that opened its mouth and drank the blood of Abel, his brother. Therefore, the earth can no longer bear fruit for him. The earth mourns. The earth chokes in blood, and cannot respond to Cain. The earth can no longer converse with him. The earth can no longer return anything to him. Cain's relationship to the land is ruptured".[24]

Cain also comes under a second curse. "He must be a wanderer, a vagabond, in the world. Nod is a 'state of mind' in which one wanders forever. Cain must live as someone who has no goal. Never again will he be at rest. Never again will there be fixed ground, a known place, beneath his feet. Never again will there be a place where he belongs, where he is at home".[25]

Having followed the contours of the text Boesak then relates his reading to "us", and more specifically to the South African situation.

> What does that mean for us? I think the story meant to tell us that oppressors shall have no place on God's earth. Oppressors have no home. Oppressors do not belong to, are not at home in God's objectives for this world. They have gone out of bounds. They have removed themselves from the world. Cain did not only break his relationship to the land, but also his relationship to God. Because Abel is no longer there, there is no longer a relationship to God. This is what the story says. When Abel no longer lives and Cain is 'brotherless,' then Cain immediately is 'Godless.' 'Look,' he says, 'you hide your face from me. You send me from your presence.' Oppressors have no place, no rest for their souls.[26]

Later he adds, "those who take another's life can never again be certain about their own life. They continue to wonder when the hour of vengeance will toll for them". The "violent and oppressive are very anxious, uncertain, frightened people. They live in anxiety and fear because they are the constant cause of anxiety and fear in others. They must live with their own conscience. They do not sleep well. It may appear that they do, but that appearance is deceptive. They do not have rest for their souls".[27]

Boesak goes on to say that he could "give countless illustrations of this from South Africa".[28] After a number of illustrations he sums up.

> And so whites remain anxious and fearful. They live in anxiety because they never know what might happen next. The really frightened ones who are eaten up with anxiety, are those who think that peace lies in the insecurity and oppression of the other; those who

think that peace lies in the ability to destroy the other; to take the life of the other; those who think that to intimidate the other and to threaten the death of the other constitutes their own security and certainty.[29]

Boesak then continues with his reading of the story. "Cain continues to live. He continues to live, I suspect, to make it clear that his type of life—a life of restlessness, uneasiness, uncertainty, violence, ceaseless wandering, a life in which there is no peace with God and one's fellows—is not what is intended for those who earnestly seek God". "There is a second reason", he continues, "why Cain remains alive: God gives Cain an opportunity to ask forgiveness".[30] Boesak does not offer any support for the latter contention from the story; instead he goes to the New Testament and the example of Jesus who forgives the murderer on the cross.

Boesak then returns to the story and follows its final form through the "Lamech story". "History moves on. Does Cain's generation learn anything? Does it improve? Or do we learn, rather, that Cain's generation cannot change, cannot improve? It seems that things cannot change".[31] However, once again he draws on the New Testament. "Here, again, we can see what a difference Jesus of Nazareth makes in human history: the words of Lamech are reversed by Jesus. Lamech says that he will be avenged seventy-seven times over. But Jesus tells his followers to forgive others not seventy-seven times, but seventy times seven times".[32]

The South African situation is addressed once more. "Is it possible to transcend our present situation in South Africa? Can it still happen? I do not know. I do not know how to tell Blacks in South Africa to forgive seventy times seven times— those who have seen their own children shot and killed in the streets. I do not know how to tell them this".[33] Boesak goes on to catalogue other examples of black suffering and oppression. In the face of such oppression, he argues, "We ought not to speak too hastily about forgiveness and similar matters". "And yet", he continues, "we read these words of the Lord, words that we cannot avoid. Ought we to believe that what is impossible for us is possible for God? With God all things are possible, including forgiveness welling up out of the hearts of suffering and oppressed Black South Africans. That too. Precisely that".[34]

Boesak concludes his reading of the Cain and Abel story by following the final form of the text through to its end in the birth of Seth.

> The story of Cain ends with the report of a joyful event. Adam and Eve have another son. His name is Seth. Eve says, 'God has given me another son in the place of Abel who Cain killed.' She does not repudiate history. She does not bypass this tragic event as if it had not happened. She does not ignore reality. She knows this, only this: with this child God wishes to begin all over again with her— and therefore also with other people. The story ends not in tragedy but in words of hope: 'At that time men began to call upon the name of the Lord' (Gen. 5:26). After murder, after death, after anni- hilation and inhumanity, God begins again.[35]

"That, brothers and sisters, is, I think, the most hopeful word in the gospel of Jesus Christ. After oppression, mur- der, terror, inhumanity, apartheid, and the gobbling up of the profits of apartheid, and finally death—after all this, God still wishes to begin all over again with us".[36]

In his reading of the Cain and Abel story Boesak does not advocate an explicit methodology underlying his mode of read- ing. Although he refers to the author he shows no interest in the author's intentions except as these are manifest in the text. Also, he gives no evidence here of any interest in the usual historical-critical concerns.[37] Throughout his reading of the Cain and Abel story he follows the final form of the text with careful attention to literary detail and the central themes. In other words, Boesak reads the text and in front of the text.[38]

However, the way in which Boesak describes his mode of reading another text, *Revelation*,[39] may be useful here in clari- fying his reading methodology. He rejects a number of inter- pretive approaches for two reasons: either they are too his- torical and so lack relevance for today or they are too sym- bolic and so show little concern for the historical context of the text. He advocates, rather, a *"contemporary-historical understanding"* of this text. Such an approach argues that this text cannot be understood outside of the historical and political context of its time.[40] But this approach also argues that the book has relevance in more than one historical mo- ment; in other words, "we see with some astonishment how truly, how authentically, that John, in describing his own time, is describing the times in which we live".[41] In sum, Boesak is interested in the broad historical and political context to which *the text* refers and so draws on historical-critical research. However, he always reads the text in its final form and always has his focus on the text or in front of the text rather than on the historical (and sociological) particularities behind the text. Although he is here dealing with a rather different genre of text, I would argue that what he calls a contemporary-historical understanding sums up his approach to the Cain and Abel story as well.

There are three interpretive procedures which consistently underlie his mode of reading. A crucial interpretive procedure in Boesak's mode of reading is to read this text from within a particular community of struggle, the oppressed black South African community. This interpretive procedure is quite explicit in his reading of the Cain and Abel story.[42]

A related interpretive procedure is evident in the link Boesak establishes between this story and the community of struggle. In his initial reflections on this story he argues that we ought not to regard the story of Cain and Abel as either remote from or irrelevant to us today.

> The story of Cain and Abel is a story about two types or kinds of people. It is a very human story that is still being enacted today. This story does not tell us in the first place what happened once upon a time; rather, it tells us about something that happens today. Because this story is a human story, we find very human elements in it and elements from our own human history.[43]

Boesak's second interpretive procedure, then, is to advocate a common humanity connecting this "very human story" with "our own human history". This identity or commonality between story and reader is what enables understanding to take place, and what bridges the hermeneutic gap between "then" and "now". However, expressing this connection in these general, universal terms is not sufficient. Boesak goes on to make it quite clear that his specific concern is in the connection between the situation of struggle in the text and the situation of struggle in South Africa.

Third, it should be quite clear by now that Boesak's focus is on the text. He reads the final form of the Cain and Abel story with careful attention to its literary and thematic characteristics. In addition, he not only reads the text as a self-contained story but also as part of the Christian canon, a characteristic feature of reading in front of the text.

But there are a number of features of Boesak's mode of reading which are not clear. As Boesak does not articulate a clear methodology underlying his mode of reading it is not clear *why* Boesak adopts this particular mode of reading.[44] Also, it is not clear whether the focus for Boesak is on the struggle of the *characters* within the narrative or on *real people* who are represented in the narrative.[45]

We turn now to the relationship between Boesak's mode of reading and the struggle for liberation in South Africa. Throughout his reading he allows the story to speak to us today. His concern is not "what happened once upon a time" but rather that "it tells us about something that happens today".[46] The link between the text and the liberation struggle today is based on two factors: first, a general commitment to read the text from within *a particular situation of struggle*, and second, *an analogy of struggle* which links the present South African situation of struggle with a past situation of struggle, a situation of struggle which is located *in the text* and *in front of the text*.

Reading behind the text

Mosala's reading of the Cain and Abel story arises out of his response to Boesak's reading of the story.[47] My concern at this stage is not to examine Mosala's critique of Boesak's reading but to construct from his comments his own reading of the Cain and Abel story.

Having briefly summarized Boesak's reading of the Cain and Abel story, Mosala briefly outlines his own reading. He begins by arguing that the "category of social struggle as a biblical hermeneutical tool necessitates a historical-critical starting point for an exegesis of Genesis 4". The questions which emanate from this approach are, among others: "What historical point is reflected by the discursive practice this text represents? What are the social, cultural, class, gender, and racial issues at work in this text? What is the ideological-spiritual agenda of the text, that is, how does the text itself seek to be understood?"[48]

With these questions in mind Mosala outlines his own reading of the text.

It is generally accepted within biblical scholarship that Genesis 4 is part of the *J*-document of the Pentateuch. Most scholars also concur that the *J*-document is to be located historically in the Davidic-Solomonic era of the Israelite monarchy. The royal scribes of Solomon, in particular, are credited with having undertaken to write the history of the united monarchy using the traditions of the various groups. This production of the history of Israel by the royal scribes is acknowledged to be dominated in its discursive practice by the concerns of the Davidic-Solomonic state. These concerns involve such matters as the change of socioeconomic structures, for example, from the premonarchical egalitarian tribal system to the semifeudal tributary-exploitive monarchical system. They also involve the need for an ideological explanation of the creation in Israel of large estates (*latifundia*), which were privately owned, and the simultaneous large-scale dispossession of the majority of the peasant producers of Israel from their *nahalahs* (II Kgs. 21), or inherited plots of land. Included in these concerns are matters such as the development of the social division of labor on which was predicated deep class distinctions. New social struggles developed around this division of labor in the monarchy, into which the prophetic movement was to insert itself in very specific ways, most of them not necessarily revolutionary.[49]

Mosala then goes on to argue that Genesis 4 represents one such production of the royal scribes of the Davidic-Solomonic monarchy.

The question of the division of the labor is excellently inscribed in this text through the struggle between the pastoral sector and the agricultural sector of the economy. The agenda of this story seems to be the legitimation of the process of dispossession of freeholding peasants by the new class of estate holders under the protection of the monarchical state. Clearly, Cain the tiller of the soil must be seen to represent the freeholding peasantry who become locked in a life-and-death struggle with the emergent royal and latifundiary classes, represented in this story by Abel. Obviously, the text favors Abel and enlists divine pleasure on his side. The reason Abel is depicted as a pastoralist must have something to do with the division of labor mentioned above and the way in which it fed the regional specialization so important to the ruling classes . . . Expropriating the lands of the peasant producers for purposes of increasing and intensifying ruling-class herding, plowing, viticulture, and orcharding was a practice that is very well attested in Israelite traditions, not least in Genesis 4. The problem, of course, is that these traditions must be understood as ideological productions—spiritual ideological productions certainly, but ideological productions nonetheless. Thus their signification of the historical and social processes of Israel is necessarily in some way reflective of, even though not exhausted by, the class and political interests of the conditions of their production.[50]

In the case of Genesis 4, Mosala continues, "roles are changed around. The story chooses to depict the victorious and successful groups of the tenth and ninth century B.C.E., the Israelite monarchy, as the victims and vice versa, thus lending ideological legitimacy to the process of latifundialization and peasant land dispossession that took place".[51]

On the issue of whether an offering was acceptable or unacceptable to the Lord, Mosala contends, "a critical biblical hermeneutics of liberation would have immediately thought of the question of the Israelite monarchy's ruling classes' practice of exacting tribute from the village peasants. This perspective would have raised the question of the class struggle in monarchical Israel and how its reality is signified in a discursive ideological textual practice such as Genesis 4 represents".[52]

Mosala concludes his reading by arguing that there is also evidence that village peasants

> often resisted encroachments on their *nahalahs*. While no indication of their victories exist in the texts of the Bible, except in the New Testament (Matt. 21:33ff.), it is reasonable to believe that the death of Abel may stand for one such victory. But, of course, the text comes to us from the hands of the ruling class, and thus one could hardly expect a celebration of Abel's representative demise. The class and ideological commitments of Genesis 4 are unequivocal. This factor, however, is not immediately obvious to the reader. It requires a reading that issues out of a firm grounding in the struggle for liberation, as well as a basis in critical theoretical perspectives which can expose the deep structure of a text.[53]

Mosala articulates a clear methodology which underlies his mode of reading. His interpretive procedures are clear. His initial procedure as far as the text is concerned is to use historical-critical methods to determine the text and its context. For Mosala the important consequence of applying these methods is that they place the text in its socio-historical setting, which in this case is the monarchic period. With the identification of this setting Mosala then moves into a historical-materialist analysis of the text.

And here we see Mosala's focus. It is on the historical-materialist context behind the text of which the text itself is a product.[54] Mosala's materialist method incorporates two related interpretive procedures: it inquires into the material conditions of the text (which includes an analysis of the nature of the mode of production, the constellation of classes necessitated by that mode, and the nature of the ideological manifestations arising out of and referring back to that mode of production) and the ideological conditions of the text (including the class origins of the text and the class interests of the text). Underlying these inquiries is the recognition that the Bible is a site of specific historical-cultural class conflicts.[55]

Not only are these two related procedures applied to the text, they are also applied to the biblical reader. Inseparable from the material and ideological conditions of the text are the material and ideological conditions of the reader, and these need to be investigated in similar terms.[56]

> The point that is being made here is that the ideological condition and commitment of the reader issuing out of the class circumstances of such a reader are of immense hermeneutical significance. The biblical hermeneutics of liberation is thoroughly tied up with the political commitments of the reader. This means that not only is the Bible a product and a record of class struggles, but it is also a site of similar struggles acted out by the oppressors and oppressed, exploiters and exploited of our society even as they read the Bible.

> Those, therefore, that are committed to the struggles of the black oppressed and exploited people cannot ignore the history culture, and ideologies of the dominated black people as their primary hermeneutical starting point. There can be no Black Theology of liberation and no corresponding biblical hermeneutics of liberation outside of the black struggle for both survival and liberation. Such a struggle, however, requires being as clear about issues in the black community as possible.[57]

In other words, the cultural, historical, and ideological situatedness of both the text and the reader provide the hermeneutical weapons for reading the Bible. More specifically, Mosala contends that the "social-ideological location and commitment of the reader must be accorded *methodological* priority", and for this reason he sees the category of "the black struggle" from precolonial times to the present as an important hermeneutical factor. With respect to the text, Mosala attempts to draw out the cultural and ideological presuppositions inherent in the text in order to "bounce them off those of the history, culture, and class of the reader" so as to "unleash the forces of struggle that each brings in the encounter with the other". In this way "one can relive the struggle of the communities behind the texts as well as that of the communities this side of the texts as a new*practice*".[58]

However, Mosala is insistent that the struggles of the biblical communities do not appear in the Bible "as mirror reflections of the real". Rather, "they have been produced as new textual practices: they come to us as *signified practices*".[59] And crucial to Mosala's mode of reading is the identification and *critical* appropriation of such signified practices.

In summary, then, there are three major links in the relationship between Mosala's mode of reading and the liberation struggle in South Africa. There is first, a general commitment to read the text from within *a particular situation of struggle*; second, *an analogy of struggle* which links the present South African situation of struggle with a past situation of struggle, a situation of struggle which is located *behind the text*; and third, *an analogy of method* which applies a similar method of historical-materialist analysis to the present South African situation of struggle as to the analysis of the text and the situation of struggle behind the text.

Modes of reading and the context of struggle

My analysis of these two readings of the Cain and Abel story can now be taken further as we compare and contrast Boesak's and Mosala's respective modes of reading.

An important similarity is their common commitment to read the Bible from within the community of struggle in South Africa. A related similarity is the important role the analogy of struggle plays in their readings. In other words, their common commitment to the liberation struggle in South Africa provides an interpretive procedure which links the situation of struggle in the text, in front of the text, or behind the text with their own situation of struggle.

A significant difference between their respective readings has to do with where they locate the past situation of struggle. Boesak locates the past situation of struggle in the text and in front of the text, so his focus is on the text itself. Mosala locates the past situation of struggle behind the text, so his focus is behind the text. For Mosala this interpretive focus is crucial, hence what I have called his analogy of method. Boesak does not put forward an analogy of method, at least not explicitly.

So both Boesak and Mosala use an analogy of struggle to link a past struggle with their present struggle. But they differ on where this past struggle is to be located. For Boesak the focus is the struggle portrayed in the text and in front of the text, a struggle which we have access to by a careful reading of the final form of the text from the perspective of the struggle for liberation. For Mosala the focus is the struggle behind the text, a struggle which is only reflected in the deep structure of the text, a struggle which the text in most instances masks and which we only have access to by a historical-materialist reading of the text from the perspective of a historical-materialist understanding of the struggle for liberation. Phrasing it in this way makes it clear why Mosala sees the stronger challenge as an analogy of method; the actual past situation is of secondary importance while the method of analysis itself is foregrounded.[60]

I will now briefly outline some of the implications of the discussion so far. In other words, I will outline why it is that such analysis matters, particularly in the South African context.

Grounds for solidarity and dialogue

I would claim that the similarities between Boesak and Mosala, specifically their common commitment to read the Bible from within the South African community of struggle and their common use of an analogy of struggle in their respective modes of reading, are sufficient grounds for dialogue concerning their differences.

More importantly, I would suggest that such dialogue is not only possible but also vital in the South African context, particularly among those who are committed to reading the Bible within the struggle for liberation and life in South Africa. Among those sharing such a commitment are those who adopt a variety of modes of reading the Bible. At this time when the prophetic voice of the church is strangely silent, dialogue among those who share a commitment to the struggle for liberation and life in South Africa is vital.[61] Among those committed to reading the Bible within this community, notwithstanding their differences, these are not only sufficient grounds for such dialogue and critique, but, I would argue, required grounds.

So it is with a clear recognition of the important similarities in their modes of reading that I now turn to some of the questions that the differences in their modes of reading raise.

Questions arising

A question of interpretive interests

An obvious question which arises is whether a particular commitment to a particular community of struggle demands not only a commitment to reading the Bible from within and for the community of struggle but also particular interpretive interests. This is what Mosala is advocating in his analogy of method, as is clear when he argues that his fundamental objection to the biblical hermeneutics of black theology "is that not only does it suffer from an 'unstructural understanding of the Bible', but—both as a consequence and as a reason—it also suffers from an unstructural understanding of the black experience and struggle".[62] Although Mosala is here offering a critique of Boesak's mode of reading, he is not calling into question Boesak's commitment to the community of struggle.

> The problem is basically one of contradiction. It has to do with the difficult area of the interface between personal existential commitments and structural-ideological locations as well as frameworks of political acitivity. It is not enough to be existentially committed to the struggles of the oppressed and exploited people. One must

also effect a theoretical break with the assumptions and perspectives of the dominant discourse of a stratified society.[63]

Also, Mosala recognizes that interpreters like Boesak are clearly correct "in detecting glimpses of liberation and of a determinate social movement galvanised by a powerful religious ideology in the biblical text". However, he argues, "The existence of this phenomenon is not in question; rather, the problem here is one of developing an adequate hermeneutical framework which can rescue those liberative themes from the biblical text. One cannot successfully perform this task by denying the oppressive structures that frame what liberating themes the texts encode".[64] So with respect to the Cain and Abel story Mosala argues that "Boesak's reading of this story is in complete ideological collusion with the text and its rhetorical intentions: to legitimate the process of land expropriation by the ruling classes of David's monarchy from the village peasants in the hill country of Palestine in the 10th century B.C.E." Mosala then exclaims,

'Kgakgamatso! Mohlolo! Isismanga! What a miracle!' Africans would say. The story of the oppressed has been stolen by the oppressors and is being used as an ideological weapon against the oppressed in subsequent histories. The point is that there is no historical basis in this period of Israel's history to support the argument that the oppressors were made homeless, wanderers, and vagabonds. Neither is there any historical evidence in previous or subsequent epochs to support the assertion that oppressors can be made homeless, even by their murder of the oppressed.[65]

In other words, "existential" or "contextual" modes of reading like Boesak's,

cannot be allowed to substitute for a theoretically well-grounded biblical hermeneutics of liberation. The reason for this is that, while texts that are against oppressed people may be co-opted by the interlocutors of the liberation struggle, the fact that these texts have their ideological roots in oppressive practices means that the texts are capable of undergirding the interests of the oppressors even when used by the oppressed. In other words, oppressive texts cannot be totally tamed or subverted into liberating texts.[66]

So, like Terry Eagleton's "revolutionary cultural worker", biblical interpreters in the community of struggle must not only be "projective" and "appropriative" but also "polemical" in their reading of the Bible.[67]

But are Mosala's interpretive interests the only ones we
ought to use in the South African context of struggle? Certainly there are those interpreters in the community of struggle who argue that the text, or more of it than Mosala would
accept, does not mask but in fact reflects the struggle behind the text. For example, Gunther Wittenberg argues that
"during the Solomonic era theologians responded in different ways to the challenges posed by the political dispensa-
tion. Theologians at the court were eager to legitimize Solomon's rule and to develop a state theology". But, he continues, this "theology from above" was challenged by a resistance theology "from below" both in Israel and in Judah.[68]
More significantly, Wittenberg argues that the primeval history (Genesis 2-11) is not "an effort in royal theology" but in
fact the opposite, "it is an unmistakable critique of the
Jerusalemite state theology".[69] He uses the Cain and Abel
story as an example. Following B. Oded and Gottwald he
argues that the genealogy of Noah "reflects the basic division
between the city and the countryside. The key variables, according to Gottwald, in discriminating the two contrasting
forms of socio-political life are political domination versus
political decentralization, and social stratification versus social egalitarianism".[70] Wittenberg continues, "While state theology in Jerusalem has a city perspective, the author of the
primeval history leaves no doubt about where his sympa-
thies lie. His perspective is the perspective of the Judean
'people of the land'".[71]

> This basic contrast is also highlighted in the story of Cain and
> Abel. Abel is the prototype of the Judean herdsman while Cain,
> after the murder of his brother, wanders towards the east and be-
> comes the founder of a city, just like Nimrod in the genealogy of
> Ham. Cain is the ancestor of Lamech, the prototype of a man of
> violence, who boasts that he will revenge every wrong done to him
> not only sevenfold but seventy-seven fold (Gen. 4:24). The message
> of the Yahwist is clear. Violence and the upheaval in societies ema-
> nate from the strong man, the builders of cities and empires.[72]

Clearly Wittenberg is dialoguing here with Mosala on his
own terms, using a similar mode of reading.[73]

The question still remains, however; is there a "*theoretically well-grounded* biblical hermeneutics of liberation" which
could support something like Boesak's mode of reading?[74]

An attempt at such an answer might develop along post-critical lines in a literary, canonical, or a thematic/meta-phoric/symbolic direction.[75] Nothing like this has yet emerged from biblical interpreters in the South African community of struggle.

However, whether or not modes of reading similar to that of Boesak's have *a theoretically well-grounded* biblical hermeneutics of liberation, they clearly do have some form of a biblical hermeneutics of liberation, a hermeneutics which I have attempted to sketch. Given the existence of these two modes of reading, there are a number of other important questions which arise out of their differences.

A question of tradition

There is the question of the interpreter's relationship with the biblical tradition. What is the status of the biblical tradition in these respective readings? Boesak's mode of reading seems to affirm the biblical tradition while Mosala's mode of reading is suspicious of the biblical tradition or, possibly, even rejects the biblical tradition. Mosala clearly questions Boesak's uncritical acceptance of the biblical tradition, but he is not so clear on his own understanding of the status of the biblical tradition. He seems to occilate between a concern to stand in continuity with the biblical tradition and a merely pragmatic use of the biblical tradition.

Besides these important questions there is the question of what the implications are of embracing these respective readings for the ecclesiastical traditions in which we stand? For example, while it is extremely unlikely that a significant group like the African Independent Churches would ever embrace Mosala's social scientific, historical-materialist reading of the Bible, they would probably be receptive to Boesak's final form reading of the Bible. In their booklet, *Speaking for Ourselves*, they write: "We read the Bible as a book that comes from God and we take every word in the Bible seriously". "Some people will say that we are therefore 'fundamentalists'. We do not know whether that word applies to us or not but we are not interested in any interpretation of the Bible that softens or waters down its message . . . We do not have the same problems about the Bible as White people have with their Western scientific mentality".[76] In other words, what are the implications of Boesak's affirmation of the biblical tradition and Mosala's suspicion (perhaps even rejection) of the biblical tradition for these and other interpretive groupings?[77]

A question of class

A related question concerns the extent to which these respective readings are accessible to the people, or more importantly, the extent to which such readings emanate from the people. Recent research into the ways in which a cross-section of ordinary South African people read the Bible suggests that hermeneutically these ordinary interpreters are closer to Boesak's mode of reading than they are to Mosala's. One could argue that a final form or literary reading is a more egalitarian reading, whereas a socio-scientific reading is produced by a new middle-class, elitist, social scientific "priesthood".[78]

And yet research also shows that there is a considerable openness among ordinary interpreters to historical and sociological perspectives.[79] Mosala himself argues that black interpreters like Boesak and others "have been surpassed by the largely illiterate black working class and poor peasantry who have defied the canon of Scripture, with its ruling class ideological basis, by appropriating the Bible in their own way using the cultural tools emerging out of their struggle for survival".[80]

The role of the "organic intellectual" is obviously a question which arises here. Many of the middle class involved in contexts of liberation find Gramsci's conception of organic intellectuals helpful. Gramsci views organic intellectuals as leaders and thinkers directly tied into a particular community of struggle primarily by means of institutional affiliations. Organic intellectuals combine theory and action, and relate popular culture and religion to structural social change.[81]

Clearly the roles of such organic intellectuals would differ substantially within the two modes of reading. For example, the role of Carlos Mesters in *God's Project*, a sociological retelling of the Bible story which is based on the work of Norman Gottwald and others, is substantially different from that of Ernesto Cardenal in *The Gospel in Solentiname*, the recorded commentary of *campesinos* discussing various biblical texts.[82]

A question of truth

A related question concerns the truth claims of the respective readings. One could argue that the truth claims for a reading which focuses behind the text is the social scientific evidence which supports that reading, but what kinds of truth claims could one make concerning literary, canonical, or thematic/symbolic readings? Or should we go further and argue that none of these kinds of truth really matter but that what we need to do is to accept "a practical and communal knowledge, which tests the truth of a position [or reading] by asking whether and how it might apply to the practice - that is, the history - of the community"?.[83]

A question of function

Perhaps one of the most appropriate questions in a discussion of liberation heremeneutics is what function or use a particular mode of reading might have in a situation of struggle. This question is obviously closely related to the question of interpretive interests, but from a slightly different point of view. The question here, then, is what does a particular mode of reading do for the liberation struggle? What role can each play in bringing about transformation in South Africa?[84]

Such questions and other related questions form the basis of the discussion in subsequent chapters.

Grounds for challenge

I suggested in my introduction that this study has implications not only for our own South African context of struggle but also for biblical studies generally.

As literary and sociological modes of reading are among the most dominant modes of reading in biblical studies many of the issues raised in my discussion of liberation hermeneutics are pertinent to the wider debate. I will draw attention to these connections in subsequent chapters.

However, the most important challenge arises from Boesak's and Mosala's common commitment to reading the Bible from within a particular community, the community of the poor and oppressed in South Africa. Biblical studies has never been "neutral" or "objective", something which the poor, the marginalized, and the oppressed everywhere have long recognized. The challenge from the South African context of struggle is first, to affirm that one does and should have commitments in reading the Bible and, second, to argue that these commitments should be shaped by the poor and oppressed.[85]

Conclusion

The analysis of two modes of reading a particular biblical text in this chapter has, I hope, generated some insight into the central concerns of this study. The parameters of what I understand by liberation hermeneutics in the South African context should now be clearer. The analysis in this chapter has also generated a host of questions. The South African context of struggle has not only raised such questions but also demands that the questions raised here are analyzed and discussed. The remaining chapters of this study attempt to take up some of these questions in detail, the primary purpose being, as initially stated, to analyze, to clarify, and to challenge.

Two areas which require further probing have emerged with particular clarity from the analysis in this chapter. The importance of commitment to a particular community, the community of the poor and oppressed, in the work of both Mosala and Boesak raises the issue of *accountability*. That both Mosala and Boesak continue to work within the Christian tradition, albeit in different ways, raises the issue of *continuity*. Chapter four explores the former and chapter five the latter.

Chapter Four

The Reader
and the Community:
Accountability and Solidarity

Introduction

"The established methodology of First World theology—
often regarded as a universally valid norm—has recently been
challenged. The challenge comes from different quarters in
Africa, Asia, and Latin America, but it also comes from certain groups within the First World, e.g., from Christians within
the feminist and labour movements".[1] With this statement
Per Frostin begins his incisive study of liberation theology in
Tanzania and South Africa.

Like others, Frostin uses Thomas Kuhn's notion of scientific paradigms to explain the methodological shift in theologies of liberation.[2] More specifically, some interpreters within
theologies of liberation use Kuhn's phrase for scientific revolutions, "paradigm shifts", to explain the magnitude of the
methodological changes now taking place in theology and
biblical interpretation.[3] According to Frostin, who works from
a liberation perspective, "the theological debate of today is
viewed as a conflict between an established, 'hegemonic' paradigm and a counter-hegemonic approach, emerging from
what is called the periphery of power".[4]

Frostin goes on to offer a penetrating profile of the new
paradigm. He defines this new paradigm within theologies of
liberation with reference to five interrelated emphases: the

choice of the interlocutors of theology; the perception of God; the social analysis of conflicts; the choice of theological tools; and the relationship between theology and praxis.[5]

Of particular concern in this chapter as we attempt to take up some of the questions raised by the previous chapter is the first of these emphases, what Frostin calls "the interlocutors of theology".[6] I argued in chapter three that the importance of commitment to a particular community, the community of the poor and oppressed, in the work of both Mosala and Boesak raises the issue of *accountability and solidarity*.[7] This chapter, then, examines the crucial role of accountability and solidarity in liberation hermeneutics. I begin with a brief summary of the new paradigm, focusing on the question of the interlocutors of interpretation. I then analyze in some detail the black experience of struggle in South Africa and the relationship of the biblical interpreter to this context of struggle.

A new paradigm

Frostin notes that all conferences of the Ecumenical Association of Third World Theologians (EATWOT) have argued persistently for a new method of doing theology. The focus of this stress on methodology is expressed in a concern for epistemology. As early as 1976 the founding members of EATWOT declared that this new methodology was based on a "radical break in epistemology".

> The theologies from Europe and North America are dominant today in our churches and represent one form of cultural domination. They must be understood to have arisen out of situations related to those countries, and therefore must not be uncritically adopted without our raising the question of their relevance in the context of our countries. Indeed, we must, in order to be faithful to the gospel and to our peoples, reflect on the realities of our own situations and interpret the word of God in relation to these realities. We reject as irrelevant an academic type of theology that is divorced from action. We are prepared for a radical break in epistemology which makes commitment the first act of theology and engages in critical reflection on the praxis of the reality of the Third World.[8]

This quotation makes two crucial points. First, in this new methodology there is a stress on epistemology. When liberation theologians stress the question of epistemological issues, questions related to the origin, structure, methods, and validity of knowledge, "the reason is obviously that they want to explain that their reflection cannot be assessed on the basis of established epistemology. In other words, they do not understand their own contribution as a meré reform within an existing framework but as a challenge to a basic consensus".[9]

Second, in this new methodology the experience of oppression and of the struggle for liberation are fundamental.[10] The opening phrases of one of the first reflections on liberation theologies, Gustavo Gutiérrez's *Theology of Liberation*, emphasizes the role of experience as the starting point for theological reflection: "This book is an attempt at reflection, based on the Gospel and the experiences of men and women committed to the process of liberation in the oppressed and exploited land of Latin America. It is a theological reflection born of the experience of shared efforts to abolish the current unjust situation to build a different society, freer and more human".[11]

The interlocutors of theology

Frostin argues that the emphasis on the experience of oppression and of the struggle for liberation sets this paradigm off from established theology in two respects. Firstly, the choice of what Frostin calls "social relations" is seen as the crux of theology. This is in marked contrast to the tendency since the Enlightenment to choose "ideas" as the distinguishing characteristics in Western theology. "In other words, liberation theologians focus on a new issue seldom discussed in established theology: Who are the interlocutors of the theology? Or, Who are asking the questions that theologians try to answer?"[12]

Second, this question of the interlocutors is given a new answer: "a preferential option for the poor". In clarifying this point Frostin compares the new paradigm with modern Western theology in two ways. He first compares the option for the oppressed as interlocutors of theology with the influential position of Schleiermacher, who addressed the "cultured critics" of religion.[13] In an important contribution to the first EATWOT conference, Gustavo Gutiérrez interpreted modern Western theology in the light of Schleiermacher's approach. The chief interlocutor of "progressivist" Western theology, he maintains, has been the educated nonbeliever. Liberation theology, by contrast, has chosen "nonpersons" as its chief interlocutors, "the poor, the exploited classes, the marginalized races, all the despised cultures".[14]

Clearly, then, the *epistemologica ruptura*, as it is sometimes called in Latin America, distinguishes liberation theologies not only from conservative but also from progressive Western theologies.[15] This distinction between theologies of liberation and progressivist theology is expressed with startling clarity in the following text:

> A goodly part of contemporary theology seems to take its start from the challenge posed by the *nonbeliever*. The nonbeliever calls into question our *religious world*, demanding its thoroughgoing purification and revitalization. Bonhoeffer accepted that challenge and incisively formulated the question that underlies much contemporary theological effort: How are we to proclaim God in a world come of age (*mündig*)? In a continent like Latin America, however, the main challenge does not come from the nonbeliever but from the nonhuman—i.e. the human being who is not recognized as such by the prevailing social order. These are the poor and exploited people, the ones who are systematically and legally despoiled of being human, those who scarcely know what a human being might be. These nonhumans do not call into question our religious world so much as they call into question our *economic, social, political, and cultural world*. Their challenge impels us toward a revolutionary transformation of the very bases of what is now a dehumanizing society. The question, then, is no longer how we are to speak about God in a world come of age; it is rather how to proclaim him Father in a world that is not human and what the implications might be of telling nonhumans that they are children of God.[16]

In the second comparison Frostin argues that in Western theology the relation to the poor is usually an ethical question, not an epistemological question. But, he continues, "such a distinction cannot do justice to the idea of the poor as interlocutors". According to the theologians of liberation, "solidarity with the poor also has consequences for the perception of the social reality, as seen in the phrase 'the epistemological privilege of the poor,' reportedly coined by Hugo Assmann".[17] This penetrating expression suggests, continues Frostin, "that cognizance of the experience of those defined as poor is a necessary condition for theological reflection".[18]

Before moving to the experience of the poor and oppressed in the South African context it is important to develop one other aspect of this discussion, namely, the move from "cognizance" to "commitment".[19]

The advocacy stance

Schüssler Fiorenza has consistently argued that "The basic insight of liberation theologies and their methodological starting point is the insight that all theology knowingly or not is by definition always engaged for or against the oppressed". In other words, "Intellectual neutrality is not possible in a historical world of exploitation and oppression".[20] Schüssler Fiorenza is making two points here.

She argues that Kuhn's notion of scientific paradigms and heuristic interpretative models is useful for biblical and theological studies in that it

> shows the conditioned nature of all scientific investigation, and maintains that no neutral observation language and value-free standpoint is possible insofar as all scientific investigations demand commitment to a particular research approach, and are carried out by a community of scholars dedicated to such a theoretical perspective. Moreover, this theory helps us to understand that theological approaches, like all other scientific theories, are not falsified, but replaced, not because we find new 'data,' but because we find new ways of looking at old data and problems.[21]

However, it is crucial to recognize that more is being said here than a mere acknowledging of the general demise of the ideology of objectivity, important as this recognition is.[22] Schüssler Fiorenza is also making a second, more important, point. Not only do interpreters and theologians within theologies of liberation *recognize* the perspectival nature of all knowledge, they also *actively embrace or advocate a par-*

ticular perspective. In other words, not only do they recognize that there is no neutral or detached perspective, they also "take sides" or become engaged with a particular perspective, the perspective of the poor and oppressed.[23]
For example,

> The shift from an androcentric to a feminist interpretation of the world implies a revolutionary shift in scientific paradigm, a shift with far-reaching ramifications not only for the interpretation of the world but also for its change. Since paradigms determine how scholars see the world and how they conceive of theoretical problems, a shift from an androcentric to a feminist paradigm implies a transformation of the scientific imagination. It demands an intellectual *conversion* that cannot be logically deduced but is rooted in a change of patriarchal-social relationships. Such an intellectual *conversion* engenders a shift in *commitment* that allows the community of scholars involved to see old 'data' in a completely new perspective.[24]

In addition, Schüssler Fiorenza, again drawing on Kuhn, argues that such a transition can only be accomplished when the emerging paradigm has produced its own institutional structures and support-systems. So while the androcentric paradigm scholarship is rooted in the patriarchal institutions of the academy, "the feminist paradigm has created its own institutional basis in the alternative institutions of women's centers, academic institutes, and study programs".[25]

Clearly, both accoutability to and solidarity with the poor and oppressed is critical to liberation hermeneutics.[26] Doing theology or interpreting the Bible is "a second act" which is based on the experience of and commitment to the struggle of the poor and oppressed.[27] In the words of Desmond Tutu, "Our scientific strivings must make room for subjectivity, for commitment, for the intuitive comprehension of matters which are hardly comprehensible for the alienated objectivity of the non-committed".[28]

Having outlined this crucial and distinctive understanding of commitment, a commitment which includes accountability and solidarity, I now turn to the South African context.[29]

The black experience of struggle

In order to understand what accountability and solidarity mean in the South African context, it is necessary to explore the black experience of struggle. And "blackness" is still at the centre of the struggle for liberation and life in South Africa.

"There seems to be no doubt that central to the concerns of Black Theology stands the category of 'blackness'".[30] Not surprisingly, "black" in black theology has a fundamentally different meaning from "black" in apartheid legislation.

First of all the two concepts have different denotations. Apartheid legislation placed South Africans in four main racial or ethnic categories: white (or European), black (or African), coloured (or "of mixed origin"), and Asian. "Black" in black theology includes those whom apartheid legislation refers to as "non-white": black, Indian, and coloured. Yet, in terms of connotation, the black theology concept of blackness rejects the description "non-white" because it defines people from the perspective of the white person. "Black", as opposed to "non-white", is a positive description that defines people in their own terms, not in terms of others.[31]

More importantly, "black" in the South African context does not only have a genetic significance. Blackness defines socio-economic status, place of living, educational and health facilities, and job possibilities.[32] "Blackness is a reality that embraces the totality of black existence";[33] or, in the words of a black poet, "My beingness oppresses me".[34] In fact, "black" in black theology is not primarily an ethnic designation but rather a socio-economic and cultural one, signifying the oppressed in a white racist society.[35] In Boesak's words, "Blackness (a state of oppression) is not only a colour, it is a *condition*".[36]

Consequently, there are close affinities between the two concepts "black" and "oppressed". "Both refer to 'the irruption of the poor' and have the same epistemological perspective, looking at reality "from the underside of history". What is more, both concepts emphasize the bonds between those who have been divided by the ruling ideology [of apartheid], calling for unity from below".[37] What Sharon Welch calls "an epistemology of solidarity" is integral to the black experience of struggle.[38]

The concept of blackness, then, is related to the epistemological break. As we have seen, blackness involves more than just a recognition of blackness. "It is a discovery, a state of mind, a conversion, an affirmation of being, which is power".[39] Black Theology is a "reflection of faith upon the present historical realities of 'Blackness'", and for this reason a black theologian "must participate fully in the condition of 'Blackness' and be sensitive to the community's hopes, fears and anxieties at the collective and individual level".[40] Hence black theology is defined as *"a theology of the oppressed, by the oppressed, for the liberation of the oppressed"*.[41]

Mosala is equally adamant, arguing that "The particularity of the black struggle in its different forms and faces must provide the epistemological lenses with which the Bible can be read. Only this position seems to represent a theoretical break with dominant biblical hermeneutics; anything else is a tinkering with what in fact must be destroyed".[42]

It is important to recognize, however, that black experience involves more than the experience of oppression. It is indeed a critical reflection on the black situation of oppression, but at the same time it is also a critical reflection on the black struggle for justice and humanity.[43] Black theology is the "critical reflection of black Christians on their involvement in the black liberation struggle".[44] This means that its agenda is determined by "the emancipatory interests of the black community".[45] Clearly then, black theology is an *engaged* theology in the fullest sense, operating with an epistemology which regards the struggle of the poor and oppressed as the "locus theologicus".[46]

The concept of "struggle" in black experience may be further defined, following Frostin, with reference to Edward Schillebeeckx's term "contrast experience".[47]

> Contrast experience, especially in the memory of the actual human history of accumulated suffering, possesses a special epistemological value and power, which cannot be deduced from a goal-centred 'Herrschaftswissen' (the form of knowledge peculiar to science and technology), nor from the diverse forms of contemplative, aesthetic, ludic or non-directive knowledge. The peculiar epistemological value of the contrast experience of suffering as a result

of injustice is *critical*: critical of both contemplative and scientific-technological forms of knowing. It is critical of the purely contemplative perception of the whole, because this form already lives out universal reconciliation in its contemplative or liturgical celebration. But it is also critical of the world-dominating knowledge of science and technology, because this form as such presumes that human beings are only dominating subjects and ignores the ethical priority to which those who suffer among us have a right.[48]

As the quotation bears out, contrast experiences are of "peculiar epistemological value" because of their critical potential. "Underlying this notion", says Frostin, "is the proposition that the truth is often suppressed in a context of oppression and may therefore be more accessible to the oppressed".[49] Put in another way,

In the theology of modernity the established rationality seems to be the interpretative framework which defines what is understandable in the biblical texts.[50] If·one assumes, as liberation theologians do, that one may distinguish between a hegemonic and a counter-hegemonic rationality, the hegemonic rationality is, of course, less suitable for the explication of contrast experiences. Boesak's phrase of a black community that shares and experiences history 'with God' suggests that the subversive memoria (in Metz's sense) of God's revelation in Jesus Christ and of past contrast experiences of the black community is the interpretative framework of the experience that is analyzed in black theology.[51]

Commitment to the community of the poor and oppressed, therefore, includes accountability to and solidarity with the conquered living and dead. Only by taking seriously these "dangerous memories" and "subjugated knowledges" is there true accountability and solidarity.[52]

Mosala makes a similar point when he argues that the biblical interpreter, like Eagleton's cultural worker, must interpret works and events "against the grain". Mosala understands by this that the appropriation of works and events is always a contradictory process embodying in some form a "struggle". "The category of struggle becomes an important heremeneutical factor not only in one's reading of his or her history and culture but also in one's understanding of the history, nature, ideology, and agenda of the biblical texts." In other words, a biblical hermeneutic of liberation requires accountability to and solidarity with the present black struggle for liberation and with "kindred struggles that were being waged in very ancient communities".[53]

In summary, the concept of blackness is a focal point in defining black theology in South Africa. Boesak puts this succinctly:

> Black Consciousness may be described as the awareness of black people that their humanity is constituted by their blackness. It means that black people are no longer ashamed that they are black, that they have a black history and a black culture distinct from the history and culture of white people. It means that blacks are determined to be judged no longer by, and to adhere to white values. It is an attitude, a way of life.[54]

The Role of black consciousness in black theology represents an "alternative consciousness", "a counter-hegemonic perception of reality",[55] in which accountability to and solidarity with the poor and oppressed is a fundamental commitment.

When we examine more closely the relationship between black theology and black consciousness we can detect some significant differences among black interpreters which must be analyzed for a more comprehensive understanding of the relationship between the reader and the community in liberation hermeneutics.

Method and strategy in the black struggle

In his discussion of the major trends or tendencies discernible in South African black theology, Kritzinger draws an illuminating map which indicates the interplay between *theological method* and *political strategy* in black theology. He plots the field along the two axes of *method* and *strategy* to indicate the pattern of different approaches.[56] In order to elucidate his mapping, Kritzinger explains the relevant issues in method and strategy respectively.

Method

Kritzinger argues that with reference to theological method "the debate centres on biblical hermeneutics. The central question can be phrased as follows: What is the most appropriate hermeneutical approach to be followed so that Black Theology may become a truly liberating force in the black community?"[57]

During Phase I, Kritzinger argues, black theology, "characterized by a strong kerygmatic dimension, used a traditional 'Word of God' hermeneutics. Characteristic of this approach is the view that liberation is the *central message* of the *whole* Bible".[58]   Representative of this approach are Boesak and Tutu.[59]

During Phase II, Kritzinger continues, "when black theologians began using Marxist analysis in a serious way, a materialist reading of the Bible started taking root, which questions the fundamental assumptions of the hermeneutics of Phase I".[60]

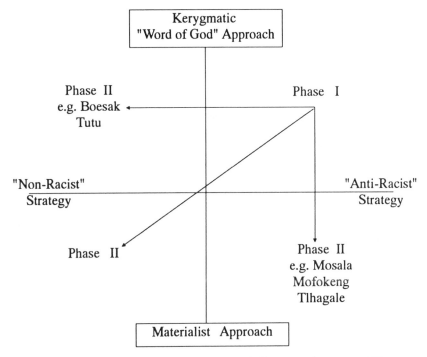

Takatso Mofokeng expresses the difference between Phases I and II very clearly when he says,

> The most commonly held approach [among black Christians] has been to accuse oppressor-preachers of *misusing* the Bible for their oppressive purposes and objectives. This misuse is based, it is argued, on misinterpretations of biblical texts to support or promote oppressive intentions.

It is clear that this critique is based on the assumption that the Bible is essentially a book of liberation. This assumption is held in spite of the obvious presence in the Bible of texts, stories and books which can only serve an oppressive cause . . . There are numerous texts which have long disqualified themselves in the eyes of the oppressed people. We can refer to the well-known Pauline position on slavery and on the social position and behaviour of women. We think that in the light of this textual reality formally trained hermeneutists and exegetes of the downtrodden should abandon the ideologically motivated concept of the unity of the Bible as well as the assumption that it is a book of liberation per se.[61]

Mofokeng and Mosala would be representative of this approach which attempts to "discover the text behind the text of the Bible - a text that has been silenced but one that speaks through this silence about the struggles of the silenced and marginalized people of the Bible".[62]

Kritzinger concludes his discussion of the method axis by summarizing its domain as follows: "The hermeneutical spectrum in Black Theology therefore stretches from a selective and critical kerygmatic use of the 'Word of God' which 'sheds its light on our path' to a materialist approach which adopts *struggle* as its hermeneutical key, searching for affinities and links between struggling black communities today and the struggling communities behind the biblical texts".[63] Although there are definitely further questions which need to be asked here, as my analysis in the previous chapter suggests, there are enough similarities between our respective analyses for Kritzinger's mapping to be useful. Of particular importance for this chapter is his *strategy* axis.

Strategy

With reference to strategy, "the central question is whether the Black Consciousness option of not entering into alliances with white 'progressive democrats' should be retained".[64] In the initial phase of black theology, Kritzinger argues, it was quite clear that black theology could not be separated from black consciousness.[65] Although there are different understandings of the relation between black theology and black consciousness, few would deny the close relationship between the two concepts. Some use black consciousness as an umbrella term which encompasses different forms of black self-affirmation, one of them being black theology. Mosala asserts that "Black Theology as a theological expression and theorisation of the black struggle for liberation cannot be understood outside the context of the Black Consciousness movement".[66] Others describe them as interrelated entities. Nyameko Pityana says that "one is the genus of the other",[67] and Mofokeng describes them as "twin sisters", "inseparably united".[68] A third position advocates a critical relationship, "understanding black theology as a theological reflection on black consciousness and black power".[69] Bonganjalo Goba speaks of black theology and black consciousness as "soul mates" or "parallel movements",[70] but proposes that black theologians need a critical perspective that will question existing categories of thought on the basis of the experience arising from the concrete struggle.[71]

Clearly, then, there is a close relationship between black theology and black consciousness. One clear indication of this intimate relationship is the role of young black *Christians* in the emergence of black consciousness.[72] In the National Union of South African Students (NUSAS), "a liberal multiracial organization",[73] white and black students were working together against apartheid. For the white liberals this kind of multiracial cooperation was *the* way of working to abolish apartheid. Among the black students, however, there was a growing dissatisfaction with NUSAS. It was at the 1968 University Christian Movement (UCM) meeting that a caucus of black students and pastors agreed on the importance of a black organization and so decided to form a separate black student organization, the South African Student's Organization (SASO). This was the first organizational expression of black consciousness.[74] In other words, a Christian organization "became the organizational ground on which the idea of black consciousness solidified" so that "SASO and thereby the Black Consciousness philosophical approach was born inside Christian circles".[75] Conversely, black consciousness organizations established black theology projects, since they regarded it as the indispensable "spiritual dimension" of the black liberation struggle.[76]

This close mutual relationship makes it possible to call black consciousness the "nerve centre" or "ideological framework" of black theology.[77] Black theology is "inseparably linked

to the Black Consciousness philosophy and based on the
Black Consciousness political praxis".[78] This view is repre-
sentative of Phase I and also of one strong tendency of Phase
II in Kritzinger's mapping.

However, Goba's concern for a critical perspective, mentioned above, arises out of his awareness of shifting strategies in the black struggle.[79] In the final paragraph of his essay on "The Black Consciousness Movement: Its Impact on
Black Theology", Goba concludes that "Black Consciousness
has played a very significant role in the development of Black
Theology". "But", he continues, "the question we have to ask
is, is it still adequate for our present situation?"[80] Responding to questions like this Mosala and Tlhagale recognize that

> The emergence of the United Democratic Front (1983) and its call
> for 'unity in the struggle through which all democrats regardless of
> race, religion or colour shall take part together' is bound to pose
> itself as a challenge to the strategy of the Black Consciousness
> Movement that excludes white people in the struggle for liberation.
> This challenge is also posed by the newly formed Congress of South
> African Trade Unions that embraces the principle of non-racial-
> ism.[81]

Kritzinger also recognizes these different strategies when
he argues that the emergence and strength of the United
Democratic Front (UDF), with its acceptance of the "non-
racial" strategy of the Freedom Charter, "put the Black Consciousness approach under pressure, and a number of black
theologians moved to the 'non-racial democratic' tendency
in the black struggle".[82]

Here, then, lies an important difference within black theology, differences relating to various perceptions of black identity and cooperation with whites in the struggle against apartheid.[83] Although the debate within black theology in this area
is not easy to describe in its complexity, particularly in this
time of transition since 2nd February 1990, there are these
two major tendencies. In broad terms the difference is between those black theologians who, like Mosala, adhere to
an exclusive black nationalism, and those who, like Boesak,
advocate a non-racial "unity in the struggle".[84]

The use of the phrase "exclusive black nationalism" may
be deceptive, however.

Even a staunch exponent of black nationalism such as AZAPO [Anzanian People's Organization] has repeatedly declared that its exclusive stance is only confined to what it terms 'the preliberation phase of the struggle'. In other words, the main concern in this tendency is not to be anti-white but to emphasize black identity. The exclusion of whites is seen as a temporary measure that is necessary in order to safeguard a platform for black thinking, issues, and programs in a certain situation. Differently put, the protagonists of both tendencies work for an egalitarian society without any racial differentiation. The dissensus is a matter of the structures of organization *before* the liberation.[85]

This qualification is immensely important because it indicates that the central point of difference within the black community, including black biblical interpreters, is among those who while sharing a commitment to black liberation differ in terms of *strategy*. And, as is now becoming clearer, this difference in terms of strategy does not only apply to the struggle against apartheid, but also the ongoing struggle for full black liberation.

In light of the above, it becomes clear that the spectrum of strategies stretches from "the traditional Black Consciousness approach to the racially broadened praxis of the nonracial democratic movement".[86] However, it should also be made clear that even the black interpreters within the nonracial democratic movement still identify themselves as black theologians who are accountable to and in solidarity with the ongoing struggle for black liberation and life.[87]

Related areas of debate

There are, of course, other areas of difference among those committed to the struggle for black liberation. Briefly, they would fall within the following areas.

There is a growing recognition that it is imperative to give clearer analysis to both the strategies and the ultimate goal of the liberation struggle.[88] Of particular importance here is the search for an adequate social analysis.[89] As we have already noted, this is an area in which Mosala is critical of Boesak. Mosala is particularly concerned about Boesak's "unstructural understanding" of the black experience and struggle.[90] A recognition of such critique results in many black interpreters drawing on socialist analysis, while preserving the concern for cultural identity.[91] The interest in socialist analysis is reflected in a more anti-capitalist stance among many black interpreters, both among advocates of non-racial cooperation and black nationalism.[92] The decline of socialist systems in other parts of the world has impacted on the South African situation, but socialist analysis still has a voice and vitality in both the townships and the Government of National Unity. What influence socialist analysis will have on government policy, particularly in the Reconstruction and Development Programme remains to be clearly seen. Economic liberation, and just what this should mean, remains a, or perhaps, the, central question of debate.

The concern to preserve an African cultural identity is reflected in the reclaiming and rewriting of black history and culture.[93] This latter concern, which encompasses the whole area of African culture and religion, has been a part of the debate among black interpreters from the beginning.[94] But now that partial socio-political liberation has been achieved, there is space for questions of Africanization and enculturation to be foregrounded. And this is happening in all sectors of society, including the church. *Ubuntu* has now moved to centre-stage. An example of this shift can be found in the growing recognition among black interpreters of the African Independent Churches (AIC) as the roots of black theology and as an important resource in theological reflection. While for many analysts the AIC have been a conservative force and have not been "in the forefront of the liberation struggle as their counterparts in North America and Latin American countries",[95] there are a growing number of analysts who emphasize the radical potential of the AIC. For example, Mofokeng argues that "black pastors of the African Independent Churches were the ones who came forward to provide the leadership [of the black struggle]. They became the first black people in South Africa to advocate a broad African nationalism and used their church organizations as the first functional bases".[96] Similarly, G.C. Oosthuizen argues that "for nearly a century South Africa has experienced Black theology—unwritten but alive—in the songs and dances, the sermons and liturgies of those outside the established churches".[97]

The ambivalence with which the AIC is viewed is explained by No Sizwe when he argues that while the AIC

> kept alive the belief that Africa belongs to the Africans and that the land should be returned . . . this was seldom given a directly political expression except by individuals in their capacity as members of political organisations of the oppressed. It was rather a general climate, a political memory that was sustained in these churches and their prayer meetings in the open veld or in the hovels inhabited by the majority of their members.[98]

A similar assessment is put forward by Constance Baratang Thetele. She argues that,

> The Independent Churches in South Africa in many ways are both pre-revolutionary and actively revolutionary at the same time. They are pre-revolutionary in the sense that they do not operate according to a set plan or strategy in trying to move society toward a definite goal. But they are revolutionary in their impact on the fabric of society, creating a change that provides the dispossessed people with a sense of hope and a vision for the future. They offer a place in society where people can begin to sense their role as creators of their own histories, rejecting a passive acceptance of the status quo and beginning to work out alternatives to dehumanization.[99]

Another related area of debate among black interpreters is the limited social basis of black theology. Even though black consciousness and black theology changed the political climate among the black community generally, "the social basis of the new type of intellectual reflection was limited".[100] In an early work on black theology Goba points to this liability. "So many of us are remote from the everyday experience of our black people. There is a gap between the black élite and the ordinary black man. We have allowed our acquired intellectualism to separate us from the ordinary people. Today when we speak of the Black Consciousness movement, we immediately think of students in the S.A.S.O. and a few clerics. The rest of the people are not involved".[101] These thoughts are echoed in a more recent book on black theology, but this time with particular reference to black theology itself. He argues here that the urban and middle class base of black consciousness and black theology are one of their central weaknesses. To address this in the area of black theology "there is a need for popular theology which reflects the total experience of our people reflected in song, poetry and their stories within the actual struggle itself".[102]

Goba's concern has been taken up in some measure by the work of the Institute for Contextual Theology (ICT) and the Institute for the Study of the Bible (ISB), where the relationship between the grassroots communities and academic black theology has been focal. Among the questions ICT asks are: "How liberating is liberation theology? [Does] Black theology really play a liberating role in our situation in Southern Africa? Are we able to measure the contribution of this Black theology of Liberation to the struggle of the oppressed masses in South Africa? Or is it just an intellectual exercise for the benefit of the Black Theologian to enhance his/her position in the academic world?"[103]

Two groups which are being foregrounded more recently are workers and women. Frank Chikane and M. Tsele argue that "Black theology should be constantly informed by those who are closer to community experiences—factory workers, community workers, etc."[104] Also, feminist concerns have been given more place in black theology in recent years. The 1984 Conference Report of the ICT reflects this concern. The Report recognizes that "Male Black theologians cannot sincerely and genuinely talk of liberation from oppression, while they continue to oppress their female partners". It also recognizes that "There are evidently structures oppressive of women inherent in both the Black community and the church. We also express our concern about the need for more critical analysis of cultural and economic forces that serve to reinforce the ideology of male dominance and humbly call upon feminist theologians to inform Black theology and forge an alliance with it".[105] The contours of the feminist-africanist debate are only beginning to become clearer.

Finally, after the suppression of black consciousness organizations, which were working within the narrow confines of South African apartheid legislation, an increasing number of the younger black Christians seriously questioned the viability of nonviolence in the struggle against apartheid.[106] The use of violence in our present context of reconstruction and development for the perceived purpose of liberation and life has been rejected by all political groupings, but there remains an ambiguity of whether certain acts of violence are criminal or political.

As we can see from these debates, debates which have been constantly reshaped since the unbanning of black political organizations and democratic elections, black theology and black liberation hermeneutics are not monolithic.[107] Yet, a common thread which is crucial to both and which is evident in their various manifestations is accountability to and solidarity with the poor and marginalized.

Conclusion

As one would expect, locating the reader in the South African context is a rather complex exercise. Nevertheless, this attempt to locate the reader in the community of struggle clarifies two crucial points. First, my analysis demonstrates an important paradigm shift in black theology which is common to all black interpreters, and those white interpreters who stand in solidarity with them. Interpreting the Bible is done from within a clear commitment to the community of struggle, a commitment which entails accountability to and solidarity with the struggle of the poor and oppressed for liberation and life in South Africa. And, as we have seen, this commitment to "black theology's political starting point in the struggles of the oppressed and exploited black people in South Africa dictates a new way of reading the Bible".[108]

Second, the analysis in this chapter clarifies the strategic differences among those committed to the struggle for liberation and life in South Africa. These differences are by no means minimal or insignificant, as this and subsequent discussion demonstrates. But it is vital to recognize that they occur within *a common framework of commitment*. This epistemological position of accountability to and solidarity with the poor and marginalized is the key factor in liberation hermeneutics.

Another important factor in a biblical hermeneutic of liberation is the relationship of continuity between the interpreter and the biblical tradition. So having analyzed the relationship between the reader and the community in this chapter, the task in chapter five is to analyze the relationship between the reader and the tradition.

Chapter Five

The Reader and the Tradition: Continuity and Solidarity

Introduction

Having discussed certain aspects of the reader pole in liberation hermeneutics, I turn now to the text. As we have already glimpsed, there is considerable disarray here. This disarray is particularly apparent with respect to the status of tradition, particularly the Bible, in theological argumentation. On the one hand we have the assertion of James Barr that "In Kantian terms, involvement with the Bible is analytic in being a Christian".[1] On the other hand we have the *postbiblical* feminist hermeneutics of Mary Daly.[2] Put briefly, there is a growing debate concerning the status of tradition in theological argumentation.[3]

This debate is part of a larger debate which arose in the Enlightenment's polarization of authoritative tradition and the freedom of reason.[4] However, the concern in this chapter is not the wider multi-faceted debate, although this will be alluded to from time to time. The focus here is on one of the issues which crisscrosses this multi-faceted debate: the status of the biblical tradition in liberation hermeneutics. More specifically, I will follow the suggestion of Linell Cady that an analysis of the status of the past in liberation hermeneutics can clarify and more accurately identify the disagreements between different methodological approaches, particularly those approaches characterized in the work of Boesak and Mosala.[5] As in previous chapters, the work of Boesak and Mosala provides the South African focus for this chapter; however, the framework for the analysis in this chapter is provided by feminist biblical hermeneutics where "one of the key issues is the relationship between past tradition and present experience".[6]

Legal hermeneutics

Cady suggests that we can begin to get some clarity about the role and status of tradition in theological argumentation by adopting Gadamer's proposal that we consider legal interpretation as the most appropriate paradigm for hermeneutical understanding.[7]

Rejecting the model of objectivity which posits a neutral, ahistorical appropriation of, for example, a text, Gadamer has attempted to show that all understanding is necessarily perspectival, influenced by the assumptions, needs, and interests of the interpreter. Developing Heidegger's model of the hermeneutical circle, Gadamer has attempted to show that all understanding takes place in and through dialogue. The interpreter brings to a text a certain preunderstanding and through a to-and-fro engagement with the subject matter attempts to develop an appropriate interpretation. Understanding is a "fusion of horizons" which is not merely a re-production of the text but a new historical appropriation of the text, a new perspective on the text.[8]

Just as understanding and interpretation cannot be separated into sequential moments, Gadamer insists that application is not a secondary practical concern but an intrinsic component of the one hermeneutic act of understanding/interpretation/application. The interpretation of a text always presupposes the horizon of the interpreter, a situation *out* of which and *for* which an interpretation occurs. Significantly, Gadamer notes that the centrality of application in hermeneutical understanding was eclipsed in the eighteenth and nineteenth centuries as historical and literary studies set themselves up as the hermeneutical paradigm. Here the emphasis was on disclosing the text in *its* historical and cultural horizon; an emphasis which obscured the recognition of the determinative influence of the interpreter's interests, questions, and assumptions.

To rectify this misleading view of the hermeneutical process Gadamer proposes that we consider legal interpretation as the most appropriate paradigm for hermeneutical understanding. In making a legal decision the judge is attempting to interpret the law as it applies to a specific concrete case and not in abstraction. By emphasizing that interpretation is shaped by situational interests and needs this model is a better illustration of the hermeneutical unity of understanding/interpretation/application.[9] Thus Gadamer writes that "legal hermeneutics is able to point out what the real procedure of the human sciences is. Here we have the model for the relationship between past and present that we are seeking".[10]

Cady pursues Gadamer's suggestion concerning the paradigmatic character of legal hermeneutics by making use of a typology of theories of jurisprudence developed by Ronald Dworkin, a philosopher of law. Through an exploration of alternative forms of legal interpretation Cady hopes to clarify various uses of the past in contemporary theological argumentation, particularly in feminist theology.[11] Cady's exploration is therefore of obvious relevance to my purpose, which is to analyze the status of the biblical tradition in the methodological approaches characterized in the work of Boesak and Mosala.

Dworkin's typology

In order to highlight the methodological assumptions embodied in diverse judicial decisions, Dworkin has developed a typology consisting of three major approaches: conventionalism, naturalism, and instrumentalism.[12] These approaches differ primarily in regard to the way in which the past functions in legal decisions.

Conventionalism is the name given to that school of judicial adjudication in which decisions are made on the basis of precedents. According to this theory, the proper task of the judge is first to identify the lawful authorities in a given society. The judge then proceeds to investigate whether such lawful authorities have established a rule which unambiguously applies to the current case. If there is such a rule, the judge is constrained to follow it. If there is no such rule, the judge may make a new ruling which becomes part of the authoritative precedents which guide later decisions. The judge, therefore, only has the leeway to make novel decisions, decisions reflecting his or her own moral and political interests, when the past does not set a precedent for how such cases are to be decided.[13]

Underlying this approach is the assumption that appropriate legal precedents can be identified in a fairly straightforward manner. However, as Dworkin carefully demonstrates, it is far from clear that judges can isolate the relevant legal precedents without an elaborate process of interpretation which inevitably involves moral and political considerations. The assumption that judges can follow relevant precedents without being swayed by moral and political interests is not supported, according to Dworkin, by historical and sociological scrutiny.[14]

The second type of judicial reasoning assumes, like conventionalism, that judicial interpretations must be based on past decisions. However, according to naturalism a precedent is never determinative in isolation but should be interpreted in as wide a context as possible in order to view it in the best moral and political light. Since all precedents require interpretation, this approach spells out the parameters which should guide the interpretive process. The best interpretation of past decisions will be the one which shows them as "coming as close to the correct ideals of a just legal system as possible".[15]

In other words, the judge will be concerned that his or her decision "fits" past rulings; however, these past rulings are not interpreted in isolation but in the widest possible context, the context which makes the best sense of law and the political order as a whole. The past constrains the judge in a naturalist theory of adjudication, but it is the past interpreted as a whole and in the light of current perceptions of what constitutes the just society. It is this latter stricture which differentiates naturalist adjudication from conventionalist adjudication.[16]

The naturalist approach recognizes that given the variety of such moral and political perceptions, two judges operating from this same methodological perspective might well disagree over which interpretation is preferable. "Beyond a certain threshold of fit, substantive ideals of justice will determine the best interpretation".[17]

Cady points out that it should be apparent from this brief description that "naturalism avoids making a radical split between the descriptive and the evaluative components of the activity of interpretation. Although distinguishing between the dimensions of fit and substantive ideals, it acknowledges that these factors are unavoidably intertwined". The political and moral assumptions of the interpreter "provide the lens through which the law is viewed. While this does not constitute subjectivism, it does call into question the fact/value dichotomy upon which conventionalism depends".[18]

However, given the significant role that moral and political values play in shaping the interpretation of the past, why should the past place *any* constraints on the judge's decision? In other words, why should a judge not decide a case solely on the basis of what will yield, according to his or her moral and political interests, the more just society? Such are the questions which the instrumentalist theory of adjudication relentlessly poses to both conventionalism and naturalism. According to the theory of instrumentalism judges should "always look to the future: to try to make the community as good and wise and just a community as it can be, with no essential regard to what it has been until now".[19]

Even though instrumentalism refuses to let the past necessarily delimit judicial decisions, this approach concedes that there may be strategic reasons for taking the past into account in making judicial decisions. So for example, the judge should not make rules which stand in direct opposition to other laws which she or he cannot overrule. "In short, judicial decisions, according to the instrumentalist theory, are based upon what will facilitate a more just society; the past has only a pragmatic role in determining the correct decision".[20]

In summary, the three main types of judicial interpretation are based on differing uses of the past. Conventionalism separates moral and political assessments on the one hand and prior decisions on the other, insisting that the latter are authoritative and should take precedence. Denying the possibility, let alone the advisability, of divorcing fact and value or description and evaluation, "naturalism deliberately combines the two in contending that prior decisions are to be interpreted in the widest possible context and weighed in terms of substantive ideals of justice. Nevertheless, judicial decisions are constrained by requiring some 'fit with the past' according to this perspective". Instrumentalism follows naturalism in allowing moral and political considerations to guide judicial decisions, but radically extends this by denying that past decisions have any intrinsic constraint upon such moral and political considerations.[21]

Feminist interpretations

Cady applies this typology to theological argumentation for two reasons. "Applying this typology not only helps sort out the alternative methodological approaches to the past in theological argumentation, it may facilitate a closer consideration of the assumptions and issues which are at stake in these diverse approaches".[22] Before I apply this typology to the work of Boesak and Mosala it is useful to remain with Cady as she applies the typology to feminist theology. Feminist theology probably offers the most incisive analysis of the status of the past in theological argumentation, and will therefore, I suggest, serve as a useful guide to the issues involved in the approaches of Boesak and Mosala.

Cady mentions that it is noteworthy, although not surprising, that feminist theology does not reflect the conventionalist approach to the past. Conventionalism tends towards a piecemeal appropriation of the past, which is viewed as the deposit of authoritative precedents.[23] So even conservative evangelical feminists have concluded that such a view inevitably "sanctifies the patriarchal distortions of the ancient Near East".[24] Reflecting this position, for example, is evangelical feminist Virginia Mollenkott who warns that "Because patriarchy is the cultural background of the Scriptures, it is absolutely basic to any feminist reading of the Bible that *one cannot absolutize the culture in which the Bible was written.* We must make careful distinctions between what is 'for an age' and what is 'for all time'".[25] In making this distinction between "for an age" and "for all time" Mollenkott, Cady argues, "is bringing her substantive ideals for justice and equality to bear in her interpretation of the Scriptures".[26] Mollenkott concludes that "we are in error to absolutize anything that denies the thrust of the entire Bible toward individual wholeness and harmonious community, toward oneness in Christ".[27] In other words, instead of citing isolated biblical texts, feminist theologians must interpret the biblical message as a whole.

Rosemary Ruether has argued a similar position in her work *Sexism and God-talk*. Ruether recognizes that there "is no question that patriarchy is the social context for both the Old and the New Testaments and this social context has been incorporated into religious ideology on many levels",[28] including the Bible.[29] "Nevertheless", she continues, "both Testaments contain resources for the critique of patriarchy".[30]

The resources within the Bible are found within what Ruether calls "the prophetic-liberating tradition of biblical faith".[31]

> Four themes are essential to the prophetic-liberating tradition of Biblical faith: (1) God's defense and vindication of the oppressed; (2) the critique of the dominant systems of power and their powerholders; (3) the vision of a new age to come in which the present system of injustice is installed in history; and (4) finally, the critique of ideology, or of religion, since ideology in this context is primarily religious. Prophetic faith denounces religious ideologies and systems that function to justify and sanctify the dominant, unjust social order.

These themes, Ruether argues, "are central to the Prophets and to the mission of Jesus. Hence the critical-liberating tradition is the axis around which the prophetic-messianic line of Biblical faith revolves as a foundation of Christianity".[32] What is more, feminism, in claiming the prophetic-liberating tradition of the Bible as a norm through which to criticize the Bible, "does not choose an arbitrary or marginal idea in the Bible. It chooses a tradition that can be fairly claimed, on the basis of generally accepted Biblical scholarship, to be the central tradition, the tradition by which Biblical faith constantly criticizes and renews itself and its own vision".[33]

While Ruether finds this prophetic-liberating tradition *within* the Bible, she also recognizes that

what is innovative in feminist hermeneutics is not the prophetic norm but rather feminism's appropriation of this norm *for women*. Feminism claims that *women too* are among those oppressed whom God comes to vindicate and liberate. By including women in the prophetic norm, feminism sees what male prophetic thought generally had not seen: that once the prophetic norm is asserted to be central to Biblical faith, then patriarchy can no longer be maintained as authoritative.[34]

So, "Feminism appropriates the prophetic principles in ways the Biblical writers for the most part do not appropriate them, namely, to criticize this unexamined patriarchal framework".[35] A crucial component of her mode of reading, therefore, is the "critical principle of feminist theology", namely, "the promotion of the full humanity of women".

Whatever denies, diminishes, or distorts the full humanity of women is, therefore, appraised as not redemptive. Theologically speaking, whatever diminishes or denies the full humanity of women must be presumed not to reflect the divine or an authentic relation to the divine, or to reflect the authentic nature of things, or to be the message or work of an authentic redeemer or a community of redemption.[36]

In words reminiscent of Boesak, Ruether argues that "This rediscovery of prophetic content,[37] and its discerning reapplication to new social situations, is precisely what the Bible calls 'the Word of God'".[38] She continues, "This, in other words, is the critical principle that Biblical faith applies to itself. It is the hermeneutical principle for discerning prophetic faith within Scripture as well as for the ongoing interpretation of Scripture as critique of tradition".[39] By this Ruether means two things. "On one level, this means that feminist theology, along with other liberation theologies, strips off the ideological mystifications that have developed in the traditions of Biblical interpretation and that have concealed the liberating content".[40] This stripping off is accomplished "as one assumes a stance of social justice rather than of collaboration with unjust powers". Not only does such a stance allow the prophetic advocacy of the poor and oppressed and the denunciation of unjust social hierarchies and their religious justifications to "leap into clear focus", but the "entire Biblical message becomes radically transformed in meaning and purpose when the full implications of the Church's social advocacy of the oppressed are grasped today".[41]

"On another level, feminism goes beyond the letter of the prophetic message to apply the prophetic-liberating principle *to women*".[42] Here feminist theology "makes explicit what was overlooked in male advocacy of the poor and the oppressed: that liberation must start with the oppressed of the oppressed, namely, *women* of the oppressed. This means that the critique of hierarchy must become explicitly a critique of patriarchy. All liberating prophetic visions must be deepened and transformed to include what was not included: women".[43] Ruether elaborates by arguing that this expansion of the biblical message to include the unincluded recognizes two factors. First, it recognizes "that not only the dominant sociology, but also the sociology of oppressed people, has its social myopias and limitations". Second, it recognizes that "the point of reference for Biblical faith is not past texts, with their sociological limitations, but rather the liberated future. We appropriate the past not to remain in its limits, but to point to new futures".[44]

Clearly, as Cady argues, "the methodological moves operative in both Ruether's and Mollenkott's positions correspond to the moves within a naturalist theory of adjudication". The interpreter has certain substantive moral and political ideals which shape the interpretation of the past. This is not to suggest, Cady argues, that the past is fabricated by the interpreter, but to acknowledge "that what is deemed important, significant, and central will be determined in large part by the interpreter's substantive ideals. In a sense, this is unavoidable given the nature of interpretation".[45]

It is important to recognize at this point that although Ruether and Mollenkott argue according to the naturalist theory of interpretation "they do not entirely share the same rationale for their approaches".[46] Ruether's appropriation of the past is based on the need "to situate oneself meaningfully in history", and because to find glimmers of truth in submerged and alternative traditions "is to assure oneself that one is not mad or duped".[47] By making the distinction between what in the Bible is for an age and what is for all

time, "Mollenkott comes close to the conventionalist rationale for basing one's position on the past".[48] Nevertheless, Cady
continues, "her self-conscious procedure in interpreting the
Bible falls within the naturalist framework".[49]

The different rationale for their respective uses of the past
suggest that it is more useful to place these differing approaches along a continuum. On a continuum from conventionalism through naturalism to instrumentalism Mollenkott
would be closer to conventionalism than Ruether.

The naturalist approach, according to Cady, "deliberately
attempts to interpret the past in the best possible light". This
entails making judgements, according to one's moral and
political interests, "about the past as a whole. It is not isolated Scriptural statements about women which must be
addressed finally but the whole biblical horizon as it relates
to the current quest for women's equality". Conventionalist
theological argumentation which rests upon isolated biblical
references "will not be considered adequate inasmuch as such
warrants are isolated elements wrenched from the total fabric of the past, and enthroned as authoritative".[50]

Cady next turns to consider the work of Elisabeth
Schüssler Fiorenza in the light of Dworkin's typology, particularly Schüssler Fiorenza's criticisms of what she calls
"the neo-orthodox" methodological approach reflected in
Mollenkott and Ruether. As I will be considering Schüssler
Fiorenza's work in more detail in the following chapter, it will
be sufficient here to discuss her critique of Ruether, briefly
outlining her own approach.

In her important work *In Memory of Her* Schüssler Fiorenza
argues against the adequacy of a feminist hermeneutic which
depends upon distinguishing between the essential and the
nonessential, form and content, or theological essence and
historical variable. More specifically, in her critique of
Ruether's hermeneutic proposal she argues that not only
does Ruether "draw a rather idealized picture of the biblical
and prophetic traditions but also she overlooks the oppressive androcentric elements of these traditions. Because she
does not analyze the classical prophetic tradition as a historical phenomenon, but uses it rather as an abstract criti-

cal interpretative pattern, she does not consider its patriarchal polemics and repression of the cult of the Goddess".[51]

A feminist biblical hermeneutic, Schüssler Fiorenza argues, "must take seriously the historical-patriarchal elements of the prophetic traditions in order to set free their liberating social-critical impulses for the struggle for women. It must retrieve them in and through a feminist critical analysis rather than elevate them to an abstract interpretative principle or criterion".[52] In the last analysis, Schüssler Fiorenza is arguing that Ruether's "reduction of the Bible to the prophetic-messianic tradition on the one hand and the concomitant reduction of this tradition to an abstract dehistoricized critical key on the other hand" does not go far enough towards developing a feminist critical hermeneutic.[53]

In order to move towards such a feminist critical hermeneutic Schüssler Fiorenza insists that women must move behind the text to a historical reconstruction of the context from which the text emerged. This is essential because the patriarchal texts do not mirror the historical and social context from which they came but offer a selective and perspectival picture of the early Christian communities. As Schüssler Fiorenza tries to demonstrate through historical reconstruction, women can move beyond the silences and backlashes against women found in the Bible to an awareness and appreciation of the participation and leadership of women in the life of the early Christian communities.[54] The biblical portrait of women in the early Christian movement is the "tip of the iceberg"; "what is necessary is a systematic interpretation and historical reconstruction able to make the submerged bulk of the iceberg visible".[55] In other words, "Only a movement behind the text can enable women to retrieve their heritage, and see their Christian foresisters not merely as victims but as victims and participants in the struggle for liberation".[56]

Although Schüssler Fiorenza rightly distinguishes her feminist hermeneutic from the approaches characteristic of Mollenkott's and Ruether's positions, there are fundamental similarities between these feminist alternatives. From the perspective of Dworkin's typology, Cady argues, "her position must be included within the naturalist type".

We have seen that the naturalist hermeneutical style rejects conventionalism for extracting isolated bits and pieces of the past rather than for interpreting it as a whole. Schüssler Fiorenza's argument can be construed similarly, as a criticism of feminist hermeneutics which does not adequately interpret the past 'as a whole'. By resting with suspicion and retrieval of a text, such feminist hermeneutics is neither radical enough in its suspicion of the androcentric texts nor able to retrieve the heritage of women which lies behind the texts. Schüssler Fiorenza, therefore, is not rejecting the naturalist approach but making very important contributions to an adequate understanding of what is entailed in interpreting the past 'as a whole'. [57]

For Schüssler Fiorenza the crucial point is, in the words of Cady, that "a contemporary interpretation of the past as a whole must not limit itself to the world of the text but must consider the historical and social context of the Christian communities".[58]

As in the case of Mollenkott and Ruether, however, the rationale for Schüssler Fiorenza's appropriation of the past is important. She cites with approval the arguments which Elizabeth Cady Stanton, the initiator of *The Woman's Bible*, gave for a corrective feminist interpretation of the Bible, and states that they are still valid today:

i. Throughout history and especially today the Bible is used to keep women in subjection and to hinder their emancipation.   .

ii. Not only men but especially women are the most faithful believers in the Bible as the word of God. Not only for men but also for women the Bible has a numinous authority.

iii. No reform is possible in one area of society if it is not advanced also in all other areas. One cannot reform the law and other cultural institutions without also reforming biblical religion which claims the Bible as Holy Scripture. Since 'all reforms are interdependent', a critical feminist interpretation is a necessary political endeavor, although it might not be opportune. If feminists think they can neglect the revision of the Bible because there are more pressing political issues, then they do not recognize the political impact of Scripture upon the churches and society, and also upon the lives of women.[59]

On their own such arguments tend towards the strategic or pragmatic view of the past associated with instrumentalism. Certainly Schüssler Fiorenza's position leans in this direction. However, like Ruether, Schüssler

Fiorenza refuses to abandon what she considers to be "authentic" within biblical religion.[60] She argues that a postbiblical feminist stance is in danger of becoming ahistorical and apolitical because it "too quickly concedes that women have no authentic history within biblical religion and too easily relinquishes women's feminist biblical heritage".[61] The point she is making here is that while androcentric texts may erase women from historiography, they do not prove the actual absence of women from the center of patriarchal history and the Bible.[62] So, while a feminist hermeneutical understanding that is orientated not simply towards an actualizing continuation of biblical traditions but towards a critical evaluation of them must uncover and reject those elements within biblical texts and traditions "that perpetuate, in the name of God, violence, alienation, and patriarchal subordination, and eradicate women from historical-theological consciousness", "*[a]t the same time*, such a feminist critical hermeneutics must recover *all* those elements within biblical texts and traditions that articulate the liberating experiences and visions of the people of God".[63]

In the same way, then, that Ruether's hermeneutic attempts a feminist recovery of the biblical principles or patterns of the prophetic-liberating tradition,[64] so too Schüssler Fiorenza's hermeneutic attempts a feminist recovery of "the biblical heritage of women".[65] In other words, both Ruether and Schüssler Fiorenza find something, a situation of struggle, which is potentially empowering for women in the struggle for liberation *in the biblical tradition*. The difference is that Ruether finds it primarily in the text while Schüssler Fiorenza finds it primarily behind the text.[66]

I say "primarily" because for both Schüssler Fiorenza and Ruether the status of the biblical *text* is more complex.[67] Schüssler Fiorenza accepts that "Most of women's early Christian heritage is probably lost and must be extracted from androcentric early Christian records", including the canonical biblical text.[68] Indeed, it is the "inconsistencies" *in the text* which indicate "that the early Christian traditioning and redactional processes followed certain androcentric interests and perspectives".[69] In other words,

> The canonization process of early Christian writings has preserved not only the patriarchalizing texts of the New Testament but also those earliest Christian traditions and texts that still permit us a glimpse of the egalitarian-inclusive practice and theology of early Christians . . . The canon thus does not function simply as perpetrator of women's secondary status in Christianity but also as a theological critique of this status.[70]

Similarly, in her discussion of the New Testament, Ruether argues that unlike the prophetic texts of the Old Testament, the egalitarian vision was not preserved "as the normative tradition in the New Testament".[71] In seeking an "alternative", "egalitarian", "countercultural" vision in the New Testament it must be "read between the lines", it must be "ferreted out", it must be brought to the surface, it must be rediscovered.[72]

> If this egalitarian, countercultural vision is accepted as the true norm of Christianity, then the authority of the official canonical framework is overturned. The conflict between liberating and patriarchal norms must be seen as existing in the New Testament in an even more radical way than in the Hebrew Scriptures. In the New Testament a suppressed tradition must be brought to the surface to criticize and refute the dominant hermeneutical line established by those who shaped the written canon.[73]

In other words, in the bulk of her discussion Ruether is dealing with prophetic-liberating "traditions", "patterns", "contents", "principles", "ideas", "imagery", "symbols", "paradigms", "themes". All these terms form a semantic field which obviously has its focus on the text. However, when it comes to the New Testament Ruether is not as clear. On the one hand she says that the countercultural character of the Jesus movement "has been reconstructed by the New Testament scholar Elisabeth Schüssler Fiorenza";[74] on the other hand she talks of "a suppressed tradition" and "fragments preserved under the surface of the New Testament".[75]

The point I am making here is that while Schüssler Fiorenza's primary focus is behind the text, she still recognizes empowering elements within the biblical text itself. Conversely, while Ruether's primary focus is on the text, she still recognizes empowering elements behind the biblical text. This does not minimize the important difference of emphasis between them. With reference to the biblical *text*, Schüssler

Fiorenza's position would tend more towards the instrumentalist position than Ruether's.

At this point it is necessary to consider once again the objection the instrumentalist approach raises about the use of the past, even with the important modification which Schüssler Fiorenza contributes. Is it not irrational, as well as immoral, to allow past interpretations to determine, in more than a strategic way, the most adequate interpretation in the present? As Cady recognizes, this is the most serious challenge facing theology and one which has been powerfully made by feminists.[76] However, it is not only feminists who have made such a challenge. It should come as no surprise to find a similar challenge confronting black theology in the South African context. So it will be instructive to refer to this context before returning to the challenge posed by instrumentalism.

Black Theology, the Bible, and Liberation

Mosala's essay on "The Use of the Bible in Black Theology" is a particularly significant essay in that for the first time in the South African context of liberation there is a clearly articulated questioning of the status of the biblical *text*.[77] Mosala levels similar criticisms at black theology as Schüssler Fiorenza levels at feminist theology, and like her also seems to lean towards an instrumentalist position.

Mosala's basic critique is directed at black theology's exegetical starting point which "expresses itself in the notion that the Bible is the revealed 'Word of God'".[78] He traces this view of the Bible as "an absolute, non-ideological 'Word of God'" back to the work of James Cone.[79] He finds it even in the work of the "most theoretically astute of black theologians", Cornel West. More importantly, "South African black theologians are not free from enslavement to this neo-orthodox theological problematic that regards the notion of the 'Word of God' as a hermeneutical starting point".[80]

Mosala underlines the pervasiveness of this view of the biblical tradition by subjecting Sigqibo Dwane, Simon Gqubule, Khoza Mgojo, Manas Buthelezi, Desmond Tutu, and

Allan Boesak to a similar critique. Mosala cites the following from Boesak as an example: "'In its focus on the poor and the oppressed, the theology of liberation is not a new theology; it is simply the proclamation of the age-old gospel, but now liberated from the deadly hold of the mighty and the powerful and made relevant to the situation of the oppressed and the poor'".[81] Mosala recognizes that, like Cone and Cornel West, Boesak insists on there being a biblical truth according to which God sides with the oppressed in their struggle for liberation. Mosala is willing to admit that this is true as far as it goes. But

> as any hermeneutics deriving from the crucible of class struggle will attest, the biblical truth that God sides with the oppressed is only one of the biblical truths. The other truth is that the struggle between Yahweh and Baal is not simply an ideological warfare taking place in the minds and hearts of believers but a struggle between the God of Israelite landless peasants and subdued slaves and the God of Israelite royal, noble, landlord, and priestly classes. In other words, the Bible is rent apart by the antagonistic struggles of the warring classes of Israelite society in much the same way as our world is torn asunder by society's class, cultural, racial, and gender divisions.[82]

Accordingly, black theology "needs a *new* exegetical starting point if it is to become a material force capable of gripping the black working class and peasant masses", and, as Mosala goes on to argue, "The social, cultural, political, and economic world of the black working class and peasantry constitutes the only valid hermeneutical starting point for a black theology of liberation".[83]

It should be made clear, however, that Mosala is here primarily discussing black theology's *starting point.* His contention, then, is that most of the Bible "offers no certain starting point for a theology of liberation within itself". For example, he argues that the book of Micah "is eloquent in its silence about the ideological struggle waged by the oppressed and exploited class of monarchic Israel". "In short, it is a ruling class document and represents the ideological and political interests of the ruling class". As such there "is simply too much de-ideologisation to be made before it can be hermeneutically straightforward in terms of the struggle for liberation".[84] The biblical text, therefore, cannot be the hermeneutical starting point of black theology. Rather, those committed to the struggles of the black oppressed and exploited people "cannot ignore the history, culture, and ideologies of the dominated black people as their primary hermeneutical starting point".[85]

However, this does not mean that Mosala totally rejects the biblical text. While the biblical text cannot be the primary starting point for black theology "there are enough contradictions within the book [of Micah, for example,] to enable eyes that are hermeneutically trained in the struggle for liberation today to observe the kin struggles of the oppressed and exploited of the biblical communities in the very absences of those struggles in the text". The Bible is, therefore, "a product and a record of class struggles".[86]

Mosala recognizes, in other words, that "black theologians are correct in detecting glimpses of liberation and of a determinate social movement galvanised by a powerful religious ideology in the biblical text". But, he continues, it "is not the existence of this which is in question. Rather, the problem being addressed here is one of developing an adequate hermeneutical framework which can rescue those liberative themes from the biblical text".[87] We will return to this important question in the next chapter. The point that is being made here is that, like Schüssler Fiorenza's, Mosala's approach falls within the naturalist hermeneutical type. This will become clearer below.

In a later essay Mosala sets out the arguments for his appropriation of the biblical tradition. He identifies two sources of black theology, "the biblical and the African roots of Black Theology".[88] Once again he makes the point that the entire Bible is not on the side of the black oppressed people of South Africa, but that on the contrary "there are significant parts of the Bible that militate against the struggle for liberation and are usable as ideological support for maintaining the interests of the ruling class".[89] Nevertheless,

> Black Theology has roots in the Bible insofar as it is capable of linking the struggles of oppressed people in South Africa today with the struggles of oppressed people in the communities of the Bible. The oppressed people in the Bible did not write the Bible. Their struggles come to us *via* the struggles of their oppressors. Thus Black Theology needs to be firmly and critically rooted in black

history and black culture in order for it to possess apposite weapons of struggle that can enable black people to get underneath the biblical text to the struggles of oppressed classes.[90]

Having reiterated his understanding of the status of the biblical tradition he develops his rationale for appropriating it. He continues, "Dialectically, Black Theology needs to be firmly and critically rooted in the Bible in order to elicit from it cultural-hermeneutical tools of combat with which black people can penetrate to the underside of black history and culture on the one hand, and beneath contemporary capitalist settler colonial domination on the other, to the experiences of oppressed and exploited working class black people".[91]

Unfortunately, this is about as explicit as Mosala gets with regard to his rationale for using the biblical tradition. However, his approach to the past does not appear to be merely pragmatic or strategic.

For further clarity on this issue it is useful at this point to consider an essay by another black interpreter who draws on Mosala's work and who elaborates on this issue.

In an essay, "Black Christians, the Bible, and Liberation",[92] Takatso Mofokeng argues that in the contemporary black South African context the Bible is both a problem and a solution. The "external" problem of the Bible is the oppressive and reactionary use of the Bible by white Christians. "When Black christians see all these conservative a[n]d reactionary efforts and hear the Bible being quoted in support of reactionary causes they realize that the Bible itself is indeed a serious problem to people who want to be free".[93]

Mofokeng outlines and critiques two main responses by black readers to locate and solve this problem. "The most commonly held approach has been to accuse oppressor-preachers of *misusing* the Bible for their oppressive purposes and objectives. This misuse is based, it is argued, on misinterpretation of biblical texts to support or promote oppressive intentions".[94] Also, in many cases "the problem of the Bible has been transferred to the area of ethics or the practical concretization of biblical teaching". Here "many downtrodden Christians have accused many preachers and racist whites of not practising what they preach".[95] It is clear,

Mofokeng argues, that these responses are "based on the assumption that the Bible is essentially a book of liberation".[96] While Mofokeng concedes that these responses have a certain amount of truth to them, the crucial point he wants to make is that there are numerous "texts, stories and traditions in the Bible which lend themselves to only oppressive interpretations and oppressive uses because of their inherent oppressive nature". What is more, any attempt "to 'save' or 'co-opt' these oppressive texts for the oppressed only serve the interests of the oppressors".[97]

Young blacks in particular, Mofokeng states, "have categorically identified the Bible as an oppressive document by its very nature and to its very core" and suggest that the best option "is to disavow the Christian faith and consequently be rid of the obnoxious Bible". Indeed, some "have zealously campaigned for its expulsion from the oppressed Black community", but, he notes, with little success.

The reason for this lack of success, Mofokeng argues, and here his argument sounds decidedly instrumentalist, is

> largely due to the fact that no easily accessible ideological silo or storeroom is being offered to the social classes of our people that are desperately in need of liberation. African traditional religions are too far behind most blacks while Marxism, is to my mind, far ahead of many blacks, especially adult people. In the absence of a better storeroom of ideological and spiritual food, the Christian religion and the Bible will continue for an undeterminable period of time to be the haven of the Black masses par excellence.

Given this situation of very limited ideological options, Mofokeng continues, "Black theologians who are committed to the struggle for liberation and are organically connected to the struggling Christian people, have chosen to honestly do their best to shape the Bible into a formidable weapon in the hands of the oppressed instead of leaving it to confuse, frustrate or even destroy our people".[98]

Such explanations would seem to tend towards instrumentalism, where strategic or pragmatic reasons for taking the past into account may be used. However, although this tendency is clearly present in Mofokeng, he does recognize that

> when many Black Christians read their history of struggle carefully, they come upon many Black heroes and heroines who were

inspired and sustained by some passages and stories of the Bible
in their struggle, when they read and interpreted them in the light
of their Black experience, history and culture. They could consequently resist dehumanization and the destruction of their faith in
God the liberator. It is this noble Black Christian history that helps
to bring out the other side of the Bible, namely, the nature of the
Bible as a book of hope for the downtrodden.[99]

He continues, significantly, by stating that "A careful reading of the experiences and witness of the early church con-
firms the correctness of the experiences of our people concerning the usefulness of the Bible as a book with a message
of survival, resistance and hope".[100]

It is for these reasons that Mofokeng argues that it is a
"viable option" for black theologians "to insist on finding and
controlling the tools of opening and interpreting the Bible as
well as participating in the process of interpretation itself".[101]
Again, the point that must be made here is that the methodological moves mentioned here by Mofokeng correspond
to the moves within a naturalist theory of adjudication.

On a continuum, then, Mofokeng and Mosala could be
placed within naturalism but tending towards
instrumentalism. But what about Boesak? Does the critique
of Mosala and Mofokeng mean that Boesak is a conventionalist?

In a perceptive discussion of the differences between
Boesak and Mosala, Frostin states that "a crucial aspect of
the dissension between Boesak and Mosala is to be found in
different concepts of 'Word of God'".[102] Frostin argues that
when Mosala discusses Boesak's and other black theologians'
notion of the Bible as the "Word of God", "he is primarily
thinking of the Word of God as the books of the Bible".[103] As
we have noted already, Mosala argues that the Bible offers
no unequivocal message of God and consequently cannot be
the fundamental criterion in theology. He critiques black
theology's understanding of the Bible as the "Word of God"
because

> the Word of God cannot (by definition) be the object of criticism.
> Furthermore, the Word of God cannot be critiqued in the light of
> the black experience or any other experience. The only appropriate
> response is obedience. At best, the black experience can be seen in
> the light of the Word of God but not vice versa. Does the definition
> of the Bible as the Word of God, therefore, mean that even the 'law

and order' God of David and Solomon cannot be the object of criticism in the light of the black experience? Does it mean that the black struggle cannot be hermeneutically connected with the struggles of the oppressed and exploited Israelites against the economic and political domination of the Israelite monarchical state, which was undergirded by the ideology of the Davidic-Zionist covenant (II Sam. 7)? Does it mean that no hermeneutical affinity can be established between working-class blacks and landless peasants, exploited workers, and destitute underclasses that made up the followers of Jesus? One cannot select one part of the 'Word of God' and neglect others.[104]

Mosala's critique is clearly directed towards a conventionalist appropriation of the biblical text. To what extent, then, is this critique applicable to Boesak?

Boesak does maintain that "Black theology deals with Black realities *in the light of,* and under the critique of, the word of God". In other words, for Boesak "Black theology itself falls under the judgement of the word".[105] Boesak cautions against Cone's notion of reflection "in the light of the black situation". He fears "that Cone attaches too much theological import to the black experience and the black situation as if these realities *within themselves* have revelational value on a par with Scripture". Rather, Boesak claims, God "reveals himself *in* the situation. The black experience provides the framework within which blacks understand the revelation of God in Jesus Christ. No more, no less".[106] So Boesak wants to emphasize both the theological importance of the black experience and its limits. "The black situation is the situation within which reflection and action take place, but it is the Word of God which illuminates the reflection and guides the action".[107]

However, for a clearer idea of just what Boesak understands by "Word of God" we need to ask with Frostin, what does the "Word of God" denote, when, for example, Boesak calls black theologians to cultivate "self-critical examination under the Word of God"? Frostin argues that "Even though 'Word of God' sometimes is used as a synonym of 'Scripture' and the Bible, it is also used in a less biblistic meaning. A close reading of the texts establishes that 'the self-critical reflection under the Word of God' demands that one test one's own programs by 'the criteria of the gospel of Jesus Christ,' defined as liberation, justice, and the wholeness of life".[108] In other words, while Boesak is reluctant to *identify* the black struggle for liberation with "the gospel", and while he argues that "an ethic of liberation . . . does not arise out of the situation", he does affirm that it arises "in the situation",[109] a situation of struggle which clearly shapes his understanding of the gospel as "liberation, justice, and the wholeness of life".[110]

Given this understanding of Boesak's use of "Word of God" (or "gospel") it would seem that Boesak too falls within the naturalist form of interpretation of the past. Unlike Mosala, however, Boesak would tend towards the conventionalist side of the continuum.

So while the instrumentalist challenge does shape liberation hermeneutics, there is a fairly clear commitment to a naturalist position among the interpreters we have been discussing.[111] I have already indicated some of the reasons for such a position, the most important being the need for continuity and solidarity with past struggles. In the next section I analyze this continuity and solidarity more carefully, once again using Cady as a guide. In her response to the challenge of instrumentalism Cady, who continues to use legal hermeneutics as her paradigm, elaborates on the naturalist's use of the past.

Reclaiming the past

In using Dworkin's work Cady realizes that the move from constitutional law to theology is not a simple one, but argues, using the work of Clifford Geertz, David Tracy, and Alasdair MacIntyre,[112] that there are significant parallels between them.

> While there is no exact equivalent to a political order within the domain of theology, there is, in my judgment, a comparable element which justifies the naturalist's use of the past. The theologian does not deal primarily with a political order but rather more specifically with a symbolic order (religious world view) which locates the task of theological interpretation, a task which includes a critical reading of the past as well as a reconstruction for the present. Since symbolic orders are maintained in large through

shared memories, the theologian's interpretation of the past is an essential element in the sustenance and transformation of such symbolic worlds.[113]

As noted earlier, according to the naturalist methodology the past is taken into account in order to sustain and to modify an existing symbolic order. This symbolic order is not elevated as an authority which requires the theologian to relinquish his or her critical judgement, a charge which is applicable to the conventionalist model. "On the contrary, *this existing symbolic order is only taken into account if it still possesses the power to orient life in a meaningful, truthful, powerful way.* The same could be said in terms of judicial law. The political order is not sustained if it appears morally and politically bankrupt. It is sustained if it continues to possess the resources to orient societal life".[114]

This brings us back to Gadamer. One of Gadamer's central concerns is to free us from the Enlightenment's "prejudice against prejudice". Gadamer argues that the Enlightenment's polarization of "authoritative tradition" and the "freedom of reason" has proved inadequate, particularly as the claim to be free of all prejudices has itself been unmasked by historical consciousness as an illegitimate prejudice.[115] The sense that an authority or a tradition may indeed be disclosive of the truth was not sufficiently acknowledged. With the rejection of the authority of the past went the elimination of the past as a possible source of genuine insight. As Mark Brett argues, Gadamer does not, however, "simply return to a dogmatic position which would uphold the legitimacy of tradition over against every reasonable argument which is brought against it. On the contrary, such a dogmatism would maintain the very polarity of tradition and reason which he is anxious to overcome; it would amount to an irrational preservation of tradition". According to Gadamer we must reclaim the past not as that to which we abdicate our own critical reason but as that which has the power to unmask our own prejudices and to disclose new truths.[116]

Developing Gadamer's point, Tracy persuasively argues that the privatization of religion and morality in contemporary culture is the continuing legacy of the Enlightenment's radical suspicion of tradition and authorities.

> Any attempt at an autonomy so pure that it is unaffected by the
> tradition in which we, willingly or unwillingly, stand is the final
> form of a general privatization which plagues our culture. If the
> terms 'socialization' and 'acculturation' mean anything, if 'finitude'
> and 'historicity' are other than empty abstractions, then one must
> restore a nonauthoritarian notion of authority and norm as well
> as a nontraditionalist notion of tradition to their legitimate place
> in all human reflection.[117]

In sum, according to Cady, "The naturalist model of
hermeneutics may be viewed as that type which continues
to view the past as disclosive of truth but which refuses
uncritically to capitulate to it".[118]

Cady recognizes, however, that there may be good reason
to judge a tradition bankrupt, or, so distorted, that standing
in continuity with it is deemed morally and intellectually
unacceptable. And, she goes on to argue, some feminist theologians have made extremely persuasive cases for such a
judgement.[119] In particular she mentions the work of Carol
Christ and Mary Daly who argue that there are intrinsic patriarchal distortions within Judaism and Christianity which
cannot be overcome given the symbolic roots of these traditions.[120] However, and this is the crux of Cady's argument,
"What differentiates their positions from, say, Ruether's and
Schüssler Fiorenza's, is not a refusal to invest the past with
heteronomous authority but a different judgement about the
potential resources of these existing symbolic orders to orient human life in a meaningful, truthful, and powerful
way".[121]

I would concur with Cady's reading of Ruether and
Schüssler Fiorenza. Both Ruether and Schüssler Fiorenza·
argue persuasively that it is feminist romanticism to abandon the reformation of a tradition in favour of discovering or
creating alternative traditions.[122] Schüssler Fiorenza argues
that a postbiblical feminist position is in danger of becoming
ahistorical and apolitical because it not only too quickly concedes that women have no authentic history within the biblical tradition and not only too easily relinquishes women's
feminist biblical heritage, but also because such a stance
does not "do justice to the positive experiences of contemporary women within biblical religion". Insofar as the Bible is
still influential today and insofar as it forms a part of many

women's personal, cultural, or religious Christian history, a cultural and social feminist transformation of society must take into account the biblical story and the historical impact of the biblical tradition. "We will either transform it into a new liberating future or continue to be subject to its tyranny whether we recognize its power or not".[123]

Similarly, Ruether argues that to express contemporary experience in a cultural and historical vacuum is both "self-deluding and unsatisfying".

> It is self-deluding because to communicate at all to oneself and others, one makes use of patterns of thought, however transformed by new experience, that have a history. It is unsatisfactory because, however much one discards large historical periods of dominant traditions, one still seeks to encompass this 'fallen history' within a larger context of authentic and truthful life. To look back to some original base of meaning and truth before corruption is to know that truth is more basic than falsehood and hence able, ultimately, to root out falsehood in a new future that is dawning in contemporary experience. To find glimmers of this truth in submerged and alternative traditions through history is to assure oneself that one is not mad or duped. Only by finding an alternative historical community and tradition more deeply rooted than those that have become corrupted can one feel sure that in criticizing the dominant tradition one is not just subjectively criticizing the dominant tradition but is, rather, touching a deeper bedrock of authentic Being upon which to ground the self. One cannot wield the lever of criticism without a place to stand.[124]

Again, Schüssler Fiorenza argues that feminists cannot afford an ahistorical or antihistorical stance "because it is precisely the power of oppression that deprives people of their history".[125] "Thus to reclaim early Christian history as women's own past and to insist that women's history is an integral part of early Christian historiography imply the search for roots, for solidarity with our foresisters, and finally for the memory of their sufferings, struggles, and powers as women".[126] Drawing here on the work of Johann Baptist Metz,[127] Schüssler Fiorenza insists that "Rather than *abandon* the memory of our foresisters' sufferings and hopes in our common patriarchal past, Christian feminists *reclaim* their sufferings and struggles in and through the subversive power of the 'remembered past'". Such a "subversive" or "dangerous memory" not only keeps alive the suffering and hopes of Christian women in the past but "also allows for a universal solidarity of sisterhood with all women of the past, present, and future who follow the same vision".[128] Standing in solidarity and continuity with these dangerous memories and subjugated knowledges is crucial to liberation hermeneutics.[129]

We find similar arguments in Mofokeng. He argues that by using the appropriate analytical tools, black Christians

> as members of a silenced, marginalized and sometimes ignored race . . . discover the silenced, ignored and marginalized people in the Bible and develop an affinity with them. They also discover the text behind the text of the Bible—a text that has been silenced but one that speaks through this silence about the struggles of the silenced and marginalized people of the Bible. As members of a people whose story of pain, fears and hopes has been suppressed, they are enabled, by their physical and psychological scars, together with the analytical tools they have chosen, to discover the suppressed and forgotten stories of the weak and the poor of the Bible. These seem, according to them, to be the stories wherein God is identifying with the forgotten and the weak and is actively retrieving them from the margins of the social world. It is through these stories that God the creator of humans is manifested as the God of the oppressed and accepted as such. This creator God acts incarnately in Jesus to end the rampant enmity in creation and restore real humanity to people. Only the reading of these stories of the downtrodden God among the downtrodden of this world strengthens the tormented faith of the oppressed of our time, as well as enhancing the quality of their commitment to the physical struggle for liberation. This discovery constitutes the liberation of the Bible from the clutches of the dominant in the Christian fold who impose the stories that justify their victories onto the oppressed.[130]

Mosala too recognizes that the "progressive traditions of the Bible" are disclosive of truth, provided we accept that there is no such thing as a politically and ideologically neutral reading of the Bible and so take up "the struggle to liberate the Bible so that the Bible can liberate us".[131]

Similarly, Frostin notes that Boesak's phrase of a black community that shares and experiences history "with God" suggests that the subversive memory, in Metz's sense, of God's revelation in Jesus Christ and of the past contrast experiences of the black community, experiences of suffering as a result of injustice, is the interpretive framework in black theology which defines what is understandable in the biblical texts.[132] For Boesak, then, the subversive and dangerous memories of past black struggles stand in continuity with the subversive and dangerous memories of the Cain and Abel story. Furthermore, standing in continuity with these past struggles is crucial to the reading of biblical texts by the present community of struggle.

So in the liberation hermeneutics of both Boesak and Mosala there is a commitment to stand in continuity with the past struggles of the poor and oppressed. Standing in solidarity with the poor and oppressed requires, then, not only accountability to present communities of the poor and oppressed but also continuity with past communities of the poor and oppressed.

Conclusion

Cady recognizes that viewing theological argumentation through the lens of Dworkin's typology will not eliminate all the methodological variations that have been identified.[133] "Methodological perspicuity will not resolve the fundamental disagreements which separate Daly from Schüssler Fiorenza and Ruether, for instance. It should, however, enable us to identify more adequately what in fact divides them".[134] This is the central contribution of Cady's analysis. As Cady has demonstrated, the differences between instrumentalists and naturalists "do not revolve around the problem of authorities and how they operate in theological argumentation. Their methodological divergences are rooted in conflicting assessments of the capacity of the resources of their inherited symbolic world to orient life adequately".[135]

More specifically, Cady's analysis ensures greater clarity in the debate between interpreters who hold differing positions with respect to the biblical text by identifying just where the disclosive and transforming power of their inherited symbolic world lies. Her analysis demonstrates, for example, a significant similarity in the positions of Boesak and Mosala, a similarity which has not been previously identified with any clarity.[136] Both Boesak and Mosala find resources in past situations of struggle within the biblical *tradition* which are potentially empowering for the poor and oppressed in South Africa. Furthermore, they are both committed to standing in solidarity with these past struggles. Continuity between past and present struggles and solidarity with past (and present) struggles form a crucial part of their respective modes of reading. Continuity and solidarity, then, locate the reader in the tradition.

So for both Boesak and Mosala, as for many feminists, the Bible is an important source for their theology of struggle.[137] Even in their more instrumentalist moments Mosala and Mofokeng acknowledge the empowering role of the biblical tradition and text, particularly for the ordinary reader.[138] They also both find, though to different degrees, empowering elements within the biblical *text* itself. However, a significant difference between Boesak and Mosala lies in their *primary* location of the empowering past situation of struggle. Boesak finds the struggle primarily in the text while Mosala finds it primarily behind the text.[139] The task of the next chapter is to explore this difference more carefully, while also considering how their respective modes of reading function in the liberation struggle.

Reading the Text, Behind the Text, and In Front of the Text: Interpretive Method and the Struggle

Introduction

In the previous chapter I argued that interpreters with different modes of reading find in the biblical tradition a situation of struggle which is potentially empowering for the poor and marginalized. The purpose of this chapter is to take up another of the questions raised in chapter three, namely, whether any particular mode of reading has a privileged relationship to the context of struggle. More specifically, the question in this chapter is about the relationship between an interpreter's interpretive interests and the liberation struggle. A closely related question which also arose in chapter three concerns the function of a particular mode of reading within the struggle for liberation and life.

In attempting to answer these questions this chapter analyzes three modes of reading and their respective relationships with the situation of struggle: reading the text, reading behind the text, and reading in front of the text. Each of these modes of readings is used within contexts of liberation. As in previous chapters, I will draw substantially on the work of Mosala and Boesak. I will also draw on the work of other interpreters from other contexts of liberation, including feminist and Latin American interpreters. However, before I begin this analysis it is important to distinguish between interpretive interests and moral and political interests. It is also important to examine the relationship between these interests.

In order to bring some clarity into discussions about textual interpretation Jeffrey Stout proposes that we use a form of Quinean explication with regard to the problematic term "meaning". Explication can be seen "as a means for exchanging more troublesome for less troublesome terms. Good explications . . . tell us how to translate theories from familiar but confusing idioms into idioms better suited to our purposes".[1]

What, then, might our concerns be when we inquire about the meaning of a text? We might, returning to the examples above, be interested in the author's intentions in a text, or in the narrative shape of a text, or in a text's "situatedness" within a particular mode of production. So, "What originally might be counted as evidence of drastic disagreement on a single topic now seems to show only that there are too many distinguishable topics present to sustain much substantive disagreement at all".[2] In other words,

> when we eliminate references to meanings, treating each theory's explication of meaning as a rule for replacing the term, the theories seem to lack a common topic. It goes without saying, of course, that they all bear in one way or another on the interpretation of texts. But they do not pick out the same aspect or feature of texts as the common topic for inquiry. This is what preoccupation with meaning tends to hide, and also what leads me to believe that much of the conflict among the theories can be dissolved.[3]

The aim, then, of explicating meaning in terms of interpretive interests is to show that some of our most intractable disagreements about textual meaning are not really disagreements about the same thing. What we thought to be one topic is really several topics.[4]

Stout's proposal, then, is that we dissolve disputes about the meaning of texts by explicating these disputes in terms of interpretive interests.[5]

Stephen Fowl argues that clarifying talk about meaning by explicating it in terms of interpretive interests should not,

however, lead us to think that we have resolved all our interpretive disagreements. What it does, though, is to enable us
to work with a clearer and more manageable set of disagreements of a much more substantive nature.[6]

At this point it is important to recognize and resist a common temptation. Having become aware of differing and conflicting meanings of a text, or having been persuaded of a
plurality of interpretive interests, interpreters may want to
insist that their particular interpretive interest is *the* right
one. Stout, and he is not alone in this as chapter one indicates, notes that we really have no epistemological grounds
for adjudicating between competing conceptions of textual
meaning or competing interpretive interests. We may have
other reasons for making such a plea but they are not based
on some epistemologically privileged position.[7]

We return now to the type of disagreements which are
likely to remain once we have explicated discussions of meaning in terms of interpretive interests. Fowl identifies and discusses a number of areas in which disagreement will remain.[8]
A particular area of disagreement central to this chapter concerns which interpretive interests to adopt in any particular
situation. Fowl suggests that there are at least three possible ways of dealing with this question. More importantly, he
acknowledges that none of these options "exists in abstraction from the social and political arrangements within which
one does one's interpretation".[9] I will return to this later in
the chapter.

Fowl explains each of the three options as follows. First,
there are those who having recognized that the term "meaning" has effectively worked to obscure the plurality of interpretive interests and that there are no grounds for granting
any particular interest epistemological privilege go on to
embrace and encourage the maintenance of a plurality of
interests.[10] "For pluralists, the only criterion for pursuing an
interpretative interest is that it is interesting to sufficient
numbers of an interpretive community to sustain its practice".[11] As has already been stated, such a position raises
ethical and political issues and "can only be coherent within
a particular social and political context".[12]

Second, there are those who while willing to accept that there can be no epistemological privilege between interpretive interests wish to argue that there are ethical or political reasons for adopting particular interpretive interests rather than others. Within this group, Fowl suggests, we can identify two perspectives. The first can be called a (universal) social responsibility position.[13] This view claims not only that interpreters do not practice their craft in a vacuum but that they have responsibilities to society.[14] Here, as opposed to the pluralist whose only criterion for pursuing an interest is that it is interesting, criteria such as social justice are invoked as those that should guide interpreters in their choice of interpretive interests. For this position these criteria are framed in universal terms. For example, Fowl argues that this position rests on some notion of a global *polis* and an ahistorical, trans-cultural, universally recognizable notion of social justice.[15]

Third, the second of the perspectives mentioned above, there are those who consciously draw their interpretive interests from a particular community. This position, which Fowl calls a "communal or collective position", shares with the social responsibility position the view that while no interpretive interest could claim epistemological privilege, there are ethical and political reasons for pursuing some interests over others in particular situations. This communal position, however, rejects the universal, trans-cultural, and ahistorical criteria of the social responsibility position.[16] For example, interpreters within the Latin American context might have their interpretive interests shaped by their commitment to a particular historical base-community. From within such a community justice would not be abstract and ahistorical.[17]

> Rather, it would receive specification and embodiment in concrete discussions and practices within the community. Having specified what justice is and how biblical interpretation is relevant to attaining it, such an interpretative community could then order its interpretative interests towards achieving such an end in any particular situation.[18]

This second position, the position of those who while willing to accept that there can be no epistemological privilege between interpretive interests wish to argue that there are ethical or political reasons for adopting particular interpretive interests rather than others, poses the crucial question in this chapter. Are some interpretive interests more appropriate to the struggle for liberation than others? This question, first raised in my analysis of the work of Mosala and Boesak, is answered in the affirmative by Mosala, Schüssler Fiorenza, and Gottwald.

Mosala, Schüssler Fiorenza, and Gottwald argue that a behind the text mode of reading is the appropriate mode of reading for contexts of liberation. More specifically, they argue that only a behind the text mode of reading provides a theoretically well-grounded hermeneutics of liberation. This chapter analyzes their arguments.

In the light of this analysis I then consider Phyllis Trible's close reading of the text and José Severino Croatto's in front of the text reading in order to establish whether these modes of reading can also provide a theoretically well-grounded hermeneutics of liberation. Finally, this chapter begins to address another of the questions raised in chapter three by considering the role of the ordinary reader in liberation hermeneutics.

Reading behind the text

Mosala contends that the impotence of black theology as a weapon of struggle comes from the enslavement of black theology "to the biblical hermeneutics of dominant ideologies".[19] More specifically, black theology's impotence comes from embracing "the ideological form of the text".[20] As we have already noted, for Mosala existential commitment to the struggle in South Africa "will not substitute for scientific analysis of the valence of a tradition in the class struggle".[21]

> Existentialist uses of the Bible in the struggle for liberation cannot be allowed to substitute for a theoretically well-grounded biblical hermeneutics of liberation. The reason for this is that, while texts that are against oppressed people may be coopted by the interlocutors of the liberation struggle, the fact that these texts have their ideological roots in oppressive practices means that the texts are capable of undergirding the interests of the oppressors even when used by the oppressed. In other words, oppressive texts cannot be totally tamed or subverted into liberative texts.[22]

More specifically with respect to Boesak's mode of reading, Mosala argues that to the extent that Boesak's existential appropriation of the Bible is founded on questionable
historical and theoretical grounds it must be asserted in
agreement with Assmann that there is a

> need to reject a 'fundamentalism of the Left' composed of short-
> circuits: attempts to transplant biblical paradigms and situations
> into our world without understanding their historical circum-
> stances. It is equally false to state that the whole biblical frame-
> work, with its infinite variety of paradigms and situations, is an
> adequate basis for establishing a satisfactory dialectics of
> hermeneutical principles.[23]

Mosala also cites Norman Gottwald who makes a similar
point to Assmann when he argues that

> while invoking biblical symbols of liberation, liberation theologians
> seldom push those biblical symbols all the way back to their socio-
> historic foundations, so that we can grasp concretely the inner-
> biblical strands of oppression and liberation in all their stark mul-
> tiplicity and contradictory interactions . . . A thinness of social
> structural analysis and a thinness of biblical analysis combine to
> give many expressions of liberation theology the look of devotional
> or polemical tracts . . . The picking and choosing of biblical re-
> sources may not carry sufficient structural analysis of biblical so-
> cieties to make a proper comparison with the present possible.
> Likewise, those most oriented to biblical grounding for liberation
> theology may lack knowledge or interest in the history of social
> forms and ideas from biblical times to the present, so that
> unstructural understanding of the Bible may simply reinforce and
> confirm unstructural understanding of the present.[24]

In an earlier work, *The Tribes of Yahweh*, Gottwald elaborates on this concern. "There is but one way in which those
religious symbols can be employed today in anything like
their full range and power, and that is *in a situation of social
struggle where people are attempting a breakthrough toward
a freer and fuller life based on equality and communal self-
possession*". Having said this, Gottwald immediately draws
a further implication from his discussion. "Even then it is a
risky business to 'summon up' powerful symbolism out of a
distant past unless the symbol users are very selfconscious
of their choices and applications, and fully aware of how their
social struggle is both like and unlike the social struggle of
the architects of the symbols".[25]

In sum, rather than naively assuming an overt or necessary connection between these inherited religious symbols
and our social aspirations and struggles, Gottwald argues
that

> it is imperative from moment to moment in the course of conflict
> that we determine the operational inter-ties between the predomi-
> nant religions and the current forms of social struggle. In particu-
> lar, we must assess to what degree and in what respects inherited
> religion converges on and reinforces social struggle and precisely
> which social sectors and tendencies religion validates and moti-
> vates and which social sectors and tendencies religion invalidates
> and discourages or obstructs.

> It should now be evident that efforts to draw 'religious inspiration'
> or 'biblical values' from the early Israelite heritage will be romantic
> and utopian unless resolutely correlated to both the ancient and
> the contemporary cultural-material and social-organizational foun-
> dations.[26]

Similarly, Mosala's fundamental objection against the biblical hermeneutics of black theology is that not only does it
suffer from an "unstructural understanding of the Bible" but,
both as a consequence and as a reason, it also suffers from
an "unstructural understanding" of the black experience and
struggle.[27] Central to Mosala's hermeneutics of liberation is
the search for a theoretical perspective that can locate both
the Bible and the black experience within appropriate historical contexts.[28] For Mosala a historical-materialist understanding of struggle provides the tool for reading both black
history and culture and the Bible. Crucially, a historical-
materialist understanding of struggle for a *critical* appropriation of black history and culture and the Bible.[29]

> The category of struggle becomes an important hermeneutical fac-
> tor not only in one's reading of his or her history and culture but
> also in one's understanding of the history, nature, ideology, and
> agenda of the biblical texts. Consequently, a biblical hermeneutics
> of liberation, using the same tool of struggle as was used to inter-
> rogate the reader's history, culture, and ideology, must now ad-
> dress the question of the material conditions that constitute the
> sites of the struggles that produced the biblical texts.[30]

In other words, Mosala is arguing for both a critical and
structural analysis of the black struggle and a critical and
structural analysis of the Bible around the issues of race,
class, gender, and age.[31]

In order to undertake this kind of analysis, Mosala argues, black interpreters must be engaged in the tasks of Terry Eagleton's "revolutionary cultural worker". Eagleton summarizes the tasks of the revolutionary cultural worker as "projective, polemical, and appropriative".[32] While Mosala recognizes that there is no doubt that black theology is "projective" and "appropriative", albeit vaguely and loosely, in its use of the Bible,[33] it is "certainly *not* polemical - in the sense of being critical - in its biblical hermeneutics".[34]

The point Mosala is making here is that black theology has not interrogated the text critically in class, cultural, gender, and age terms.[35] Black theology has not asked in what code the biblical text is cast and so has read the biblical text as an innocent and transparent container of a message or messages.[36] Mosala argues that underlying Boesak's mode of reading there is just such an assumption, namely, that "there exists a 'gospel' that all social classes, genders, and races can recognise equally as representing the essential message of Jesus of Nazareth". This perspective, continues Mosala, "derives from seeing and regarding the entire biblical text as encoding, in an unproblematic way, God's message and intention to and for the world".[37]

The Bible, according to Mosala's analysis, is a complex text best understood as itself a "*signified practice*". "As such, the Bible is coded differently in literary, political, cultural and ideological terms. It cannot be reduced to a simple socially and ideologically unmediated 'Word of God'. Nor can it be seen merely as a straight forward mirror of events in Ancient Israel. On the contrary it is a *production*, a remaking of those events and processes".[38] More specifically, some "parts", or more accurately "layers",[39] of the Bible are cast in "hegemonic codes" which represent social and historical realities in ancient Israel in terms of the interests of the ruling classes. Other parts of the Bible are encoded in "professional codes" which have a relative autonomy, but which still operate within the hegemony of the dominant code. Other parts of the Bible are signified through "negotiated codes" which contain a mixture of adaptive and oppositional elements, but which still take the dominant codes as their starting point. Still other parts of the Bible represent "oppositional codes" which are grounded in the interests and religious perspectives of the underclasses of the communities of the Bible.[40]

The main point here, of course, is that a critical and structural analysis of the biblical text requires that black theology identify the reference-code in which a particular text is encoded. For it is only by recognizing the particular encoding of a text that an interpreter can prevent herself or himself from colluding with the hegemonic and dominant. Moreover, it is only by recognizing the particular encoding of a text that the interpreter can then interpret the text "against the grain".

In other words, the polemical task of the interpreter is vital because it enables the appropriative task. A critical analysis of the biblical text ensures that black theology appropriates the text against the grain. "This means that it is not selective. It does not engage in 'proof-texting' in favour of one ideological position against another. It eschews monolithic positions. Rather, it advocates an analytic approach to the text of the Bible that exposes the underlying literary and ideological plurality in the text without denying the hegemonic totality or shall we say unity of the final product".[41]

This phrase of Eagleton's, "against the grain", seeks to remind us, Mosala argues, "that the appropriation of works and events is always a contradictory process embodying in some form a 'struggle'". As we have already seen, "struggle" is a key category in developing a biblical hermeneutics of liberation. The struggle in this context is, depending on the class forces involved, "either to harmonize the contradictions inherent in the works and events or to highlight them with a view to allowing social class choices in their appropriation".[42] The problem, according to Mosala, is that Boesak's readings exemplify how hermeneutically ill-equipped many black theologians are for this critical task.[43]

The crucial point here is not that Boesak *cannot* read any text, no matter what its encoding, against the grain, but that Boesak *ought* not to do this without *recognizing* what he is doing.[44] Mosala's primary concern, then, is that there ought to be a *critical consciousness* in the modes of reading of Boesak and other black theologians.

Mosala accepts that interpreters like Boesak are clearly correct "in detecting glimpses of liberation and of a determinate social movement galvanized by a powerful religious ideology in the biblical text". However, he argues, "The existence of this phenomenon is not in question; rather, the problem here is one of developing an adequate hermeneutical framework that can rescue those liberative themes from the biblical text". "One cannot, Mosala continues, "successfully perform this task by denying the oppressive structures that frame what liberating themes the texts encode".[45]

To summarize, three major concerns shape Mosala's arguments above. He is concerned that interpreters recognize the ideological nature of the text; he is concerned that readers develop the critical skills to analyze the text (and society) which will enable them to arrive at this identification;[46] and he is concerned that such an analysis should be theoretically well-grounded. His own answer to these concerns is a historical-materialist sociological reading of biblical texts (and society).

Similar concerns can be found in Schüssler Fiorenza's critique of Phyllis Trible and other feminist interpreters whose modes of reading focus on the text or in front of the text.[47] Schüssler Fiorenza begins her critique of Trible by arguing that Trible "shares with Russell and Ruether an understanding of the hermeneutic process that is rooted in neo-orthodox theology". What worries Schüssler Fiorenza is that "for Trible the voice of God is ultimately identical with the biblical text" and that in order "to find out the intention of God the biblical exegete must 'listen' to and interpret the text as accurately as possible".[48] Behind comments such as these is Schüssler Fiorenza's concern that Trible "is in danger of using a feminist perspective to rehabilitate the authority of the Bible, rather than to rehabilitate women's biblical history and theological heritage".[49]

Schüssler Fiorenza's concern here seems misplaced, because in a section that Schüssler Fiorenza herself quotes, Trible makes it quite clear that she is not interested in authorial intention;[50] and she never mentions "the intention of God". Her interest is the text itself, the Bible as literature. She wants to "explore the literature to discover its vitality". "This artistic pursuit", she continues, is neither isolated from nor opposed to a religious interest, neither superior nor subordinate. Although aesthetic and religious modes of experience can surely be distinguished 'at their more obvious levels,' nevertheless, 'they discover in their depths unexpected resonances and harmonies out of which a common music may be made.' In the totality of interpretation, their visions fuse. Thus, the Bible as literature is the Bible as scripture, regardless of one's attitude toward its authority. And conversely, the Bible as scripture is the Bible as literature, regardless of one's evaluation of its quality.[51]

In other words, far from rehabilitating the authority of the Bible Trible is concerned that her emphasis on the Bible as *literature* may be construed as not "religious" enough. Whether or not one fully accepts her "convergence of the aesthetic and the religious", Trible is clearly not basing her methodological approach on the authority of the Bible.[52] The problem of the authority of the Bible is more Schüssler Fiorenza's than Trible's.

More illuminating is the question of Trible's understanding of the status of the past. In terms of the previous chapter, which explicated talk of authority in other terms, both Trible and Schüssler Fiorenza would be naturalists. Both find elements of a feminist struggle in the biblical tradition which are worth recovering. Where they differ is in their primary location of this struggle. Trible locates the struggle primarily in the text, while Schüssler Fiorenza locates the struggle primarily behind the text.

With this rather unsubstantial critique out of the way I now come to Schüssler Fiorenza's more substantive critique. Taking up Trible's definition of feminism as "critique of culture in light of misogyny", Schüssler Fiorenza argues that

she does not engage in such a feminist critique of Scripture's misogynist stamp and character as a document of patriarchal culture because her method allows her to abstract the text from its cultural-historical context. If 'historical background, archaeological data, compositional history, authorial intention, sociological setting or theological motivation' are extrinsic to interpretation and only a 'supplement' to the textual understanding of the biblical interpreter, then feminist analysis as a cultural critique can really not inform her work. Patriarchal culture and patriarchal religion need not be addressed because they are extrinsic to the *meaning* of the biblical text for today. Trible therefore never raises the question of whether the female imagery and traditions about women are really feminist 'countervoices' or whether they are only remnants of the patriarchal repression of the Goddess and of women's religious powers. Since she focuses on the text and its interpretations, she also does not raise the political implications of biblical interpretation.[53]

In addition, "a method divorcing the language and text of the Bible from its socio-cultural patriarchal conditions cannot provide a model for the reconstruction of women's history as members of biblical religion".[54]

The crux of Schüssler Fiorenza's critique here is that Trible is not interested in what lies behind the text and that she *ought* to be. She ought to be, Schüssler Fiorenza argues, for two reasons. First, she ought to be because *the text* bears, as Trible admits, a permanent patriarchal stamp. In other words, Schüssler Fiorenza argues that there are no authentic feminist countervoices *in the text*, there are only patriarchally encoded "remnants of the patriarchal repression of the Goddess and of women's religious powers". The second, related, reason is that she ought to be because by focusing on the text Trible is unable to reconstruct and rehabilitate women's biblical history and theological heritage.

In order to more clearly understand Schüssler Fiorenza's argument it is necessary to consider her own approach in more detail. As we have already seen, she agrees with Ruether's argument that it would be "feminist romanticism" not to reappropriate and transform patriarchal culture and androcentric texts. However, the crucial question then becomes, "How and on what grounds is such a reappropriation possible and what makes such a reappropriation feminist?".[55]

Schüssler Fiorenza's starting point is Cady Stanton's insight that not only biblical interpretations but the biblical texts themselves are androcentric.[56] So

> it must not be overlooked that the marginality and invisibility of women in biblical history is produced by androcentric texts and linguistic reconstructions of history insofar as androcentric texts tend to erase women as active participants in history. Regardless of how androcentric texts may erase women from historiography, they do not prove the actual absence of women from the center of patriarchal history and biblical revelation.[57]

In other words, "Androcentric texts and linguistic reality constructions must not be mistaken as trustworthy evidence of human history, culture, and religion. The text *may* be the message, but the message *is not* coterminal with human reality and history".[58] What Schüssler Fiorenza calls a feminist critical hermeneutic must, therefore, "move from androcentric texts to their social-historical contexts".[59]

The need for this focus behind the text is necessary, Schüssler Fiorenza argues, because of the nature of the biblical text itself. First, biblical language is without question androcentric.[60] Second, early Christian authors have selected, redacted, and reformulated their traditional sources and materials with reference to their androcentic interests and perspectives.[61] Third, the textual and historical marginalization of women is also a by-product of the "patristic" selection and canonization process of the Bible.[62]

In addition, this focus behind the androcentric text is necessary, Schüssler Fiorenza argues, because the androcentric text misrepresents the life and ministry of Jesus and the discipleship community called forth by him, and because a feminist reconstruction of history recovers the early Christian movements as a discipleship of equals and the reality of women's engagement and leadership in these movements.[63]

In sum, we must find ways to break the silence of the text; rather than

> take androcentric texts as informative 'data' and accurate 'reports', we must read their 'silences' as evidence and indication of that reality about which they do not speak. Rather than reject the argument from silence as a valid historical argument, we must learn to read the silences of androcentric texts in such a way that they can provide 'clues' to the egalitarian reality of the early Christian movement.[64]

In order to do this a feminist critical hermeneutic of the Bible

> must develop theoretical interpretative models that can integrate the so-called countercultural, heretical, and egalitarian traditions and texts into its overall reconstruction of scriptural theology and history. Although the canon preserves only remnants of the nonpatriarchal early Christian ethos, those remnants still allow us to recognize that the patriarchalization process is not inherent in Christian revelation and community but progressed slowly and with difficulty. Therefore, a feminist biblical hermeneutics can reclaim early Christian theology and history as women's own theology and history. Women had the power and authority of the gospel. They

were central and leading individuals in the early Christian movement.[65]

Like Mosala, Schüssler Fiorenza critiques many of the traditional models of historical and sociological reconstruction.
She argues in favour of the developing feminist sociological
models for the reconstruction of history.[66] Such feminist sociological models for the reconstruction of history

> using the patriarchal household and family structures as heuristic
> categories are helpful to explore the a-familial character and the
> love patriarchalism of the early Christian movement. Moreover, they
> combine such a heuristic concept with a class analysis that makes
> the social setting of androcentric texts and symbolizations intelli-
> gible. Finally, they show that the definitions of sexual role and
> gender dimorphism are the outcome of the social-economic inter-
> actions between men and women but that they are not ordained
> either by nature or by God.[67]

Having briefly outlined Schüssler Fiorenza's approach we
will now analyze the link between her interpretive method,
historical and sociological reconstruction, and the feminist
struggle to which she is committed.

Schüssler Fiorenza summarizes her interpretive method
when she says that a feminist reconstitution of the world
behind the text requires "a feminist hermeneutics that shares
in the critical methods and impulses of historical scholarship on the one hand and in the theological goals of liberation theologies on the other hand".[68] So, on the one hand, a
feminist critical hermeneutics "not only challenges
androcentric reality constructions in language but seeks to
move from androcentric texts to patriarchal-historical contexts"; on the other hand, a feminist critical hermeneutics
"seeks to develop not only a textual-biblical hermeneutics
but also a historical-biblical hermeneutics of liberation. It
challenges biblical studies as 'objective' textual interpretations and value-neutral historical reconstructions fundamentally".[69]

> Such a historical reconstruction and theological revisioning is in-
> spired not only by scholarly theoretical goals but also by practical
> interests in the liberation of women from internalized biblical pa-
> triarchal structures and doctrines. It is concerned not only with
> analyzing the historical oppression of women in biblical religion
> but also with changing the social reality of the Christian churches

in which the religious oppression and eradication of women takes its specific historical patriarchal forms.[70]

Once again, as with Mosala and Gottwald, there is a clear *analogy of struggle*. Like them Schüssler Fiorenza also locates this struggle *behind the text*. While this is clearly her focus, Schüssler Fiorenza accepts that the biblical text remains a crucial and critical source for feminist reconstructions. So the ambivalence towards the biblical text so evident in Mosala and Mofokeng is also present in Schüssler Fiorenza. In words reminiscent of Mofokeng she states: the Bible as "the source of our power is also the source of our oppression".[71]

Although Schüssler Fiorenza recognizes that she has to work with the biblical text as a source for her reconstructions her focus is clearly behind the text. This is so for two reasons. First, her interpretive interests are historical and sociological. Hence her concern to reconstruct and rehabilitate "women's biblical history", and hence her concern for Trible's lack of such interests. Second, and more importantly, she argues that the feminist struggle requires such interpretive interests. She rejects the approaches of Ruether, Trible, and others because they are *selective*; they are "attempts to isolate the liberating Tradition from the androcentric-patriarchal texts of the Bible, to distill the feminist kerygmatic essence from its culturally conditioned androcentric expressions, and to separate social-critical prophetic traditions from the patriarchal oppressive biblical traditions".[72] Such views, she continues, are "in danger of reducing the ambiguity of historical struggle to theological essences and abstract, timeless principles".[73]

In sum, Schüssler Fiorenza has a problem with the text because, it would seem, and this is not absolutely clear, even the "inconsistencies" and "critiques" in the text are thoroughly patriarchal. The text is merely a clue, and a patriarchal clue at that. It is only behind the text that we can find "women's biblical history and theological heritage". In the words of Mosala and Gottwald, Schüssler Fiorenza is concerned that Trible's lack of interest in the history of social forms and ideas from biblical times to the present will produce an uncritical and unstructural understanding of the Bible which will simply reinforce and confirm an uncritical and unstructural understanding of the present.[74] In addition, Schüssler Fiorenza's continual critique of the alleged "selectivity" of Trible and others suggests a concern for what Mosala calls a *theoretically well-grounded* hermeneutic of liberation.

The question, then, is whether a mode of reading which has its focus on the text can respond to these concerns for a critical and structural reading of the Bible and a related structural and critical reading of society in a coherent and theoretically well-grounded way. Although Trible does not herself respond to this question, I have constructed a reply which arises from her reading practice. Such a reply clearly has relevance for aspects of Boesak's mode of reading.[75]

Reading the text

Trible recognizes that feminism, as a critique of culture and faith in the light of misogyny, as a prophetic movement which examines the status quo, pronouncing judgement, and calling for repentance, engages the Bible in various ways.[76]

One approach, similar to that of Schüssler Fiorenza, documents the case against women historically and sociologically. A second approach, characteristic of Trible's *God and the Rhetoric of Sexuality*, "discerns within the Bible critiques of patriarchy. It upholds forgotten texts and reinterprets familiar ones to shape a remnant theology that challenges the sexism of scripture". Yet a third approach, found in Trible's *Texts of Terror*, "recounts tales of terror *in memoriam* to offer sympathetic readings of abused women. If the first perspective documents misogyny historically and sociologically, this one appropriates the data poetically and theologically. At the same time, it continues to search for the remnant in unlikely places".[77]

Central to Trible's approach is the metaphor of the "Bible's journey": "The Bible is a pilgrim wandering through history to merge past and present".[78] What she understands by this is that "Composed of diverse traditions that span centuries, it embraces claims and counterclaims in witness to the complexities and ambiguities of existence. Similarly, it engages struggles and perplexities outside itself to generate varied applications throughout the ages". This metaphor of the "journey" of the Bible yields hermeneutical, methodological, and topical "clues" for her particular approach. "By exploring these clues we join the peregrinations of a text from an ancient to a contemporary setting".[79]

The first clue in Trible's mode of reading is the "hermeneutics functioning within scripture". By tracing the "pilgrimage" of a text Trible finds that "A single text appears in different versions with different functions in different contexts. Through application it confesses, challenges, comforts, and condemns. What it says on one occasion, it denies on another. Thus, scripture in itself yields multiple interpretations of itself".[80]

> Furthermore, this hermeneutic does not employ a single set of principles to achieve meanings. As our proclamation wandered through the centuries, it provided no map of its peregrinations. Seldom did it disclose precisely how it got from one time to another, from one setting to another, or from one meaning to another. Yet it did provide glimpses of numerous methodologies, such as compression, displacement, additions, omissions, and irony. Interpretation, then eschews systematizing. It invites participation in the movement of the text, and it requires risk on the way to application. Though mute, a text speaks to attentive hearers in particular contexts. In turn, these hearers construe the text variously.[81]

It is from this "inner hermeneutics" of the Bible that Trible derives a clue to "the pilgrimage of the Bible in the world".[82]

Trible's second clue is the interaction between the Bible and the world. Her emphasis here is the recognition of "a pilgrimage of understanding that is application". In other words, Trible recognizes that readers "understand scripture from the perspective of contemporary issues".[83] Here too there are multiple interpretations, which leads Trible to argue that

> All these contemporary interactions between the Bible and the world mirror the inner dynamics of scripture itself. The interpretive clue within the text is also the clue between the text and existence. Hence, the private and public journeys of the pilgrim named scripture converge to yield the integrity of its life. As the Bible interprets itself to complement or to contradict, to confirm or to challenge, so likewise we construe these traditions for our time, recognizing an affinity between then and now.[84]

For Trible "hermeneutics encompasses explication, understanding, and application from past to present. Subject to the experiences of the reader, this process is always compelling and never ending. New occasions teach new duties".[85] Among these "new occasions" is feminism "as a critique of culture in light of misogyny",[86] a perspective from which Trible is committed to read selected biblical texts.[87]

However, while Trible demonstrates the thesis of interaction between the Bible and world, she argues that this interaction "does not mean that the Bible has an 'answer' for every contemporary issue or even speaks specifically to it". "Nor", she continues, "does the fact of interaction per se legitimate an interpretation. Not all interpretations are valid, and not all valid interpretations are equally so". A major criterion for the evaluation of interpretations, according to Trible, is methodology.[88]

Trible accepts that "hermeneutics employs many acceptable methodologies", but herself chooses rhetorical (or literary) criticism. "According to this discipline, the major clue to interpretation is the text itself".[89] This "literary approach concentrates primarily on the text rather than on extrinsic factors such as historical background, archaeological data, compositional history, authorial intention, sociological setting, or theological motivation and result".[90] Unlike some, however, Trible is not here rejecting these "external concerns".[91] "To be sure, these external concerns supplement one's understanding so that the critic never divorces herself or himself from them". Yet, for Trible the "stress falls upon interpreting the literature in terms of itself".[92]

More specifically, she views the text as "a literary creation with an interlocking structure of words and motifs. Proper analysis of form yields proper articulation of meaning".[93] In other words, her accent is upon "the inseparability of form, content, and meaning; the rhetorical formation of sentences, episodes, and scenes as well as overall design and plot structure; and the portrayal of characters".[94]

As already mentioned, Trible recognizes that "since all methodologies are subject to the guiding interests of individual users, the application of a single one may result in multiple interpretations of a particular passage. Specifically, not all rhetorical studies yield the same results". However, following Ricoeur she argues that "while multiple readings are not per se mutually exclusive, not all interpretations are thereby equal". This is where the evaluative criterion of the particular methodology comes in. "The text, as form and content, limits constructions of itself and does, in fact, stand as a potential witness against all readings".[95]

The third clue Trible finds in the Bible is a topical clue. "Throughout the centuries, interpreters of scripture have explored the male language of faith, full and overflowing. Yet the Bible itself proclaims another dimension that faith has lost—female imagery and motifs",[96] and forgotten female characters.[97]

To sum up, within the Bible her topical clues are forgotten or neglected texts concerning women. To interpret this topic, her methodological clue is rhetorical criticism. Outside the Bible, her hermeneutical clue is an issue: feminism as a critique of culture. These clues meet as the Bible again wanders through history to merge past and present.[98]

In other words, the crucial aspects of Trible's mode of reading are the following. First, she argues that the text yields multiple interpretations of itself. Her emphasis here is less a question of the plurality and ambiguity of language than it is a question of context and application. This emphasis leads, second, to her argument that the interests and experiences of the interpreter guide and shape interpretation. Here she not only recognizes her own feminist interests and questions, she also embraces them. Third, she argues that within the Bible there are countervoices, untold tales of terror, and neglected themes. And fourth, she argues that this counterliterature can be recovered via a rhetorical-critical methodology to inform a feminist perspective.

Having briefly outlined Trible's approach, I can now analyze the link between her interpretive method, rhetorical (or literary) criticism, and the feminist struggle to which she is committed.

From the outset Trible recognizes that a focus on the stylistic and rhetorical features of the text presents problems for the feminist perspective.

Hebrew grammar employs masculine pronouns for God. Though grammatical gender decides neither sexuality nor theology, these distinctions are difficult, if not impossible, to maintain in our hearing and understanding. Consequently, masculine pronouns reinforce a male image of God, an image that obscures, even obliterates, female metaphors for deity. The effect is detrimental for faith and its participants. In my own writing, I avoid pronouns for deity; an occasional resulting awkwardness of style is a small price to pay for a valuable theological statement. As yet, however, I do not know how to resolve the dilemma posed by grammatical gender for deity in the scriptures themselves, since translation must answer to both grammatical accuracy and interpretive validity.[99]

This problem is reiterated more starkly in her conclusion where she states, "Clearly, the patriarchal stamp of scripture is permanent".[100]

But, she maintains, and here we see the link between her methodological approach and the feminist struggle, just as clearly, interpretation of the Bible is forever changing, "since new occasions teach new duties and contexts alter texts, liberating them from frozen duties and constructions".[101]

The crucial factor then is the feminist experience and the feminist questions which Trible brings to the text. Clearly, then, the hermeneutic clue between the text and world plays a significant role. Equally clearly, the hermeneutic clue within the text also plays a significant role. But what of the text itself? Does the text itself validate such feminist readings? In other words, does the text as form and content "witness" to such feminist readings?[102]

Trible responds in the affirmative. "In various ways they [the discussed texts and themes] demonstrate a depatriarchalizing principle at work in the Hebrew Bible. Depatriarchalizing is not an operation which the exegete performs on the text. It is a hermeneutic operating within Scripture itself. We expose it; we do not impose it".[103] In the conclusion of her *God and the Rhetoric of Sexuality* she restates this argument: "Moving across cultures and centuries, then, *the Bible informed a feminist perspective*, and correspondingly, a feminist perspective enlightened the Bible. Shaped by a rhetorical-critical methodology, this interaction resulted in new interpretations of old texts; moreover, *it uncovered neglected traditions to reveal countervoices within a patriarchal document*".[104]

Trible is making two related points here. First, she claims that there is a depatriarchalizing principle at work in the Bible itself. This depatriarchalizing principle operates "through themes which implicitly disavow sexism" and through careful exegesis of passages specifically concerned with female and male.[105] "For our day", Trible argues, "we need to perceive the depatriarchalizing principle, recover it in those texts and themes where it is present, and to accent it in our translations".[106] Second, she claims that feminist interests and questions can appropriate the Bible in new ways because the "meaning and function of biblical materials is fluid".[107]

In making these claims Trible realizes that this interaction between the text and feminist readers does not "eliminate the male-dominated character of scripture"; such a task, she continues, "would have been both impossible and dishonest".[108] Her task is more modest. She does not argue that the perspectives given in her readings dominate the scriptures. Instead, she has accented what she considers to be neglected themes and a counterliterature. "Using feminist hermeneutics, I have tried to recover old treasures and discover new ones in the household of faith. Though some of these treasures are small, they are nonetheless valuable in a tradition that is often compelled to live by the remnant".[109]

So, sharing similarities with Boesak's mode of reading, Trible finds an *analogy of struggle*, both a feminist and a wider liberation struggle,[110] *in the text*. While accepting that the dominant form of the text is patriarchal, she nevertheless finds clues to a feminist struggle, or remnants of such a struggle, *in the text itself*. Trible is also concerned to recover and appropriate this struggle for the feminist struggle today. Indeed, it is her very *situation of struggle* which brings her specifically feminist experiences, interests, and questions to the text. The interpretive method that links the biblical context of struggle with her context of struggle is a close reading of the surface structure of the text.

But what of the concerns of Mosala, Gottwald, and Schüssler Fiorenza? Have they been answered? As we have already noted, Trible acknowledges that the patriarchal nature of the Bible is evident and permanent![111] However, within

this patriarchal literature she finds a "counterliterature".[112]
She is not arguing here that this counterliterature is non-
patriarchal; she is arguing that *within* patriarchal literature
there are counter-discourses. What I am arguing, and this
is not necessarily Trible's understanding, although it reflects
her practice, is that Trible is *deconstructing* the biblical text.[113]

David Jobling argues that deconstruction expresses both
an attitude of mind and determines a method of interpretation.[114] "The attitude of mind is one which senses that human systems, and in particular the complex system which is
'western culture', are built on arbitrary but established cer-
tainties which become near-impregnable defenses against
alternative ways of being, doing, and thinking". "The method
is to analyze a system, eventually 'the system', from a perspective of what it must exclude in order to maintain itself
as a system, and then to demonstrate its failure to achieve
this exclusion".[115] The problem, as Jobling notes, is "that we
can only analyze within terms the system gives us . . . We do
not escape the system".[116] In other words, "Deconstruction
is an insistent *problematization* of human constructions from
within".[117]

Jobling's discussion indicates a distinction between two
emphases within deconstruction.

> On the one hand, it [deconstruction] may emphasize the
> *ungroundedness* of a system, its lack of justification outside of ar-
> bitrary axioms; this emphasis has much in common with a
> 'hermeneutic of suspicion'. On the other hand, it may emphasize
> the *endlessness* of the process of interpretation, suggesting (de-
> pending on the analyst) one of two extremes: a terror of the 'abyss'
> of meaninglessness, or a joyous self-abandonment to the 'free play'
> of meanings.

Jobling adds that "Though these emphases must eventually come together, their distinction is very important for
analysis".[118]

These emphases, I would argue, do come together in
Trible's mode of reading. In her work, as has been shown, we
find both the "ungroundedness" of the patriarchal system
and the "endlessness" of the process of interpretation. What
keeps Trible from the nihilism of meaninglessness and the
play of pluralism is her social and political commitment, her
commitment to the feminist struggle.[119]

Trible, then, conjoins two discourses: "liberation" and "deconstruction". In the words of Jobling,

These two discourses, liberation and deconstruction, embody demands for freedom which are revolutionary vis-á-vis the established system. Liberation embodies the demand from the dominant culture's political and economic 'Other', both from the geographical outside, the Third World, and from within (movements of sociopolitical and personal liberation in the West).[120] Deconstruction embodies the demand from the withinest of within, setting out to interpret what is really going on in freedom from the dominant culture's most basic assumptions, assumptions so deep that the culture doesn't notice them. The 'Other' which deconstruction makes heard is what has aptly been called the 'political Unconscious' of the West, the assumptions which generate our sociopolitical structures, and which these structures serve to conceal.

"Revolution from without and from within; these discourses belong together";[121] something Trible's work demonstrates.

In summary, I am arguing that working within the system of the patriarchal literature of the Bible Trible uncovers and recovers a counterliterature which deconstructs the dominant patriarchal tradition.[122] She does not claim that the perspectives given in her work dominate the Bible. Instead, she has given prominence to what she considers neglected themes and counterliterature.[123] In so doing she enables marginalized discourses and marginalized groups to become counter-discourses and counter-movements![124] Trible's selectivity is not a search for non-patriarchal "essences" but an uncovering of those texts which deconstruct, and so render unstable, the patriarchal system. It is, to use Gottwald's phrase, a "restructuring of consciousness",[125] with respect to both the past text and present society. Trible's mode of reading is certainly not an "unstructural understanding of the Bible" nor is it an "unstructural understanding of the present". Her literary-feminist reading of the text is a theoretically well-grounded hermeneutic of liberation which challenges the reader and the dominant methods in much the same way as the modes of reading of Mosala, Gottwald, and Schüssler Fiorenza.[126]

In saying this I realize that the meaning of "structural" shifts somewhat between Mosala and Gottwald on the one hand and Schüssler Fiorenza on the other,[127] and then between Schüssler Fiorenza on the one hand and Trible on the other. Nevertheless, there is significant overlap in their common commitment to a critical approach to the text and society, and this, I would argue, is the crucial issue. This is in line with Gottwald's positive assessment of Schüssler Fiorenza's work and his general positive assessment of feminist theology's "critical" appropriation of the Bible.

In other words, as far as Gottwald is concerned, the crucial issue is a critical reading which constantly mediates "between the patriarchal overlays and the feminist outcroppings within the Bible" and so incorporates a "principle of canonical criticism driven along by a preunderstanding of the presence of divided and contradictory social and theological currents in the biblical testimonies themselves".[128] Trible clearly practises such a critical mode of reading.

Trible does not foreground method in quite the same way as Mosala, Gottwald, and Schüssler Fiorenza. She acknowledges, as we have already noted, that her mode of reading is one among other useful and appropriate modes of reading.[129] The final "respondent" in this chapter, however, does foreground method. In addressing similar concerns to those of Mosala, Gottwald, and Schüssler Fiorenza, José Severino Croatto, a Latin American interpreter, articulates and advocates a mode of reading *in front of the text.* Croatto articulates with some clarity "a theory of reading" which would support aspects of Boesak's mode of reading. For this reason, and the related reason that his mode of reading is the most coherent and theoretically well-grounded of those interpreters who focus on the text within contexts of liberation, I will discuss his mode of reading in some detail.

Reading in front of the text

Croatto's hermeneutic begins by affirming a commitment to both the Bible and to his context of liberation. This is captured succinctly in the earliest of his three studies on biblical hermeneutics:

So this little book seeks to orchestrate a method for re-reading the Bible from the standpoint of our own situation in Latin America. The aim of our method is to enable us to construct a *theology* of liberation and to avoid the opposite danger—the danger of flatly denying the relevance of the Bible, insofar as it is a text from the past, as a message of liberation *for us.*[130]

Again and again these two commitments are affirmed. Croatto dedicates his most recent work on biblical hermeneutics to "all who make their lives a living witness of the word of God, rereading it from the vantage point of their commitment to the dispossessed",[131] and rejects the attitude of a great number of Christians committed to the struggle against unjust structures which relegates the Bible "to a secondary level, as a 'deactualized' text, a text no longer speaking to the present".[132]

Croatto does not, however, minimize the question underlying this attitude: "Does the gospel say anything*new* to us?" He recognizes that the question is a sincere one, but argues that "it reflects a methodological flaw, emerging from a traditional reading of the Bible that has alienated it from the real history of men and women".[133] It is therefore "a matter of urgency", Croatto argues, "to acquire the theoretical instrumentation that will enable us to reread the Bible in such a way as to tap its 'reservoir of meaning'" so that it "speaks to us in the present".[134]

And this is the central purpose of Croatto's hermeneutical work, to articulate a "theoretical instrumentation" which answers the crucial question of "how does a message expressed in another age, for a people of another cultural and social milieu, become effective in our time and place?"[135]

Croatto, who bases his mode of reading on the work of Paul Ricoeur and Hans-Georg Gadamer,[136] summarizes his mode of reading as follows:

> we can speak of a circular dialectic between event and word, and, by the same token, between kerygma and situation, between the biblical word on liberation and our processes of liberation. But a hermeneutic reading of the biblical message occurs only when the reading *supersedes the first contextual meaning* (not only that of the author but also that of the first readers). This happens *through the unfolding of a surplus-of-meaning disclosed by a new question addressed to the text.*[137]

The Bible as Language

The first strand in Croatto's hermeneutic is his understanding of the Bible as language. In both his later works on biblical hermeneutics Croatto begins with the Bible as *language*.[138] He draws on de Saussure's distinction between *langue* (language as system) and *parole* (language as speech) and Chomsky's distinction between competence and performance in order to establish that in the move from "language to speech, from competency to performance, from system to use, a first *distantiation* occurs"; that is, a "closure" of meaning takes place.[139]

Briefly, he is arguing here that in the act of discourse, in the speech act, which is made up of a sender, a receiver, and a context or horizon of understanding, "there must be a *closure* of the potential polysemy residing in the words or sentences" for communication to take place.[140] Put in another way, the system of signs which is language (*langue*) must be "activated" by having it "*used to say something about something*". Speech (*parole*) is "the *act* executing the given possibilities residing within a system of signs" in which the three factors, sender, receiver, and context, contribute to the "closure of meaning".[141]

Language, however, is not exhausted in this step. A new distantiation, which Croatto calls a "second distantiation" occurs "when discourse crystallizes in a transmitted 'text'".[142] Croatto makes two important points here with regard to texts. "The first is the capacity of a text to bestow meaning in virtue of what it is - the *coding* of a message". The point here is that a text is something which has definite limits within which structured internal relationships produce a meaning.[143] The importance of this point will emerge more fully later.

The second point is that a text "is open to a new understanding thanks to the second distantiation, that between 'speech' or the act of discourse and the inscription of meaning in such or such a text".[144] This distancing takes place because of significant changes in the three factors that have previously contributed to the closure of meaning, which now contribute to the opening of meaning. The original sender disappears in a text;[145] the original receiver is no longer present; and the context of the original discourse disappears.[146]

These two characteristics of the text (emphasized in Ricoeur's work) shape Croatto's understanding of the hermeneutic process and he returns to them again and again. He summarizes this understanding as follows: "The meaning is now in the text, not in the mind of the author. But it is not in the text as a separable entity; rather it is 'coded' in a system of signs constituting the account and 'saying something about something' by virtue of its manifestation as*this* discourse".[147] And it is this "autonomy" of the text which conditions the hermeneutic openness of the act of reading.

> The author's finite horizon is replaced by a textual infinitude. The account opens up again to a polysemy, and not only a *potential* polysemy, as on the level of 'language', but a *potentiated* polysemy, made possible by the network of significates or meanings that constitute a work. This textual openness awaits new addressees, with their own 'world.'[148]

The role of the reader

The final sentence of this quotation introduces the second strand in Croatto's hermeneutic: the role of the reader. For Croatto "any reading is the *production* of discourse, and thus of a meaning, from a point of departure in a text".[149] This production of discourse is generated by the relationship between the text as text, on the one hand, and the readers in their context, on the other. Croatto explains this relationship as follows:

> This [production of discourse] is possible, first, because discourse engages a plurality of codes, which each reading selects and organizes. Secondly, because, as we know, the author 'dies,' is 'erased', leaving only what he or she has written: henceforth it is the text that contains within itself not only the moment of reading, or interpretation, but the moment of production as well. In other words the text becomes polysemic, even from a purely semiotic viewpoint. It contains a surplus-of-meaning, which wells up and spills over when the text is read.

But there is another facet: any and every reading of a text is done *from and in a given situation*—from and in a context that is no longer that of the first addressees of the text. The reader interrogates the text from and in the reader's own being and concerns—not in order to *impose* an *extraneous* meaning, but in order to interpret *the text itself*. To this end the reader mobilizes the semantic potential of the text by selecting codes that correspond to his or her own situation and context.[150]

We will return to this strand of Croatto's hermeneutic from a slightly different perspective later.

The canonical process

A third strand in Croatto's hermeneutic is his understanding of the canonical process, or what he calls the move from event to text. Croatto argues that "The point of departure of a text is an experience of some kind—a practice, an important event, a worldview, a state of oppression, a liberation process, an experience of grace and salvation, or the like. Any of these may be called an 'event'".[151] In the move from event a crucial hermeneutic phenomenon is at work: "the word springing from the event, in order to narrate it or celebrate it, effectuates a selection, prioritizing one experience and leaving many others in shadow. This is a form of closure, and therefore of interpretation".[152]

With this understanding of an event producing meaning Croatto goes on to argue that "this meaning can be manifested in other events, aligned with the first". The first event, then, is seen as "originary" with respect to the others. "It is now understood as the 'founding' event". But, and this is important, it is seen to have been foundational "only at a distance—in light of its projections in new events".[153]

The canonical process flows from this dynamic. "An 'originary event' broadens its meaning in readings made of it at a distance, as it incorporates new events".[154] These readings are then transformed into a living "tradition". Tradition in all its many forms, from determinate practices to oral or written texts, "is the organized rereading or earlier readings of founding events". Tradition, then, is a form of closure. However, "At a certain stage, tradition, representing the closure of an earlier reading of originary events, tends to become polysemous—open to interpretation".[155] But, continues Croatto, the very concept of "tradition" implies a limiting and controlling context, so that rereading will frequently generate tension. "When a tradition arrives at the moment of greatest tension in its growth of meaning, one of two possible solutions generally results. Either it divides or it 'closures' in a *canon—which will also exclude aspects of tradi-*

tion, *thus being tantamount to originating a certain division*".[156] Put a little differently, "At a determinate moment in the course of this process, a 'cut-off', a delimitation occurs, with respect to the (oral or written) texts representing*the* interpretation of the events that have given rise to this tradition".[157]

So this closure which comes about in the canon is part of a long hermeneutic process; a process which does not end with the canon. Although the canon is a closure which does not admit a reopening, or the inclusion of new traditions, the canon "will be polysemous". This is so because the canon is a *text*, and a text which embodies polysemous processes.[158] The interpretive process cannot be closed off, and generates a variety of literary products: translation, targum, *pesher*, midrash, commentary, sermon, or theological and philosophical systematizations. "Thus the canon, which in the moment of its constitution was an expression of 'closure of meaning', ironbound and authoritarian, becomes polysemous, in virtue of being a text, in virtue of the distance between it and the successive generations who read it, and in virtue of the life of the community that harbors it".[159]

The originary event

The fourth strand of Croatto's mode of reading elaborates on the "originary event" itself. For Croatto the origin of the Bible lies in the Exodus event. The Bible's origin, "in the origin of the Israelites as a people, was *in a liberation process*".[160] From this moment forward, "it is this liberation experience that will be the 'referent' in the historico-salvific project of Israel". "Jewish religious institutions—the festivals, the prophetical critique of breaches of the covenant, the heralding of a new order of justice, the messianic hope, Jesus' proclamation—all these, too, recall and retrieve the 'memory' of the exodus as liberative content".[161] So even with its contextual transfer, "the liberation message permeates the pages of the New Testament. And the theology of the exodus—sometimes, to be sure, at a distance—echoes once again".[162]

What Croatto is here asserting is that the reading of the Exodus event and its subsequent rereadings "constitutes a 'semantic axis' on the level of text, which becomes, at the proper moment, a 'kerygmatic axis' on the level of message"[163] In other words, one of the "axes of meaning" in the Bible as a

totality is "the kerygma of the liberation of the oppressed".[164]
There are other "axes", for example, justice, love and fidelity,
hope, the covenant, God's presence as grace, judgement, freedom, and so on, which are part of the kerygmatic continuum
and which confirm and reinterpret the "core-of-meaning" of
the Exodus as it reaches *us* by passing through them.[165]

The context of the reader

As the emphasis in the last sentence above indicates,
Croatto is always concerned with the appropriation of meaning "for us". Integral to the strand of the readers' production
of meaning discussed above is the context of the readers.
This fifth strand is also closely related to the previous one.
Because the Bible's origin "was marked by profound experiences of suffering and oppression, liberation and grace, in
which Israelite faith could recognize the savior God in a
liberative dimension", therefore "the lowly of the earth are on
a 'horizon of understanding' that renders the biblical kerygma
'pertinent' to them". Put more strongly, "Inasmuch as the
generality of human experience is that of suffering, wretch-
edness, sin, and oppression, it is not difficult to recognize
that the most adequate 'ownership' of the Bible, the most
adequate 'pertinency' for rereading the kerygma of the Bible,
is with the poor. The kerygma belongs to them 'preferen-
tially'—first and foremost". There is a common frame-of-ref-
erence between the "horizon of production" and the "horizon
of understanding".[166]

But this is not all. Croatto has more to say concerning the
readers' context. "One of the 'semantic axes' of the Bible", he
argues, "is precisely that God is primarily revealed *in the
events* of human history".[167] So just as the Exodus event
was taken up in literary symbols and narrative codes which
express the interpretation of faith,[168] so too God is saying
something *new* in the struggles of the oppressed, in the process of liberation today.[169] Human events, in other words, are
not only illuminated by a text but also by the meaning that
faith discovers in these present human events.[170] "The text,
then, is the vehicle of a message because it continually incorporates its own rereading, called for by practice and by
the work of faith, which continues to discover the ever new
God of history".[171] "*Recontextualization*" of the biblical mes-

sage requires a reading of the "signs of the times",[172] and a reading from a particular praxis.[173]

Bringing the strands together: the fusion of horizons

Having outlined the hermeneutic process as Croatto understands it is important to recognize that

> This hermeneutic process is *part of the very message of the Bible.* That is to say, the Bible, taken as 'product' of a hermeneutic process, favors us with an important reading key: that its kerygmatic meaning is bestowed only in the prolongation of the same hermeneutic process (the 'two-way street' from event to word and back) that has constituted the Bible. Thus, to lay claim to 'fixing' its meaning once and for all at the moment of its production is to deny its *open meaning.* When, by contrast, the Bible is read from out of socio-historical reality—political, economic, cultural, religious, and the like—it reveals dimensions not previously seen, helped by beams of light not captured in earlier readings. What is unsaid in what a text 'says' is said in a contextualized interpretation.[174]

"Actualizing" the biblical message means rendering the biblical kerygma effective for our situation. This is done by (1) applying the laws of the linguistics of discourse (strand one), (2) by recalling the process of the event-become-word, in which a meaning unfolds in the biblical text, a meaning that overflows its first referent (strands three and four), and (3) by recognizing that there is not one route only, emerging only *from* the biblical text, but that hermeneutic circularity implies a "return trip", in which the praxis of faith in a determinate social context also has a contribution to make to the "meaning" of the Bible, opening it up precisely as "word of God" (strands two and five).[175]

In summary, like the others in this chapter, Croatto emphasizes the interests and questions of the interpreter in the interpretive process. Like Trible, he insists on readings being warranted by the text. However, while Trible focuses on the literary characteristics of the text, and Schüssler Fiorenza, Gottwald and Mosala focus on the reconstructed situation behind the text, Croatto focuses on the major themes, metaphors, and semantic axes in the text.[176]

Clearly, then, Croatto presents a coherent and *theoretically well-grounded* biblical hermeneutic of liberation. But

like Mosala, Gottwald, and Schüssler Fiorenza Croatto goes
further and argues that we *ought* to read the text in this way.
In other words, he too advocates particular interpretive interests, and so a particular mode of reading.

Text versus behind the text

Croatto's emphasis on "text as text" is the underlying argument of his mode of reading, and while I have already discussed his understanding of language, it is important to recognize the important role of "text" in his mode of reading.
Also, it is in connection with his discussion of the Bible as
text that he discusses the role of the historical-critical and
sociological methods (and so dialogues with Mosala, Schüssler
Fiorenza, and Gottwald).

Croatto's emphasis throughout is on the Bible as text.
The historical-critical methods attempt to recover the "behind" of the text, the life situation that originated it or the
author that intended it, where the "priority is finally assigned
to the referent—an extralinguistic factor— over the meaning
and import of the text itself". "But", insists Croatto,
"*rereadings flow from the text, not from the referent*".[177]   In
addition, it is not historical people, authors, or events but
the canonical *text* which has been handed down by tradition
and held to be the word of God. Hence the supreme importance of any reading as "a *reading of a text*".[178]

The problem with the historical-critical approaches, according to Croatto, is that they seek to read the facts and
thus rob the accounts of "the hermeneutic distance that has
restructured their meaning". And here lies a central understanding of Croatto's. There is no such thing as "pure fact",
"no such thing as 'pure' chronicle, without interpretation".[179]

So all we have is interpretation and it is precisely in interpretation that we have meaning or "*theological* significance".[180]
Historical-critical exegesis seeks to understand the production of texts, "whereas the theological reading done from
within a faith experience concentrates on the text produced,
exploring its reservoir of meaning as linguistic phenomenon
and as word of God".[181]

So an event only has "meaning" insofar as it is interpreted and becomes "meaning-event", which is in turn "subsumed into a meaning-*text*, which has the status of *scripture*". The vehicle of meaning is now a *text*.[182] In other words, we always return to the plane of language.[183]

This does not mean that Croatto totally rejects the historical-critical methods, although he is very clear about their limitations. He dismisses their aspiration to isolate the "objective, *historical* sense of a biblical text" as illusory.[184] Furthermore, he states that it is not "such a simple matter to get at what is 'behind' the text". But his fundamental critique is that these methods "run the risk of shutting up the message of the Bible in the past" by focusing on the "behind", the archaeology, of a text, or by "clinging to the *intention of the author or redactor* as the sole meaning". The historical-critical methods offer a *history* of the text rather than an exploration of its meaning for today.[185]

However, he does see an "urgent", but partial, role for them. In answering the objection that his mode of reading is subjective he responds by arguing that

> the hermeneutics of a text is conditioned *by the text itself.* The text indicates the limit (however broad) of its own meaning. Textual polysemy does not mean simply what-you-will. *A text says what it permits to be said.* Its polysemy arises from its previous *closure.* Hence the urgency of situating it in its proper context, by means of historico-critical methods, and of exploring its capacity for the production of meaning (according to the laws of semiotics), in order thus to cause its 'forward' to blossom from within life.[186]

This quotation states his position succinctly. He recognizes the importance of locating a text in its context of production and so refuses to go along fully with a reductionist structural analysis which "abstracts from the 'life' of a text— its history, its cultural, social, or religious milieu".[187] He also accepts that a text's meaning is limited by these factors.[188] And yet he still wants to affirm the fertility of the "literary structure" of a text "inasmuch as it gives us certain reading keys emerging from the codification of a text".[189]

Most importantly, he wants to argue, as we shall see in more detail below, that our Bible is "a process Bible" in which the process of intratextual rereading is part of the very message of the Bible, a process which the historical-critical methods, even redaction criticism, fails to explore.

For Croatto, then, the significative possibilities of a text do not end with historical-critical methods. Moreover, "For a theology of oppressed peoples, especially, this approach offers only a partial solution. Its importance is undeniable. One must pass this way. But one must not rest here".[190]

As I have already suggested, Croatto is here reacting primarily to the failure of historical-critical approaches to complete the hermeneutic circle. He is also, however, arguing for an interest in the text itself, an interpretive interest which those committed to a context of liberation should have. In this respect Croatto shares a fair amount in common with a large number of interpreters who advocate reading the final form of a text.[191] However, more controversially, Croatto goes on to argue that not only should we read the final form of the text but that we should read the final *canonical* form of the text. Croatto's focus on the final canonical form of the text arises from a cluster of arguments, some more overt than others.

Reading the canonical form of the text

The central concern in this cluster of arguments is an overt concern for the ordinary reader. Croatto argues that a reading of the Bible from the "grassroots", from the "base", entails certain disadvantages. He points out two disadvantages. First, the Bible "is a very long book. It contains 'a bit of everything', and one can find pretty much whatever one would like". This is clearly a disadvantage when one acknowledges, as Croatto does, that the poor and oppressed usually have little say in what "bits" have traditionally received attention. Second, "the Bible is a book put together and structured, by and large, by a comfortable middle class generally alienated from the people". The disadvantage here is clear, the Bible is largely the product of the oppressors. So, the ones most in need of the liberative message of the Bible, the poor and oppressed, are those who have least access to it. Croatto then asks, "Do narrative semiotics and hermeneutics have a contribution to make here?" The answer, according to Croatto, is clearly yes.[192] The arguments outlined below are Croatto's answer to this concern and so to the needs of poor and oppressed ordinary readers.

Canonical form as a single text

As has already been mentioned, Croatto argues that the hermeneutic process which he finds in the canonical process is part of the message. A crucial aspect of this canonical process is the move from "*inter*textuality" (the relationships among texts which are understood in light of one another in the same community) to "*intra*textuality" (these relationships which now obtain within one larger text). From a linguistic standpoint they now constitute a single new text.[193]

Croatto supports his argument by referring to "narrative semiotics" which "teaches us that the message of a text is not in a fragment of the account, but in its totality, as structure codifying meaning". Even when one account "is woven, 'textured,' with another, a *new* account is produced that is not the sum of its parts, and the meaning will be in this new codified totality, now constituting one text, and not in the sum of the literary units or their original significations".[194]

In answering the question, "Which text ought we to read today?", he answers "Surely, the current form, however little it may be to our taste". The reason he gives here is that any "addition" to earlier layers of the text are now "*no longer* an addition in the text as it has been handed down. It is a new text, and it produces meaning *as it is*".[195] For example, he recognizes in the canonical form of *Amos* that the final oracles of salvation "*modify* the narrative positioning, and thereby the signification, of the oracles of punishment", but he still wants to maintain that "the Book of Amos as we have it today is *a single text*, and must be read as such if the reader is to grasp its message. It matters little that it is no longer the text of the historical Amos. But it is a *text of Amos*".[196] In a similar way he argues that "*the Bible is a single text*", especially from the moment it constituted a fixed canon of literary compositions.[197]

Canonical form as extended semantic axis

As an extension of the previous argument Croatto goes on to argue that "If the Bible, then, is a *single* text, it is not the

cumulative sum of a plurality of literary units. It is the uni-
fication of a linguistically coded central kerygma. Henceforth
it is possible to recognize, in this one, *extended* account, the
'semantic axes' orientating the production of meaning that
is our reading of the Bible".[198]

The significance of this is clear when we recall Croatto's
contention that one of these "axes of meaning" in the Bible
as a totality is "the kerygma of the liberation of the oppressed".[199] This quest for "semantic axes" in the Bible as a
totality is in many ways the crucial contribution of Croatto's
hermeneutic reading of the final canonical form.

He recognizes that there are contending ideologies in the
Bible,[200] and he recognizes that "the Bible is a book put together and structured, by and large, by a comfortable middle class generally alienated from the people";[201] *but*, he insists, these factors only become foregrounded when we read
the Bible's separate texts. When we read the totality of the
Bible the originary liberative event and its many appropriations and rereadings are foregrounded, forming a semantic
axis.

For example, "There are texts that reject authority, and
others that extol obedience to authority. In the totality of the
Bible, however, is not power—the king's, a judge's, and so
on—an instrument to save the weak, to help those who do
not have power and therefore are exploited, who do not have
power and therefore cannot free themselves?".[202]

Another example shows that Croatto is fully aware of the
"ideological" issues involved. He recognizes the risk of
"decontextualization" that reading the final form entails.

> Let us take the case of 1 Corinthians 14:33b-35. In writing to a
> Greek church, surely Paul may not have considered it opportune
> suddenly to negate a cultural praxis, doubtless based on an Orphico-
> Platonic worldview, that idealized men and scorned women. A
> decontextualized universalization of this text elevates to a 'doc-
> trine' what may have been a circumstantial indication. This would
> save Paul—but not the text! And we do not read *Paul* today, but
> the *text* he wrote!

Yet, "At the linguistic level this account is within another
account—the Bible as a totality" and in "this single text we
have another Pauline affirmation: 'There does not exist among
you . . . male or female. All are one in Christ Jesus. Further-

more, if you belong to Christ . . . you inherit all that was promised' (Gal. 3:28-29). This time we have a more radical principle, subsuming the other".[203]

Croatto is not clear on why this text subsumes the other, but in line with his earlier arguments there are two important factors which could support this. First, the latter text forms part of the central axis in the Bible, the liberation axis; and second, this priority of one text over another arises from the reader's commitment to a context of struggle.

Croatto is quite clear that is how we *should* read the Bible. "At our distance, our own rereading should take up the whole Bible once more in its character as a new intratextuality, so that we may discover its new semantic axes, and be able to read it from within our own lives".[204]

In the remainder of his arguments for reading the final canonical form Croatto's concern for the ordinary reader is foregrounded even more clearly. I emphasize this concern of Croatto's because the ordinary reader has been subliminally present throughout my discussion in preceding chapters, but now this presence must be brought to the fore.

Canonical form as normative for ordinary readers

One of the reasons for Croatto's "should" in the last quotation is his view of the final form of this single text as normative. He argues that a text becomes normative and archetypal within a community that lives in its atmosphere, and, he continues, the Christian community of faith asserts that the Bible is "our paradigmatic text as the word of God".[205] As Croatto implies, this would be true particularly for ordinary readers.

Canonical form as viewpoint of the oppressed

There are one or two places in Croatto's work where he seems to be arguing that the final form reflects the viewpoint of the oppressed; this notwithstanding his argument that the Bible is by and large a book put together and structured by a comfortable middle-class alienated from the people.[206] Perhaps the phrase "by and large" is the clue here, because he argues that the final form of the Pentateuch, closing as it does without narrating the fulfillment of the promise, "was closured from the viewpoint of the oppressed" in that "the promise to the fathers is *still open*". In other words, in its final form the Pentateuch "is the relaunching of hope in the fulfillment of a promise".[207] However, it is not clear here whether Croatto is only offering a creative rereading of the final form of the Pentateuch or whether he is also arguing that the oppressed actually had a role in the final form of the Pentateuch. Clearly if the semantic axis of liberation is as pervasive as Croatto affirms it is, then he may be arguing along the latter lines.

Canonical form as accessible to the poor

A more important argument concerns the accessibility of the Bible to the poor and oppressed. Here Croatto argues that the understanding that the poor, the suffering, and the marginalized have of the Bible as their book and as a message concerning them first and foremost "falls under the rubric of a totalizing reading of the Bible through its 'axes of meaning,' which it offers in its condition as *single text*, or extended account". Croatto is here arguing that "understanding the Bible does not require expertise, but the grasp of great lines of meaning".[208] The importance of this point cannot be stressed enough. For too long the Bible has been possessed, controlled, explained, interpreted, only by representatives of a dominant stratum of society, the church hierarchy, professional theologians and exegetes, the educated.[209] For too long have the "knowers" and the "rulers" mediated the reading of the Bible.[210] In order for the Bible to return to the readings of the poor and the oppressed to whom it "belongs" and "pertains"[211] we need to recognize that

> Our reading of the Bible in our Christian education and upbringing, in liturgy and preaching, in seminaries and theology departments, is a piecemeal fragmentation of a single text, rendering it a multitude of texts, leaving us with a 'heap' of different meanings. Doubtless these meanings are valuable. But they sidetrack our understanding of the totalizing meaning, our understanding of the 'axis' of which I have been speaking, which is more easily identified by grassroots Christians.

In other words, returning the Bible to the poor and the oppressed "suggests a reading of the Bible as a *single text*, whose meaning is now simplified vis-à-vis the plethora of little accounts composing it".[212]

Canonical form as the mode of reading of the poor

Not only does a reading of the Bible as a single text make it more accessible to the poor and the oppressed but this is in fact how they *do* read the Bible. And, Croatto argues, when the people do approach the Bible (often forbidden) without the mediations of the "experts" "its reading is one of unsuspected fecundity". In a sense Croatto's entire hermeneutic is an answer to the question of what happens when the people read the Bible in a liberation process, or some other situation in which the people or a community is the subject both of history and of its own reading of the Bible.[213]

For the intellectual committed to reading the Bible from the viewpoint of the poor and oppressed, as Croatto is, the challenge is clear.[214]

> The Bible . . . must be read as a single text. And not as the sum of its many literary units, but as the unification of a central, linguistically coded, kerygma. In this one great account, one may recognize those 'semantic axes' that orient the production-of-meaning constituted by our reading of the Bible in Latin America. This too is one of the tasks of the theology of liberation in its exegetical component. It is a hermeneutical task and a function, in this particular case, of an understanding of the Bible as (semiotically) one great text, whose theme is God's salvific project, and whose key is the concept of liberation.[215]

In summary, Croatto is arguing that to read in front of the text, as so many interpreters within contexts of liberation do, is incomplete unless one reads the Bible as a single text. In his own terms, then, he too is opposed to "selective" or "unstructural" readings. It could be argued that in the same way that Trible's close literary reading recovers a counterliterature that deconstructs the "patriarchal stamp" of the Bible, so too Croatto's reading in front of the text identifies an extended semantic axis of liberation that deconstructs the "comfortable middle class" construction and structuring of the Bible. For both Croatto and Trible this deconstruction is a product of a distanced, committed, and critical stance.

Ideology, the ordinary reader, and canon

While I think there are problems with Croatto's insistence on a final form canonical reading of the Bible as *the* mode of reading, we must recognize that the majority of Croatto's arguments for this mode of reading arise from his explicit concern for the ordinary reader, particular the poor and oppressed. And this concern we must hear.

However, there are at least two problematic arguments in Croatto's cluster of arguments. First, there is his argument that not only is there a clearly identifiable, unambiguous, liberation axis in the Bible but that it is also the central semantic axis in the Bible. Mosala, Gottwald, and Schüssler Fiorenza clearly differ with Croatto here as to how much of the Bible is unambiguously liberative. Second, there is his argument concerning the normative character of the canonical text. Once again, Mosala, Gottwald, and Schüssler Fiorenza raise serious questions concerning the socio-political interests of those "winners" who construct, shape, and constitute canonical literature.

Both Mosala and Schüssler Fiorenza would agree with Gottwald when he argues that "Both canonical process and canonical shape are ways of underscoring the ideological component of Israelite society and religion" and that "Literature, especially canonical literature, is not disinterested. Every text has its social matrix and represents one or more social interests, whether we can easily identify them or not".[216]

Gottwald would be willing to concede to Croatto that the canonical process has left us with a single text and that this canonical process has blurred and obscured the original sociological factors behind the development of biblical texts.[217] However, for Gottwald the crucial question is the methodological significance attached to this blurring and obscuring of origins. According to Gottwald

> one of the prime reasons for obscuring the identity of those who advocate authoritative decisions and interpretations is to make their judgments look unquestioned and ancient, even timeless, and certainly descended from divine authority. To overlook this psychosocial reality of ideology and mystification in religious assertions, canonical assertions included, is to deliver theology into an uncritical subjection to the unexamined self-interests of canonizers.[218]

In other words, Gottwald is concerned with the *motives* (conscious or unconscious) of canonical editors.[219]

Croatto does not seem unwilling, however, to face up to these concerns.[220] As we have seen, he readily accepts that the Bible is a product of the middle-class;[221] *but,* he insists, these factors only become foregrounded when we read the Bible's separate texts. When the poor and oppressed read the totality of the Bible the originary liberative event and its many appropriations and rereadings are foregrounded. So in stressing the "productive" nature of interpretation Croatto, like Gadamer, is able to take seriously both the truth claims of an ancient text as well as the claims of modern *Ideologiekritik.*[222]

While Gottwald, Mosala, and Schüssler Fiorenza might feel that he does not take their ideology critique seriously enough, the real question for me is whether the poor and oppressed, ordinary readers, really do discern a central and unambiguous liberation axis in their reading of the Bible. Croatto invites this question because he himself implies it when giving an example of the liberation axis: "There are texts that reject authority, and others that extol obedience to authority. In the totality of the Bible, however, is not power—the king's, a judge's, and so on—an instrument to save the weak, to help those who do not have power and therefore are exploited, who do not have power and therefore cannot free themselves?"[223] The question mark raises the question, a question that I will address in the next chapter.

Conclusion

In this chapter I have attempted to do four things. First, I have analyzed three modes of reading the Bible in contexts of liberation. I have also analyzed the relationship between the respective modes of reading and the liberation struggle. In so doing I have also analyzed how a particular mode of reading functions in a context of liberation. Second, I have constructed replies on behalf of modes of reading which focus on the text and modes of reading which focus in front of the text to the concerns of the behind the text modes of reading of Mosala, Schüssler Fiorenza, and Gottwald. While I have not been able to analyze the theoretical aspects of Boesak's mode of reading in any great detail, I have analyzed two modes of reading which have much in common with his mode of reading. I have established, I would argue, that these two modes of reading also can provide a critical, structural and theoretically well-ground hermeneutics of liberation. Third, I have provided a detailed account of two such modes of reading, and therefore some resources for such modes of reading in the South African context of liberation. And fourth, I have foregrounded a concern for the ordinary reader.

The discussion in this chapter has shown, I suggest, that there is no one mode of reading which has a privileged relationship to the context of struggle. While there is certainly more to be analyzed here, and while there are a number of questions still to clarify, each of these modes of reading, whether focusing behind the text, or on the text, or in front of the text, offers a coherent and theoretically well-grounded hermeneutic of liberation.

Moreover, and this must be stressed, each of these modes of reading is a *critical* reading.[224] Each offers *a* structural reading of the biblical text, although the respective emphases differ.

Another important similarity is that their appropriation of biblical elements, whether behind the text, in the text, or in front of the text, is a *critical appropriation*.[225] While this may not always be true for Boesak's readings, it is true of the modes of reading of Trible and Croatto. From Boesak's readings it may appear that there is a relatively straightforward access to and appropriation of the struggle within the biblical text; however, for Trible and Croatto, as for Mosala, Gottwald, and Schüssler Fiorenza, the struggle within the biblical text can only be accessed and appropriated critically. For both Trible and Croatto the interpretive task involves both suspicion and retrieval, which is how the interpretive task is described by Schüssler Fiorenza.[226]

However, fascinating as this discussion has been, and will continue to be, and important as it has been to show that "literary" and "symbolic/metaphoric/thematic" readings can meet the challenges posed by "socio-scientific" readings,[227] it has been largely a discussion among trained readers. Perhaps the most important contribution of Croatto's theory of reading is his *explicit* concern for the ordinary reader.[228] Given that interpreters within contexts of liberation have argued for the epistemological privilege of the poor and oppressed in liberation hermeneutics such a concern is not surprising.[229]

I am suggesting that a conclusion which emerges from the discussion in this chapter is that the question of the relationship between a particular methodology of reading and the liberation struggle is not the crucial question after all. The crucial question is the question of whom we are dialoguing with when we consider such questions. As Gottwald has continually argued, the liberation theology agenda demands collaborative work.[230] Where Gottwald is not as clear as he ought to be is that this collaborative work must include the poor and oppressed, those ordinary readers who read "from below". In the next chapter I take this challenge seriously and so, in accordance with the liberation paradigm, open the discussion to those necessary (within the liberation paradigm) yet neglected interpreters, ordinary readers.

Chapter Seven

The Role of the
Ordinary Reader
in Liberation Hermeneutics

Introduction

Much of the discussion so far has been centred around the interpretive work of trained readers. It is their questions and concerns which have shaped most of the discussion. And yet, the ordinary reader has always been present, if not always foregrounded. But, I would argue, the ordinary reader must be foregrounded if we are to understand liberation hermeneutics adequately and appropriately. I would also argue that the thrust of the discussion so far moves us in this direction.

I noted in chapter one that there has been a rediscovery of the role of the reader in biblical interpretation. While most of the discussion in chapter one dealt with theoretical considerations, these theoretical considerations themselves led interpreters like Cornel West to foreground the need for an active and transformative solidarity with ordinary readers, particularly the poor and oppressed. In discussing the interpretive crisis in South Africa in chapter two a similar concern emerged. Not only was there acknowledgment that academic biblical studies is removed from ordinary readers, there was also the call by Mosala and others for black theology to be based in the wider black community, especially in its most oppressed sectors. One of the questions which arose from the analysis of Mosala's and Boesak's readings of the Cain and Abel story in chapter three was specifically the extent to which their modes of reading emanated from and are accessible to ordinary people in a context of liberation. In chapter four the need for accountability to and solidarity with ordinary readers was stressed. Here too the crux of the liberation paradigm, the epistemological privilege of the poor and oppressed, was affirmed. The concern for the ordinary reader in chapter five was evident in the commitment of interpreters within contexts of liberation to the neglected ordinary voices in the biblical tradition. In addition, even those interpreters with reservations about the biblical tradition recognized its importance for the ordinary reader. Finally, in chapter six the analysis of different modes of reading and their functions in contexts of liberation foregrounded the ordinary reader.

More pragmatic factors have also played a role in foregrounding the ordinary reader.[1] A factor which has particular relevance to the South African context is the growing recognition that "the people" must be allowed to speak for themselves. For too long the "experts" have spoken on their behalf or, worse, prescribed for them. So the purpose of this chapter is to allow ordinary readers to speak for themselves.

This chapter consists of a number of case studies, each of which investigates ordinary readers reading the Bible. Once I have discussed each case study I will explore the relationship between the ordinary reader and the three modes of reading analyzed in the previous chapter.

Case study 1: Readings in Anglican parishes

Introduction

Despite this renewed interest in the reader, it is a curious fact that what has been done up to now in the field of biblical studies was almost exclusively concerned with *theoretical* aspects of reader research. *Empirical* reader research of biblical material is still virtually non-existent, although many opportunities present themselves.[2]

Previous work in this area in the South African context has tended to focus on trained or semi-trained readers reading as individuals.[3] Our focus, however, differs in two respects. Our central concern was to have a record of *ordinary people* reading the Bible *in an authentic and familiar context.*[4] We were also concerned to have a wide range of readers involved. We therefore based our analysis on transcripts of a Bible study (Mark 10:17-22) which was done in Bible study groups within most Anglican parishes in Pietermaritzburg.[5]

The researchers who went out into the parishes were all senior biblical studies students who had received some training in the role of facilitating group discussion. They had participated in a pilot study in which these skills and the research material were evaluated. The research material consisted of a Group Profile Questionnaire and a Bible Study Outline. The Group Profile Questionnaire was designed to provide a detailed profile of individual group members and of each group. The Bible Study Outline was designed to facilitate group discussion of two questions: (a) "What do you think this story meant in the time of Jesus?" and (b) "What do you think this story means for us today?"

The use of the word "facilitate" in the above paragraph reflects our concern for as authentic a group response as was possible in such circumstances. In order to minimize the sense of intrusion which a researcher and a tape-recorder would introduce, the individual researchers worked in those parishes with which they shared a similar background.

The analysis of the group profile questionnaire provided no serious difficulties.[6] The analysis of the group Bible study transcripts was more difficult in that it entailed a more subjective approach.[7] However, all of our findings were independently verified. We also invited our researchers to respond to our observations and incorporated their comments.[8]

It is important to note that this research took place in a context of conflict. While this conflict has very little affect on white parishes it has a marked affect on black parishes.[9] Our researchers were met with suspicion from various sections of the black community and often found themselves in situations of tension and conflict.[10] Obviously this affected the research. For example, in group 13, a black group, the researcher notes that the people were suspicious about his coming. During the study one participant refused to elaborate on what he or she meant by "the situation" which made and kept people poor in South Africa. The researcher notes that this person was scared to elaborate on this point.

More generally, researchers from the university, armed with tape-recorders and asking questions aroused some apprehension if not suspicion in most groups. We anticipated this response and so made our objectives as clear as possible, reassuring group leaders that we had no hidden agenda in our research. In fact, we expressed our concern to feed back our research into the parishes.[11] Understandably, however, our assurances did not always dispel every apprehension.

Some findings on the reading of Mark 10:17-22

In the analysis that follows our emphasis will be on the hermeneutics of the groups: on their modes of reading the biblical text. We will begin with some observations arising from the groups as a whole.

Applying the text to today

It is hardly surprising that Bible study groups should be willing to apply their readings of the text to their lives. Being a Christian means, among other things, being linked in some way with the Bible. In each of the groups researched there was a readiness to apply their understandings of Mark 10:17-22 to their own lives. Moreover, there was a feeling that the Bible study would have consequences on the way they lived their lives. And, we suggest, this is in fact a highly significant hermeneutic factor. James Barr recognizes this when he asks,

> One must wonder whether the great question as posed by twentieth-century biblical hermeneutics was not wrongly conceived. It was often said that, given our knowledge of the original historical meaning of texts, the great hermeneutical task was to enable us to move from there to the meaning for today, to show how in some sense this could be meaningful and relevant for the life of the church today, how it could be seen also as an effective Word of God. Was this not an immense straining to accomplish something that was actually there all the time? Was not the special status of scripture both given and accepted throughout, in spite of the new angles introduced by modern criticism? Was not the real question this:

not, given the historical meaning, how do we move from it to the meaning as Word of God for today, but, given the church's readiness to hear the scripture as Word of God for today, how is that hearing to be modified, refined, and clarified through our knowledge of the actual character of the biblical text, as mediated through critical, historical, and other sorts of knowledge?[12]

Our research clearly supports Barr's contention that there is a readiness in the church "to hear the scripture as Word of God for today", although his "real question" needs more analysis.[13]

A related point is the relative freedom the groups had in reading and applying the text without the assistance of "expert" knowledge. It is often assumed that unless people have the types of knowledge mentioned by Barr they will be unable to read and appropriate a text. However, the people in these groups were quite able to interpret the biblical text with little or no knowledge of this sort. Even in the group which was most clearly looking for "expert" guidance from our researcher (group 13), a group which was not familiar with corporate Bible study and was used only to being taught by an "expert", there was still that readiness to read and appropriate the text. Perhaps the question of some is whether people *ought* to interpret biblical texts without "expert" knowledge?[14] But it is important to point out that this is a different question from whether they *can*.

How did ordinary people read Mark 10:17-22? The following questions were used to facilitate a careful reading of the text.

General Bible study questions.
(a) What do you think this story meant in the time of Jesus?
(b) What do you think this story means for us today?

The following questions may help you to answer these two general questions:

The wealthy man.
(a) What do we know about this man who spoke to Jesus?
(b) What do you think he did for a living?
(c) Why do you think he owned many possessions?

(d) Why do you think he spoke to Jesus?

The commandments.
(a) Why do you think Jesus talked about the commandments?
(b) Why do you think Jesus used these particular commandments?
(c) What do you think the commandments that Jesus used have in common?
(d) Why do you think keeping these commandments was not enough to gain eternal life?
(e) Which do you think is more important to Jesus, to keep the commandments or to give to the poor?

The challenge.
(a) Why do you think Jesus told the man to sell his possessions and give to the poor?
(b) Why do you think Jesus told the man to do this before he could follow him?
(c) Why do you think the young man did not obey Jesus?
(d) What do you think Jesus meant by "treasure in heaven"?

The poor.
(a) Who do you think Jesus meant by "the poor" in this story?
(b) Why do you think they were poor?

Today.
(a) Does this story say anything to us today?
(b) Who do you think are similar to the wealthy man today?
(c) Why do you think they are wealthy?
(d) Who do you think are the poor today?
(e) Why do you think they are poor?
(f) What do you think Jesus' challenge means to us?

The context of the story.
(a) After Jesus speaks to this man he speaks to his disciples about how difficult it is for the wealthy to

enter the kingdom of God. Do you think this is important to the story?

(b) After Jesus speaks to this man and after he speaks to his disciples he promises Peter and the other disciples that they will be rewarded for what they have given up in order to follow him. Do you think this is important to the story?

(c) Mark says that Jesus was going on a journey. He was on his way to Jerusalem. Do you think this is important to the story?

Matthew's story (Matthew 19:16-22).
Matthew tells the same story but in a different way. Some of the differences are:

- Mark says the man comes and kneels before Jesus and Matthew says the man just came and spoke to Jesus.
- Mark says that the man calls Jesus "good" teacher and Matthew says that the man just calls Jesus teacher.
- Mark says that that this is a man and Matthew says that this is a "young" man.
- Matthew includes a commandment that Mark does not have: "You shall love your neighbour as yourself".
- Mark says that Jesus felt a love for the man and Matthew does not mention this.
- Mark says that the man went away grieved and groaning/gloomy and Matthew says he went away grieved.

(a) Why do you think there are these differences?
(b) What difference do these differences make to the two stories?
(c) What do you think really happened, what Mark says or what Matthew says?

The analysis of the responses that follows provides a preliminary profile of how ordinary readers read the Bible.

Reading the text historically

Besides the information in the text there was generally very little awareness of historical and no awareness of sociological information. However, in most of the groups there was someone who offered some historical information, although this was usually vague. This "external" information was generally appreciated because it assisted the group to form a fuller picture of the situation portrayed by the text. For example, in question 7 which probed the differences between the Matthian and Markan versions of this story the groups were generally eager to have access to historical information which would help them understand the differences. Most of the information volunteered was of a historical rather than a source-critical nature although there was some of the latter. For example, people were interested in whether Mark and/or Matthew had been eye-witnesses, whether Mark recorded Peter's account, which account had been written first, etc. The basic historicity of the story was never in question and the differences were either minimized or explained as differences in individual point of view. In no group was there hostility to this question. In groups 12 and 13, both black groups, there was no response at all to these questions but it is difficult to know how to interpret this silence.[15] Incidentally, most of the groups that explored the differences identified more with Mark's account because they felt that it was more sensitive and compassionate.

While it is clear that historical information was valued and that the basic historicity of the story was affirmed, the scarcity or vagueness of this sort of information was not perceived as a serious problem in the groups' appropriation of the text.

Reading the text as a literary unit

During the course of discussion members of the group would often refer back to the text in order to establish whether a particular reading was warranted. However, on the whole this close or literary reading of the text was not sustained. In other words, there was never in any group a concerted effort to read the text as a whole in its own right. Various parts of the text were often read as unrelated to the other parts. For example, there was virtually no exploration of the narrative

link between the particular commandments Jesus enumer-
ated and his challenge to the man to sell all he possessed
and give to the poor.

Reading the text canonically

In most groups the text was read "canonically", that is, it
was read as a part of the Christian scriptures.[16] On a number
of occasions in various groups people would read this text in
the light of other parts of the Bible. People clearly felt quite
comfortable with reading the text in this way, which supports Wuellner's claim that a religious classic like the Bible
is often seen by the religious community as "a single rhetorical unit".[17] In other words, the readers attempted to understand this particular text in terms of their understanding of
the central message of the Bible.[18]

However, in none of the groups was there any sense of
Mark as a distinct literary unit in itself. Question 6 of the
Bible Study Outline encouraged the groups to see this story
in its wider literary context, which generally the groups were
able to do. Question 7 explored some of the Markan characteristics of this story, which again the groups were able to
recognize. However, this input never developed into any discussion on Mark as a whole.

Reading existentially

It is probably fair to say that what can be called an existential reading dominated each groups response to the text.
Peoples' experiences differ, particularly in a society such as
South Africa, and this was reflected in the research. While it
is important to note that in many instances the differences
between groups were also present within a group, there were
clear differences in interpretation which seem to correlate
with the different experiences associated with a particular
population group. In other words, people come to the text
with different pre-understandings. For example, only black,
Indian, and coloured groups (groups 9, 10, 11, 12, 13) expressed a sense of suspicion with how the wealthy man in
the story acquired his wealth. This was expressed in various
ways but underlying each was a feeling that this wealth may
have been acquired through the oppression of others. Another example which shows the different pre-understandings
which people bring to the text is reflected in the various re-

sponses to wealth today (question 5). In most of the groups wealth was not seen as an evil thing in itself, provided it was shared with others and provided one did not worship it. However, in the two black groups (groups 12 and 13), which also shared the above views, there was the additional perception of wealth alienating the classes within a community.

There were also some differences in appropriation which seem to correlate with the different perceptions associated with a particular population group. In all the groups questions 5 (a) ("Does this story say anything to us today?") and 8 ("What have you learned from this study?") were taken up personally. In other words, people felt individually challenged in their personal lives to share what they had, to see to it that wealth was not an idol in their lives, etc. However, one group, an Indian group (group 11), also responded on a communal level. The group felt that the church should lead the way in breaking down the barriers that divide people and should stop using apartheid to maintain separate parishes in different group areas. They also felt that it was time for them as a community to stop being complacent and to join their voices with those who are calling for justice.

Reading contextually

Closely related to the above section is a contextual reading, that is, a reading which takes into account the South African context.[19] As we have already mentioned, there was one group (group 13) which did not feel the freedom to develop this particular aspect of their interpretation. However, in almost all the groups there was some degree of contextualizing. For example, in most groups there was some recognition of social structures in South Africa being directly responsible for whites generally being wealthy and blacks generally being poor. In group 11 there was an immediate application of the text to the South African context and this was sustained throughout the study. The text was read with the South African economic, ecclesiastical and political situation in mind. But in most groups the contextual reading was less analytical of the South African context. The lack of analysis in most of the groups reflects at least two things. It reflects the pervasive repressive and authoritarian nature of the South African context, and it reflects the need ordinary readers have for resources and processes which will facilitate the development of analytical skills.[20]

Reading dualistically

The last two sections raise what was clearly the central tension within every group, namely, whether to read the story materially or spiritually. This story seemed to generate a dualistic response within most groups, particularly when it came to question 5 which explored the relevance of the text for today. For example, when groups were discussing question 4 (a), "Who do you think Jesus meant by 'the poor' in this story?", there was general agreement that the poor meant the materially poor. However, when the group came to question 5 (d), "Who do you think are the poor today?", there was less agreement as to who the poor were today; for some readers they were the spiritually poor and for some they were the materially poor. Often when a comment was made someone would ask for clarification, "Do you mean materially or spiritually?" Clearly this is an area in which Bible study groups in the South African context have difficulty.[21]

Reading corporately

In all the groups, except groups 12 and 13, the two black groups, there was a familiarity with this form of corporate Bible study, although many of the groups commented that they did not usually study a passage in so much detail. However, groups 12 and 13 were unfamiliar with this corporate form of Bible study. When they did have Bible study, which was infrequently, it was more a "teacher talk" approach.

It is also important to note here that our research demonstrates the creative role that such corporate Bible study plays, particularly when one remembers that many of the differences between groups were also present within a group. In most of the groups there were those who felt that they had learned from and been challenged by the responses of others. However, the reality of apartheid South Africa (and its legacy) makes contact between people with different racial classifications extremely difficult, and so the transformative potential of corporate Bible study is restricted.

Conclusion

There is much in this case study which requires more research. We have already indicated that this research is preliminary. In fact, this research is an initial phase in a larger research project.[22] While this research has enabled us to form some general impressions of how ordinary readers in local Anglican churches read the Bible, we are concerned to develop the research by working in a more participatory manner with some of the groups. This concern for a more participatory research process arises from our commitment to a liberation paradigm.[23]

The case studies which follow are more narrowly focused than this case study, so this case study provides a useful overview of a wide range of ordinary readers reading the Bible. The next case study considers a more homogeneous sector of ordinary readers.

Case Study 2: Readings in the trades-union

Introduction

In discussing the constructing of an indigenous theology of work, James Cochrane makes some penetrating comments on workers reading the Bible.[24] He argues that besides being "the primary source of the Christian mythos", the Bible "is probably the only source of theology for most members of our churches. It is, as some have said, the people's book par excellence".[25] "However", he continues,

> we know today that the Bible is not a neutral text offering some clearly defined truth for all to read, about which no problems of interpretation will emerge. Who reads the Bible will have as much impact on a theological judgement as will the text itself. Those who have written most of the theology of our time, including any theology of work, are those who read the Bible with eyes influenced by their location in society, and by the training they have received.[26]

These trained readers bring a wide range of skills to their reading of the Bible, most of them relying on critical historical tools, sociological insights, and theoretical concepts.[27]

There is, however, Cochrane argues "no reason to think that this is how a worker will read the Bible". "The interpretation I may make of a text will not be the same as that of a worker, even if I rely on an abstracted analysis of the nature of work in the South African political economy taken from the writings of trade unionists. I will simply not see in the text what a worker might see". He concludes,

> To my mind, the task of getting that direct insight into the text from workers is the necessary first step to any effective and significant theology of work in our time. Any other resources we may bring to bear—from the tradition, from historical critical skills, and so on—will remain anaemic and impotent without a foundation built upon insights arising from the practical experience of work.[28]

Church and labour

Cochrane's argument is supported by The Institute for Contextual Theology's "Church and Labour Research Project" which offers us a useful framework for discussing workers' readings of the Bible.[29]

The Report notes that perhaps "the most interesting question of all, given the response to it, was whether or not the Bible had any significance for workers, and if so, what kind of a meaning it could have". "The answers are astonishing", the Report continues, "at least to anyone who might have thought that the general picture of a relatively high level of alienation from the Church would be echoed in this question".[30]

First, "we would not intuitively have expected that an effective 80% of our respondents would regard the Bible as significant. This is a very high positive evaluation in the light of all the other generally more negative data" concerning, for example, the relevance of the church.[31]

Second, to this positive statistical picture must be added the discursive responses of workers. The Report discerns three trends in the responses to the question: "Explain in what way the Bible means something for a worker's life". The three trends are a "master/slave" view (eight out of the forty one responding groups), a "personalist individualistic ethic" (fourteen groups), and a "prophetic focus on justice" (eighteen groups).[32]

Within the first trend six groups interpreted the Bible as encouraging obedience to the employer and mutual respect between employers and workers. A paternalistic sense of the employers' responsibility to the worker commonly accompanied this interpretation, with no critique of existing structures of power. Two groups saw the master/slave reading of the Bible as "a tool or weapon of the oppressor and management".[33]

A more frequent view was found within the second trend where fourteen groups interpreted the Bible as encouraging "the individual towards a personal morality somewhat divorced from any issue of public or social morality". From this perspective some of the characteristics of the Christian worker are holiness, perseverance, honesty, and diligence.[34]

In the third trend a variety of theological statements or images are given by eighteen groups in support of a reading of the Bible which supports struggles for justice.

> The idea of the *imago dei* (we are made in the image of God) is used to sustain the concept of equality in the workplace. Jesus is understood either as a worker, or as being on the side of the poor, the oppressed and the exploited. The image of the eye of the needle also emerges as significant for a critique of the rich, while workers rights may be located in the Genesis tradition of the so-called Yahwist redactor. Moses is also mentioned as an archetypal liberator, under God, of workers.[35]

One group here turned the prophetic viewpoint inwards upon church leadership, suggesting that "the priests themselves take the heavy things and direct it to the labourers while they carry the easy things; this is like today in what employers do to employees".[36]

One group felt that the Bible has no meaning or significance for workers.[37]

"Overall", the Report concludes here, "the most important conclusion to be drawn from this question is that the Bible is a rich source of interpretation for the worker's life, certainly of much greater significance than the liturgical and pastoral operations of the Church. Of course, the Bible is a two-edged sword, as is demonstrated by the variety of responses we obtained".

> Nevertheless, churches and their leaders need to take note of the special role the Bible might have, both to counter individualistic or spiritualized interpretations, and—more importantly—to foster the liberatory meaning and significance of the biblical message for workers. This latter task is of particular significance when considered

against the traditional lack of active empowerment of workers by
the churches in a social system which has for most of this century
sought to reduce their power and common responsibility for our
life together. Perhaps the founding concept of the *imago dei* provides the direction for a reversal of this sad history.[38]

Conclusion

Clearly, then, the Bible is significant in the life of many
workers. The diverse trends in the responses to the question
concerning the Bible and the worker's life suggest that there
is no simple correlation between workers and their interpretations. The interpretive trends discussed in the Report could
be analyzed more carefully, but that is not the task of my
study. The research on which the Report is based was participatory and so any further analysis of the data outside of
the participatory research model would be inappropriate.

An area which is not explored in this research concerns
the modes of reading of workers. In other words, *how* do
workers read the Bible? The next two case studies consider
this question. In order to avoid generalizing I will consider
two particular groups of workers: the members of a particular African Independent Church (AIC), and the members of
Young Christian Workers (YCW).

Case study 3: Readings in the YCW
(Young Christian Workers)

Introduction

Young Christian Workers (YCW) is an organization which
brings groups of young workers together to work out how
they can bring their Christianity to bear on their total working context. The YCW thus takes as its starting point the
lives of young workers, the majority of whom are black. YCW
is not a union but a movement for education situated within
the working class. The fundamental process of YCW groups
is the See-Judge-Act method. Young workers begin by
analyzing the conditions experienced by themselves and their
friends at work, at home and at school (See). They assess the
situation "in the light of the Gospel" (Judge), and then try to

improve the situation by taking appropriate action to change conditions (Act).[39]

Reading resources in the YCW

The Bible plays a significant role in the life of YCW. Some workers "started to believe in [the] bible again when they came to YCW through action".[40] In other words, the Bible becomes relevant again to these workers through the relating of action and faith in YCW.[41] In addition to the renewed relevance of the Bible in the experience of individual workers, there is also the ongoing use of the Bible in the See-Judge-Act structure of YCW reflection. In particular, a biblical text is often used in the pivotal Judge part.[42] For example, in reflecting on "wage negotiations" the YCW group studied Exodus 18:13-23 in the Judge part.[43]

Before we look at these workers' mode of reading the Bible it is important to understand something of the resources offered to them. First, as has already been mentioned, the YCW offers a context in which politicized young workers, what the YCW calls "militants", relate faith and action.

Second, the YCW offers a variety of biblical resources to assist workers in their reflections on the Bible. For example, the "History of Salvation" presents a three page sketch beginning with 1250 BC and ending with the work of Jesus. This sketch includes broad historical and sociological information.[44] This kind of information is also often integrated with particular texts. For example, in a study of Moses the biblical "story" is retold in a creative manner which includes such information.

Another important example of resource material is the booklet *Bringing the Good News to the Working Class*. "Often while preparing a group meeting a[n] idea for faith reflection would strike them. They would relate a story in the bible: 'Do you remember that one about when Jesus was feeding people . . . How is it?' 'Yes it's good . . . where is it in that big book?' 'I do not know . . . let's leave it.'" So as the YCW is short of chaplains and the young workers are "not bible experts and have little time to study the bible in order to be able to prepare faith reflections" the YCW offers this selection of texts to facilitate Bible study and faith reflection preparation and "proposes a few texts that might be useful during these preparations for reflections during YCW meetings; group meetings; study days/weekends; rallies; progress days; etc".[45] The booklet consists of biblical texts and witness accounts of young workers.

As a further resource the biblical texts in this booklet are arranged under headings or themes. For example, the first theme is: "The system and how God is condemning it", which includes the following subsections: "Racism and nationalism", "The downfall of capitalism", "God and irrelevant worship", "Greediness", and "Deception".[46]

Another resource is found in the questions which accompany most biblical passages and which shape the discussion. This will be illustrated below.

Given these resources how do workers in the YCW read the Bible? In answering this question I will consider, first, the actual reading of a specific text (Matthew 13:1-46).[47] Second, I will then summarize the responses of young workers to a number of questions under the rubric "What is the use of reading the Bible in the YCW?"

Reading Matthew 13:1-46

At a YCW formation weekend Jesus' discourse in parables in Matthew 13:1-46 was discussed. The participants were given a narrative comprising verses 1, 3, 4-8, 31-33, and 44-46 on a sheet of paper. Following the text is an introduction and questions for discussion:

> In these parables, Jesus speaks about the kingdom of heaven. Through our actions, in YCW we are trying to build a new world, a world of justice, friendship, equality and happiness.
>
> Can we say that by our actions we are trying to build the kingdom of God? Why?
>
> How can we compare our successes and our difficulties with what Jesus is saying in his parables? What do we learn from that?
>
> How can we compare the choices and commitments that we have to take in YCW with what Jesus is saying in his parables? What do we learn from that?
>
> What sort of disciples does Jesus want? What sort of militants does YCW need? What sort of faith is necessary today to build a kingdom where every young worker will be respected and able to live as a true son of God?[48]

What follows is a summary of the discussion in workshop groups. In answering the first set of questions it was said that "the kingdom of God is not in favour of bad working conditions facing the working class. That's why Jesus was always identifying himself with the poor and fighting for the poor and exploited. As a worker, a carpenter by hand, Jesus saw his work among the poor. His actions brought happiness and commitment among his followers and that was building the Kingdom of God". The work of the YCW, "challenging bad conditions at work, school", "bringing unionisation at our workplaces, fighting for health and safety, fighting to stop overtime to accommodate the unemployed etc is all part of building the Kingdom of God". "Like Jesus, in the YCW, our work and actions are for the exploited workers. We live and work among the working class people. By struggling and fighting for the right to work, we are surely building the Kingdom of God".[49]

In response to the second group of questions comparing YCW successes and difficulties with what Jesus is saying in the parables "militants said that we learn that it is not easy to build the Kingdom of God. We must expect successes and difficulties in building the Kingdom of God. In the YCW, we see lost seeds as those young workers who do not accept the commitment of the movement, those who run away from tackling concrete actions to change bad conditions at work, school". However, "Some do accept the commitment to changing bad working conditions. These are the people who produce crops. From the parable, we learn that it is not just anyone who will take the commitment of fighting conditions that exploit the working class".[50]

The third group of questions were answered as follows. "In the YCW, we choose and commit ourselves to tackling concrete actions as part of building the Kingdom of God".

> To many, our actions might appear to be very small. This is like a mustard seed which a man took and sowed in his field. It is the smallest of all the seeds, but when it has grown it is the biggest of shrubs and becomes a tree so that the birds can come and shelter in its branches. What we learn from this parable is that even if our choices appear very small, through our commitment our small actions will give rise to big changes. This is the kind of commitment we have to take in the YCW.[51]

In conclusion, and in response to the last group of questions,

> it was said that what we can learn is that we must expect difficulties in winning the minds of other young workers. It would sometimes be hard to carry on with our actions when faced with victimisation by the employers etc. However, our commitment in reflecting at the group level, [and] taking action by involving our fellow workers/students would eventually produce Jesus disciples. If we have the faith to believe that we are building the Kingdom of God by being involved in the YCW, we will create conditions where every Young Worker will be respected and be able to live as a true son of God.[52]

Rather than analyze this reading any further I will allow the young workers themselves to offer a more theorectical response.

Why read the Bible in YCW?

In the General Assembly of a Key Militants Formation Meeting in 1984 the question "What is the use of reading the Bible in the YCW?" was debated. The following are some of the conclusions of the workshop.

> The Bible reveals to us the history of the struggle, and becomes an inspiration for the liberation which has been promised by the Almighty. It reveals to the Movement the process of the struggle.[53]

> Today, in the working class, the religion is a reality. But Christianity has been falsified. With the Bible the YCW stands to bring back the faith.[54]

> The Bible helps us to link what we are doing today to what Jesus was doing.[55] We have seen the importance of reading the Bible. We have strengthened our faith. No faith without action.[56]

> We know better from the Bible that God himself fights with the poor people, through his believers and not without them.

> The Bible is also helpful to get new people into the Movement.

> The Bible gives us a discipline, such as: respect for people, love.

> We learned that Moses gave the Commandments in order to give rules of behaviour amongst the people. It is the same in the YCW: We have principles, structures, orientations in order to help us.

> In short, the Bible relates our commitment to the source of life which is love. It encourages our struggle for the liberation of the oppressed people of South Africa.[57]

The young workers also recognize that they have a certain autonomy over against the Bible.

> We saw that the Bible is not here to answer all our questions. We have to recognize that our situations are different in many ways from the situations at the times of the Bible. But the Bible shows us how the believers before us (Moses and Peter) tried to tackle their own situations, how they reflected and analyzed why they sometimes failed. This teaches us to be critically minded and operate always with the 'See-Judge-Act' method. And we must be careful not to take a statement of the Bible out of its environment. That is the way so many preachers make the Bible say everything and its opposite.[58]

Conclusion

The dominant factor in the YCW mode of reading the Bible is their commitment to reading the Bible from and for their specific context as young black workers in South Africa. That the Bible speaks, both as encouragement and challenge, into their specific context they have no doubt. They find a clear resonance between the Bible's story of liberation and their own struggle for liberation, a resonance which is facilitated by a structured approach to reading the Bible. Clearly, this structured reading environment plays a significant role in making the Bible relevant (again) to young workers.

The final case study provides a quite different picture. The mode of reading of members of the Zion Apostolic Church, most of whom are workers, is quite different from the critical and structured mode of reading of the YCW.

Case study 4: Readings in the African Independent Churches

Introduction

There is a vast amount of material *about* the AIC, only some *by* the AIC themselves,[59] and almost no material on the biblical hermeneutics operative among them. Itumeleng Mosala has recently completed some preliminary research in this area and it is this research which will form the basis of this section.[60]

Briefly, the AIC are religious formations characterized by a number of sociological and theological factors. As Mosala notes, these factors vary in their concentration in any particular one of these churches. Nevertheless, there are a number of common features. A key feature of the AIC is that their leadership is indigenous African.[61]

Another feature is that positions of leadership in these churches are not attained by either educational training or birth. "On the contrary leadership is a product of the work of the holy spirit, it is rooted in a spiritual democracy crucial to the life of these formations".[62]

Another feature they have in common is that they are "religious solidarity networks".[63]

Finally, and crucially, they represent a particular articulation of a resistance struggle.[64]

It is important, however, to recognize that there are a variety of types of AIC and consequently grouping these formations under one rubric masks crucial characteristics. The AIC arose out of different historical contexts and tend to draw their character from the historical circumstances to which they were a response.

A Zion Apostolic Church

The particular church in which Mosala conducts his research is a Zion Apostolic type. These are small groups with a relatively unstructured leadership and liturgy.[65] They are a new phenomenon produced by the conflictual convergence of two histories. Members of the Zion Apostolic churches are Africans whose African societal material base and its cultures have been eradicated by colonialism and capitalism on the one hand, and whose presence in capitalist society and culture is unwanted except as exploitable "wage-slaves" on the other hand. Mosala argues that they are an integral part of the black working class in South Africa.

Instead of being simply an anti-colonial discourse, they are a "socio-religious sub-culture that lives its relation to the contradictions of monopoly capitalism in distinctive ways".[66] Specifically, "In the era where the *commodity form* reigns supreme they have carved out a control base in which they manipulate the most important commodity in the lives of the *commodityless, the landless, the capitalless* masses of

African descent, namely the Spirit—*Moya*. If they cannot control the means of *material* production they can at least control the means of *spiritual* production".[67]

A hermeneutic of mystification

It is among these churches that the Bible plays a crucial role. However, before we come to Mosala's research on the nature of the role played by the Bible in this movement, it is important to allow the AIC to speak concerning the Bible for themselves. In their booklet, *Speaking for Ourselves*, they write: "We read the Bible as a book that comes from God and we take every word in the Bible seriously". "Some people will say that we are therefore 'fundamentalists'. We do not know whether that word applies to us or not but we are not interested in any interpretation of the Bible that softens or waters down its message . . . We do not have the same problems about the Bible as White people have with their Western scientific mentality".[68]

Remembering that Mosala is focusing on one particular type of church within the AIC, we can see an immediate link between the above remarks and Mosala's findings.[69] These comments support Mosala's initial observation that "The Bible plays a crucial role in the lives of black working class people in South Africa".[70] Mosala is here speaking about the AIC which, he argues, "are black working class churches*par excellence*".[71] More importantly, these comments of the AIC speaking for themselves support the related observation of Mosala's that being Christian and believing in the Bible are inseparable, or, in Barr's terms, analytic.[72]

A second observation of Mosala's is that "The fundamental class issue that affects the reading of the Bible in the AICs is the educational levels of the members", "They simply do not have a literate knowledge of the Bible"[73] In other words, the "source of their knowledge of the Bible is not the biblical texts themselves. Members have an oral knowledge of the Bible. Most of their information about the Bible comes from socialisation in the churches themselves as they listen to prayers and to sermons".[74] For such members of the AIC the Bible as written text makes no sense.

Third, Mosala argues that the Bible is not appropriated by workers within the AIC "in terms of what is says, but in

terms of what it stands for - a canonical authority".[75] Mosala
goes on to contrast this appropriation with that of other black
working class people outside of the AIC who appropriate the
Bible in terms of its contents. "Many *Madodana* (men's guilds)
or *Manyano* (women's guilds) while not having significantly
more education, have been assimilated into a reading culture of the Bible. Thus the authority of the Bible for them
derive[s] from its contents. For this reason a specifically black
working class hermeneutics, drawing its weapons largely from
the work place experiences, is discernible in these groups".
By addressing the contradiction of class such a working class
hermeneutic "represents a better chance of enabling its bear-
ers to find a resolution to the problematic of the entire class
of which they are members". However, this "is not so with
the sub-cultural members of the AICs who form a part of
this same class".[76]

A fourth, related point, then, is that within the AIC there
is "a more symbolically pitched attempt to resolve the problem".

> For sure it enables them to negotiate their reality and even to re-
> sist the forces of brutalisation with which the whole class is faced.
> But their hermeneutical weapons are not drawn from the concrete
> experiences of the work place and social life of its members. It is
> rather derived from the mystifications generated by the authority
> status of a basically unknown Bible . . . In short, therefore, work-
> ing class members of the AICs do not search their contemporary
> historical experience to find tools with which to unlock the myster-
> ies of the Bible. Rather, they appropriate the mysteries of the Bible
> and indeed of traditional African society in order to 'live through'
> their problematic as members of a subordinate class.

In other words, "there is neither a social nor a theological
deliberateness in the movement's manner of appropriating
the Bible from this perspective of a dominated race".[77] Similarly, "On the question of gender as on the issues of race and
class the result of our research revealed that a hermeneutics
of mystification based on a patriarchal consciousness that is
ironically foreign to the religious practice of at least the Zion
Apostolic version of the AICs existed".[78] An illuminating example of the point Mosala is making here is that of healing,
the central activity of the faith practice of the AIC. "Members
draw heavily from the Bible to make sense of the illness prob-

lems that bring so many of them to these churches. Nevertheless no connections are made between gender, illness, and social condition".[79]

This leads Mosala to a fifth, and closely related, observation. "The African symbols and discourses that exist in the AICs faith and practice are the only thing *black* in their hermeneutics".[80] Mosala is here pointing to the absence of race, gender, and class as hermeneutic factors in their appropriation of the Bible while acknowledging the "Africanness" of their appropriation.

The major conclusion to Mosala's research is that "there is no distinctive sub-cultural biblical hermeneutics among the AICs" besides what he has referred to as "the hermeneutics of mystification".[81] Because Mosala's focus is on race, class, and gender as hermeneutic factors he does not develop this notion of a hermeneutic of mystification. However, from discussion with Mosala a hermeneutics of mystification would seem to include the following. First, as I have already mentioned, the notion of "text" is problematic as many of the members are illiterate. For example, when asked by Mosala what their favourite text was, most members had only a vague idea of what was meant by the question. Some were able to give a specific text, while others were clearly not at all sure of what was in the Bible. More importantly, when asked to explain why a particular text was their favourite there was very little understanding of the particular text itself; nevertheless, something about the text appealed to them.[82] This level of mystification relates to Mosala's observation that the Bible is not appropriated by workers within the AIC "in terms of what is says", but as a symbol of God's presence and power.[83]

A second level of mystification is closely related to the first in that it relates to an interest in the "mystery" of the symbolic world of the Bible. Here the focus is not on the concrete, either in the biblical text or in the members' context, but on the symbolic.[84]

Mosala concludes that the search for a distinctive *workers'* biblical hermeneutic "will need to situate itself within the wider black working class parent culture of which the AICs are an integral part".[85]

Conclusion

Mosala's research opens up significant but almost totally ignored areas for participatory research. Unfortunately, Mosala himself stops short of exploring their interpretive strategies and categories *in their own terms.* This is clearly an area for participatory research, because we will only properly understand the liberative and transformative potential within groups like the AIC when we are prepared to learn from ordinary readers of the Bible.

Modes of reading and the ordinary reader

These four case studies clearly demonstrate that there is no "typical" ordinary reader. Equally clearly, there is need for more participatory research with ordinary readers. This research is continuing in South Africa, but with it come extremely complex and difficult questions. This becomes evident when we attempt to locate the ordinary reader in the interpretive debate of the preceding chapters.

While there may appear to be some affinities between "the ordinary reader" and the modes of reading of both Boesak and Mosala, the situation is more complex. A crucial point that needs to be made here is how different the ordinary reader's mode of reading is from that of the trained reader. While there are certainly interesting similarities, we must recognize that something fundamentally different is going on in the modes of reading of the ordinary reader. The majority of ordinary readers read the Bible pre-critically. If "pre-critical" is understood as it is usually used in biblical studies then the ordinary reader has little choice in how they read the Bible. They read it pre-critically because they have not been trained in critical methods. In other words, although there are important similarities between the modes of reading of ordinary readers and the modes of reading of "expert" readers there is nevertheless this crucial difference, namely, that ordinary readers almost by definition read the Bible pre-critically while all the other readers we have been discussing read the Bible critically, even those who choose to read the Bible post-critically. Ordinary readers do not have this choice.

The question of criticalness is crucially important. As we have already seen, Mosala argues that black interpreters like Boesak and others "have been surpassed by the largely illiterate black working class and poor peasantry who have defied the canon of Scripture, with its ruling class ideological basis, by appropriating the Bible in their own way using the cultural tools emerging out of their struggle for survival".[86] Unfortunately, Mosala does not elaborate on this. However, while there is definitely a "critical consciousness" on the part of *some* ordinary readers, as case study 3 and some responses in case study 1 have shown, this is not quite the same as the sort of historical-sociological critical approach advocated by Mosala, Gottwald, and Schüssler Fiorenza.

The ordinary reader may be "politicized" or "conscientized" and so have a general critical consciousness towards society and texts, but they do not have the historical and sociological tools to engage critically with the biblical text in the same way as Mosala, Gottwald, and Schüssler Fiorenza.

When young workers in the YCW appropriate the Bible as the story of liberation they are doing so on the basis of selected texts (and not various redactional layers) and of selected historical and sociological information (and not a systematic reconstruction of the social system behind the text). The critical consciousness of some ordinary readers may predispose them to a critical approach to the Bible, but as ordinary readers they are not there yet.

Similarly, Croatto seems to argue that the poor and oppressed actually read the Bible in the way that his thematic mode of reading articulates. But once again it is important to recognize that while many ordinary readers do read the Bible thematically in its final form as a single canonical text, this is not quite the same as the linguistic-symbolic post-critical canonical approach of Croatto (or the similar approaches of Boesak and Ruether).

When the ordinary reader reads the Bible thematically in its final form they begin with creation (and not exodus) and read selectively (and not along a semantic axis). So while ordinary readers may be predisposed to such a post-critical reading of the Bible they are not there yet.

Conclusion

It is crucial that we recognize both the difference and the complexity of the readings of ordinary readers. If the crux of liberation hermeneutics, the epistemological privilege of the poor and the oppressed, is really going to shape our readings of the Bible then we have to recognize these factors. Once we admit the poor and marginalized, ordinary readers, into the debate things will never be quite the same.

Methodological analysis and clarification among trained readers is not sufficient, particularly among those committed to reading the Bible in contexts of liberation. Such contexts demand that ordinary readers join this discussion. A first step in this direction requires a willingness to discover who the ordinary readers are and how they are reading the Bible. A second step in this direction requires that we honestly analyze the relationship between the trained reader and the ordinary reader in liberation hermeneutics. While chapter seven has made a tentative move in the direction of the first step,[87] chapter eight makes a similar tentative move in the direction of the second step.

The Interface between Biblical Studies and the Ordinary Reader

Introduction

The question of the relationship between biblical studies with its trained readers of the Bible and ordinary readers of the Bible lies at the heart of this study.

In this study we have come to a recognition of an interpretive crisis both in the wider interpretive debate and within biblical interpretation. In chapter one I outlined the shape of this crisis. I argued that the reader and the text have come under careful scrutiny. This scrutiny, I argued, exposed the limitations of objectivity and uncovered the powerful negative hermeneutic potential of moving beyond objectivism. I rejected, however, the popular postmodern options of despair or play and argued for a positive hermeneutic that goes beyond skepticism and nihilism. Finally, I argued that such a positive hermeneutic would require a prophetic vision of resistance and hope that was rooted in an active and transformative solidarity with the community of the poor and oppressed. The question chapter one did not adequately address concerned the nature of the relationship between the trained interpreter and the ordinary interpreter.

In chapter two we analyzed the biblical interpretive crisis in South Africa in both its historical and methodological dimensions. In my discussion of the historical dimension of the interpretive crisis in South Africa I argued that the Bible has been both a problem and a solution, both a collaborator and a liberator. This ambiguity is found among the oppressed. Among the poorest of the oppressed, many of whom are members of African Independent Churches, this ambiguity is particularly evident. The roots of black theology as well as the maintenance of the status quo can be found in the readings of these ordinary readers. I also argued that such ambiguity is present, although perhaps not as overtly, among the black theology of the the black educated middle-class. The penetrating analysis of Mosala exposed the ideological and theoretical enslavement of this sector to the biblical heremeneutics of dominant theologies. At precisely this point the historical dimension of the interpretive crisis merges with the methodological. In order to address both aspects of this interpretive crisis, I argued, there was a need for a theoretically well grounded biblical hermeneutics of liberation which rooted black theology in critical discourse and in the history and culture of the poor and oppressed. Implicit in this need is some kind of relationship between the trained reader and the ordinary reader. Chapter two assumed this relationship but did not analyze the nature of the relationship.

The analysis in chapter three formed the fulcrum of the study. In this chapter I analyzed Boesak's and Mosala's respective readings of the Cain and Abel story. The focus of Boesak's mode of reading, I argued, is on the text and in front of the text. There are elements of both literary and thematic/symbolic/metaphoric approaches in Boesak's mode of reading. The focus of Mosala's mode of reading, I argued, is behind the text. Mosala uses historical-critical and sociological approaches in his mode of reading.[1] I also argued that there are significant similarities in Boesak's and Mosala's modes of reading. In particular, their common commitment to read the Bible from within the South African community of struggle and their common use of the notion of struggle in their respective modes of reading are significant similarities which should facilitate ongoing dialogue among those committed to liberative readings of the Bible in South Africa. With these crucial similarities firmly established I then analyzed some of the questions that the differences in their modes of reading raised. Within each of these questions the question of the relationship between Boesak's and Mosala's respective modes of reading and the ordinary reader came up again and again in various forms. Although I argued that this was a key question I did not explore the nature of this relationship in chapter three.

In chapter four I discussed the nature of this relationship in some detail, but at a more general and political level. I argued here that an epistemological commitment which includes accountability to and solidarity with the poor and oppressed is the key factor in the liberation hermeneutics of both Boesak and Mosala. Nothwithstanding this common epistemological position there are, I argued, real strategic differences between Boesak and Mosala in their political perspectives and so in their programmes for liberation in South Africa. So while this chapter did consider some aspects of the nature of the relationship between trained readers and ordinary readers, there is still the need to analyze the nature of this relationship in more detail.

In chapter five I analyzed the relationship between the interpreter and the tradition. I argued here that both Boesak and Mosala find something, a situation of struggle, which is potentially empowering for the poor and oppressed in the biblical tradition. They are also both committed, I argued, to standing in solidarity with these past struggles. Continuity between past and present struggles and solidarity with past (and present) struggles form a crucial part of their respective modes of reading. So for both Boesak and Mosala the Bible is an important source for their theology of struggle. I also argued that even in his more instrumentalist moments, Mosala acknowledges the empowering role of the biblical tradition and text, particularly for the ordinary reader. Mosala's overt and Boesak's implicit recognition of the importance of the biblical tradition and text for the ordinary reader raises once again the question of the relationship between the trained reader and the ordinary reader.

Chapter six took up this question, but obliquely. By analyzing the relationship between particular modes of reading and the situation of struggle I was able to establish what the central concerns of biblical scholars committed to contexts of liberation were. I argued that for all the interpreters discussed, excluding perhaps Boesak, there was an explicit concern for a critical reading of the biblical text. For Trible and Croatto, as for Mosala, Gottwald, and Schüssler Fiorenza, the struggle within the biblical text can only be accessed and appropriated critically. Although they go about this task differently, they all affirm the crucial importance of a critical reading. I concluded the chapter somewhat abruptly by arguing that Croatto's explicit concern to relate his mode of reading to the modes of reading of ordinary readers was a concern that we, particularly those of us commmmitted to liberative readings of the Bible, had to hear. In other words, the analysis of chapter six could not be taken further until the ordinary reader had been heard in chapter seven.

Chapter seven provided an opportunity to analyze a number of case studies of ordinary readers reading the Bible.

The unfinished analysis of chapter six can now be continued in the light of the analysis in chapter seven. The question, therefore, is how the concern of biblical scholars for a critical reading of the Bible relates to their accountability to and solidarity with the poor and oppressed. As we have already seen in chapter six, Croatto relates his mode of reading explicitly to his accountability to and solidarity with the poor and oppressed. But does this mean that only Croatto's mode of reading is adequate to contexts of struggle? What is the relationship, for example, between Mosala's mode of reading and his committment to accountability to and solidarity with the poor and oppressed?

Modes of reading, the ordinary reader, and the struggle

In responding to this question James Cochrane argues incisively that Mosala's concerns raise

> the practical matter of facilitating a critical consciousness among oppressed people in order that they may be assisted in taking up the chains of the[ir] oppression and breaking them. This is crucial because—as in the best work of the independent black-led trade

unions—it concerns the empowerment of people who have been dispossessed and dehumanized.

Moreover, it contributes to the process of building the communicative competence necessary for a democratic society free from domination and [the] maximizing of the participation of its citizens. Mosala recognizes that critical consciousness and democratic activity is not spontaneous (though always potential), but are learned . . . One may say, therefore, that Mosala represents an approach which has taken praxis into itself as the most penetrating way of uncovering the strategies of domination.[2]

"But", Cochrane continues, "what makes Mosala's hermeneutic difficult in the context of oppression (though it would not change outside of this context, it appears) is that the vast majority of the people he has as his intended base of operations appear to read texts and events somewhat differently".[3]

Boesak's affinity with the ordinary reader, and so the strength of his mode of reading, argues Cochrane, lies in his focus on the text and on the liberation story "for though he is aware of, and has been trained in, the critical tradition, he easily sets a large part of it aside in turning to the text or the event through narrative. He relates to the narrative character of the experience, and thereby links himself to the liberative memory of the past (which may appear in the text as text despite the author) through this strategy".[4]

While Cochrane is probably right in his location of the ordinary reader with respect to the respective modes of reading of Boesak and Mosala, the really incisive point he is making is that both Boesak and Mosala show some awareness of the challenge of the ordinary reader. Their responses, however, are different. By focusing on a critical method Mosala seeks to empower the reader to develop a structural understanding of the Bible as well as a structural understanding of the black experience and struggle.[5] By focusing on the liberation story in the biblical text Boesak seeks to empower the reader to recognize the liberation axis or theme running through the Bible.

Each in their own way is clearly wrestling with the question of the role of the biblical scholar or intellectual in the South African context, a question which arises with particular urgency in contexts of liberation.

In the Latin American context Juan Luis Segundo has analyzed this question with remarkable clarity. In an important essay Segundo outlines the shift within Latin American theology between "two lines" of liberation theology, one essentially a middle class product and the other essentially the product of the "common people". Segundo captures the complexities and the tensions of these two lines. Although his two lines do not correspond exactly with my two modes of reading there are some relevant connections.

Segundo looks at the history, aims, methods, and results of at least two theologies of liberation coexisting now in Latin America. The first theology has three characteristics:

> the origin of a theology of conversion among middle class groups, the methodological trend to suspect that the customary way of understanding Christian faith was distorted at all levels of society by ideological bias that concealed and justified the status quo, and finally, the long-term aim of providing the pastoral activities of the Church with a new and de-ideologized theology capable of speaking about the common themes of Christian faith as they were at the beginning, i.e. a revelation of the humanizing and liberative will of God and of God's own being.[6]

Segundo notes that in this first theology the social sciences are used in a way similar to the use theology made of philosophy in past centuries. However, while the social sciences "provide the theologian who wants to carry out a de-ideologizing task with valuable cognitive tools" they are "tools which . . . are beyond the grasp of the majority of people".[7] In addition, the rise of popular or populist movements either outside or inside the church "had shown that common people had neither understood nor welcomed anything from the first theology of liberation, and had actually reacted against its criticism of the supposed oppressive elements of popular religion. They resisted the new pastoral trends trying to correct it".[8]

The second theology, then, comes from the common people who often did not understand or support the first.[9] "It appeared then that if theologians were still to be the 'organic intellectuals' of the common people, that is to say useful as intellectuals charged with the understanding of popular faith, they were obliged to learn how oppressed people lived their faith".[10] So theologians wanting to be in religious matters the organic intellectuals of poor and marginalized people, "began then to understand their function as one of unifying and structuring peoples' understanding of their faith, as well as grounding and defending the practices coming from this faith".[11]

Segundo, like other Latin American liberation theologians, does not totally agree with this shift. "Some still refuse to give up the first *critical* function which comes out of a suspicion that theology, like other all-pervasive cultural features, can and perhaps should be considered an instrument of oppression and, hence, as a non-Christian theology. Facts point so obviously in that direction that theologians belonging explicitly to the second line cannot but raise the same central question".[12] Segundo finds this tension in the work of Leonardo Boff. He argues that there is "an undoubtedly involuntary contradiction here [in Boff's work] between the claim of having been evangelized by the poor and taught by them, and, on the other hand, the pretension of relocating in people's minds the true meaning of the cross and suffering".[13]

In other words, how does one learn theology from the poor and oppressed and yet at the same time recognize that their theology has been predominantly shaped by the dominant theology of the oppressor? It is at this point that we "both grasp the meaning and appreciate the difficulty in the shift in Latin American liberation theology".[14]

Before we consider this question in more detail it will be useful to note a similar shift in the work of a South African interpreter. In his *Jesus Before Christianity: The Gospel of Liberation* Albert Nolan presents a critical reading of the gospels which he then relates to the daily sufferings of millions of people in South Africa.[15] In this work Nolan draws extensively on biblical scholarship and in so doing brings to light things that ordinary readers do not have access to. His purpose in using critical biblical research is clearly to serve the poor and oppressed.

However, in a recent paper on "A Worker's Theology" we can detect a shift in Nolan's approach. In this paper he too recognizes the "host of questions" raised by taking the ordinary reader seriously. In arguing that "a genuine theology of work will have to be a workers' theology, that is to say, a

theology that is constructed by workers and for workers"
Nolan recognizes that:

> If we ourselves [the trained readers] do not have the experience of
> work that we are reflecting upon in a theology of work, then no
> matter how well we know the Bible and Christian tradition, we will
> simply never be able to *see* in God's word what the workers *see* in
> God's word. No matter how well we know the Hebrew and Greek
> words of the Bible, no matter how thoroughly and critically we
> study the Bible, we will always *miss* some of the things that a worker
> will notice about what is said in the Bible.[16]

Nolan recognizes that it will be argued that the worker
does not have the theological and biblical expertise, nor the
time or leisure, nor the inclination, to construct such a theology. Nolan responds to these arguments, drawing out the
implicit tension between worker and expert.

While acknowledging some truth in these arguments,
Nolan emphasizes that workers have the *experience* of work
and that this together with their Christian *faith* and their
reading and hearing of the stories of the Bible can and do
produce "an elementary and somewhat superficial theology".
But, he continues, "if it is to have any real depth and con-
sistency it must make *use* of the experts".[17] What then, is
the relationship between workers and experts that Nolan
envisages?

The ideal situation for constructing a theology of work "is
not that the professional theology *makes use of* the insights
of workers, *but* that workers *make use of* the expertise and
technical knowledge of academics. So that it is, in fact, and
remains, in fact, a workers' theology. In practice this means
that *we* have to learn the skill of being used, of putting our
expertise into the hands of the *working class* as a service to
them. What Jesus called "learning to serve rather than to be
served".[18]

This is much more difficult to do than it might at first
appear to be, continues Nolan. "As academics, intellectuals,
biblical scholars, we are more accustomed to making use of
the insights of others than allowing ourselves to be made
use of". So such service "requires a conscious and concerted
effort to do more than just listen to what workers have to
say. In fact it requires a confident and militant group of workers who will dictate their needs and interests to us and cor-

rect us whenever we begin to dictate the pace and the requirements".[19]

In other words, such service by trained readers of the Bible requires a humility to hand over our knowledge, skills, and resources to the working class for them to use as they wish;[20] an enormous act of trust and confidence in the truth and value of the interests of the working class; a willingness for such a theology to be done at a pace the workers themselves set;[21] and a commitment to empower others to construct a theology *in their interests.*[22]

We can detect, it would seem, a shift in Nolan's emphasis. The role of the ordinary reader is now foregrounded. This shift has consequences for the reading of the Bible. "What needs to be discovered is that whereas the 'bosses' have hijacked the Bible for their purposes, in fact the Bible favours the workers as victims of oppression and sin. This means the Bible can indeed become a 'weapon' in the struggle for liberation".[23]

The interface between the trained reader and the ordinary reader

Both Mosala and Nolan, then, want the Bible to be a weapon for liberation in South Africa. For this to happen, Mosala argues, the Bible must be read critically, and so the ordinary reader must to some extent be dependent on the work of biblical scholarship. For this to happen, Nolan argues, the Bible must be read from the perspective of the poor and oppressed, and so the trained reader must to some extent be dependent on the readings of ordinary readers. In other words, for the Bible to be a weapon of liberation in South Africa there needs to be an appropriate relationship between the trained reader and the ordinary reader. Mosala stresses the role of the trained reader while Nolan stresses the role of the ordinary reader. However, Mosala does not minimize the role of the ordinary reader and Nolan does not minimize the role of the trained reader.

In order to analyze this difference in emphasis it will be useful to reconsider the dynamics and complexity of oppression and to reconsider the role of the organic intellectual. For Paulo Freire, among others,[24] "the logic of domination represents a combination of historical and contemporary ideological and material practices that are never completely successful, always embody contradictions, and are constantly being fought over within asymmetrical relations of power".[25] In other words, we find in Freire's work a discourse that begins to bridge the relationship between agency and structure, "a discourse that situates human action in constraints forged in historical and contemporary practices, while also pointing to the spaces, contradictions, and forms of resistance that raise the possibility for social struggle".[26]

In Freire's analysis of domination the poor and oppressed are not only oppressed by external structures and forces, they also internalize and thus participate in their own oppression. So Freire argues that the oppressed people's accommodation to the logic of domination may mean that they actively resist emancipatory forms of knowledge.[27] James Scott, however, offers a more nuanced analysis, arguing that theories of hegemony and false consciousness do not take account of what he calls "the hidden transcript".[28]

> Every subordinate group creates, out of its ordeal, a "hidden transcript" that represents a critique of power spoken behind the back of the dominant. The powerful, for their part, also develop a hidden transcript representing the practices and claims of their rule that cannot be openly avowed. A comparison of the hidden transcipt of the weak with that of the powerful and of *both* hidden transcripts to the public transcript of power relations offers a substantially new way of understanding resistance to domination[29].

The crucial point of Scott's detailed argument is that "[t]he public transcript, where it is not positively misleading, is unlikely to tell the whole story about power relations. It is frequently in the interest of both parties to tacitly conspire in misrepresentation".[30] Social analysis which focuses on the public transcript, as most social analysis does, is focusing on the formal relations between the powerful and weak,[31] but is not attempting to "read, interpret, and understand the often fugitive political conduct of subordinate groups"[32]. A focus on the hidden transcript, where it is accessible in the rumours, gossip, folktales, songs, gestures, jokes, and theater of the poor and marginalized, or the more public infrapolitics of popular culture,[33] reveals forms of resistance and defiance. "Unless one can penetrate the official transcript of both subordinates and elites, a reading of the social evidence will almost always represent a confirmation of the status quo in hegemonic terms".[34]

But is there still not a case for Antonio Gramsci's notion of the dominated consciousness of the working class? For Gramsci "hegemony works primarily at the level of thought as distinct from the level of action".[35] Scott turns this around. He considers "subordinate classes *less* constrained at the level of thought and ideology, since they can in secluded settings speak with comparative safety, and *more* constrained at the level of political action and struggle, where the daily exercise of power sharply limits the options available to them".[36] So he argues that "subordinate groups have typically learned, in situations short of of those rare all-or-nothing struggles, to clothe their resistance and defiance in ritualisms of subordination that serve both to disguise their purposes and to provide them with a ready route of retreat that may soften the consequences of a possible failure".[37] This is because most protests and challenges—even quite violent ones—"are made in the realistic expectation that the central features of the form of domination will remain intact".[38] So "[m]ost acts of power from below, even when they are protests—implicitly or explicitly— will largely observe the 'rules' even if their objective is to undermine them".[39] He believes "the historical evidence clearly shows that subordinate groups have been capable of revolutionary *thought* that repudiates existing forms of domination".[40] However, because the occasions on which subordinate groups have been able to act openly and fully on that thought are rare, the conflict will usually take "a dialogic form in which the language of the dialogue will invariably borrow heavily from the terms of the dominant ideology prevailing in the public transcipt". So we must "consider the dominant discourse as a plastic idiom or dialect that is capable of carrying an enormous variety of meanings, including those that are subversive of their use as intended by the dominant".[41]

The picture that emerges from this brief overview of Friere's and Scott's analyses of domination and resistance is clearly

complex. If we are to understand the meaning of liberation
we must first understand the form that domination takes,
the nature of its location, and the problems it poses for those
who experience it as both a subjective and objective force.[42]
Because there is no "average" ordinary reader, as the discussion in the previous chapter indicates, trained readers
committed to working with the poor and marginalized will
have differing emphases depending on their analysis of the
nature of domination and oppression within specfic contexts.

In Nolan's work with fairly politicized and critically conscious workers, he emphasizes the possibilities and resources
for self-emancipation. In Mosala's work with members of a
Zion Apostolic Church whom he believes have internalized
their own oppression, he emphasizes the need for critical
intervention.[43] Although analyses may differ, as in the case
of Mosala and Nolan, the starting point remains the same:
the social and historical particularities, the problems,
sufferings, visions, and acts of resistance of the poor and
oppressed constitute the starting point for the committed
intellectual.[44]

Central to an adequate understanding of the relationship
between the committed intellectual and the poor and oppressed is a redefinition of the very notion of the intellectual.
Like the Italian social theorist Gramsci, Freire redefines the
category of intellectual and argues that all men and women
are intellectuals. "That is, regardless of one's social and economic function, all human beings perform as intellectuals
by constantly interpreting and giving meanings to the world
and by participating in a particular conception of the world".[45]
Moreover, and this is perhaps the crux of the relationship
between the trained and the ordinary reader, "the oppressed
need to develop their own organic and resistant intellectuals
who can learn with such groups while simultaneously helping them to foster modes of self-education and struggle
against various forms of oppression".[46]

> In this case, intellectuals are organic in that they are *not* outsiders
> bringing theory to the masses. On the contrary, they are theorists
> fused organically with the culture and practical activities of the
> oppressed. Rather than casually dispense knowledge to the grate-
> ful masses, intellectuals fuse with the oppressed in order to make
> and remake the conditions necessary for a radical social project.[47]

But what of those who are not and cannot be organic intellectuals and yet who are committed to solidarity with and accountability to the poor and marginalized? How do I as a white, middle-class, South African male inhabit the "ongoing tension between avoiding the indignity of speaking for the oppressed and attempting to respond to their voices by engaging in social and political critique"?[48] I can only do this by moving beyond "speaking for", and beyond "listening to" the poor and oppressed, towards "speaking to/[with]" the poor and oppressed.[49]

"Listening to" presupposes the speaking voice of a wholly self-knowing subject free from ideology, while "speaking for" denies the subject status of the poor and oppressed altogether.[50] In other words, the danger of "listening to" is that we romanticise and idealise the contribution of the poor, while the danger of "speaking for" is that we minimise and rationalise the contribution of the poor. Jill Arnott argues that Gayatri Spivak uses the phrase "speaking to" to point to

> the need to occupy the dialectical space between two subject-positions, without ever allowing either to become transparent. By remaining constantly alert to, and interrogative of, her own positionality and that of her subject, and ensuring that the mediating process of representation remains visible, the feminist researcher may succeed in enabling a dialogue in which the 'testimony of the [subaltern] woman's voice-consciousness' can be heard.[51]

Clearly "such a testimony would not be ideology-transcendent or 'fully' subjective",[52] "but it would not be misrecognised as such, and it would, at least, be heard".[53] In other words, Arnott and Spivak are arguing that "speaking to/with" takes seriously the subjectivity of both the intellectual and the subaltern, and all that this entails for their respective categories and contributions. However, the power relations in the interface between the subaltern (or what I call the "ordinary reader") and the intellectual (or what I call the "trained reader") cannot be obliterated, and they must not be ignored. They must be foregrounded. Postmodern feminists like Arnott, Spivak, Elizabeth Ellsworth, and Audre Lorde emphasise the creative and constructive potential of "a genuinely dialectical interaction between two vigilantly foregrounded subject-positions".[54]

Provided the unequal power relations between ordinary and trained readers are acknowledged and foregrounded, provided the trained reader is willing to serve and to learn "from below", and provided the poor and marginalized continue to empower and be empowered, there is hope for something truly transformative emerging from the interface between trained and ordinary readers of the Bible.

The challenge to biblical studies

So there are still a number of questions to ask and to answer in the South African context of liberation, the crucial one being the nature of the relationship between the trained reader and the ordinary reader.[55] While I have argued that there is sufficient in common for a constructive dialogue to take place between the different modes of reading the Bible in the South African context of struggle,[56] unless this dialogue includes the poor and oppressed it will prove to be largely irrelevant to the transformation of our country.[57] So if it is true that the Bible is "the basic source of African theology" but only when read "in the context of our struggle for humanity",[58] then surely the voices of the poor and oppressed must be heard.[59]

In the last analysis, argues Gutiérrez, "we will not have an authentic theology of liberation unless and until the oppressed are able to express themselves freely and creatively in society and within the people of God". Explaining his argument further Gutiérrez says, "The fact is that so far this critical reflection on liberation praxis has come from sectors in which the popular classes are not present in important or decisive numbers. We must realize that there will be no qualitative leap forward to a different theological outlook until the alienated and exploited become the artisans of their own liberation and make their voices heard directly".[60]

Where the different modes of reading in the South African context of struggle, and in all contexts of struggle, clearly do converge is in the conviction that the primary function of biblical studies is to serve the community, particularly the community of the poor and oppressed. Those of us who are white middle-class males are not and cannot be organic intellectuals, but we can choose to be accountable to and to be in solidarity with the poor and oppressed. We can learn from them and we can serve them. We can choose to be partially constituted by work with them.[61] And it is with this challenge that this study concludes.

The challenge is to move away from the notion of biblical studies as the pursuit of disinterested truth to something more human and transformative, something which is shaped by a self-critical solidarity with the victims of history.[62] Put more strongly, in solidarity with the voices of the poor and oppressed in seven countries as expressed in the recently published *Road to Damascus*,[63] this study calls biblical studies to repentance and conversion.

The Institute for the
Study of the Bible

Introduction

The purpose of this Afterword is to respond to the challenge with which the last chapter concludes. The explicit challenge is to biblical studies to serve the poor and oppressed. The implicit challenge is to pursue the questions still posed by the interface between the trained reader and the ordinary reader. These two challenges are, of course, related. The Institute for the Study of the Bible (ISB) is an attempt to respond to these challenges.

The needs which led to the establishment of the ISB are South African, but some of the vision for the ISB came from a response to similar needs in Brasil.

The Bible movement in Brasil

What has been called "the Bible movement" in Brasil is an attempt at searching for answers to the challenges posed above. The Bible movement emerged with the poor and oppressed trying to read the Bible from a new perspective, a perspective which enabled the Bible to speak into their situation. Biblical scholars were drawn into this process and from the resulting interface the Centro de Estudos Bíblicos (CEBI) was formed.

The common factor that unites the work of CEBI is a Bible reading methodology. The reading methodology of CEBI involves three crucial commitments: first, a commitment to begin with reality as perceived by the organized base; second, a commitment to read the Bible in community; and third, a commitment to socio-political transformation through Bible reading. This reading methodology is referred to as the CEBI process of contextual Bible study.

The first of these commitments is critical. Fundamental to every level of CEBI is that the base "shows" reality. This is qualified, however, in that it is the organized or politicized base who present the picture of reality. This qualification is crucial because it indicates the concern for a critical consciousness among the poor and oppressed.

The second commitment highlights the importance of a communal reading of the Bible: "no-one can read the Bible alone, there must be a search for consensus in the group".[1] This commitment binds biblical scholars and ordinary readers together. While the base has in the past been suspicious of intellectuals this is not necessarily the case. Biblical scholars are continually being "called" by the people. This trust of intellectuals is reserved, however, only for those whom the people choose to speak with.

The biblical scholars who are part of the CEBI process are committed to doing biblical studies with and from the perspective of the poor and oppressed. So in CEBI there has always been a clear recognition by intellectuals of their role as servants. As all of the biblical scholars associated with CEBI are embedded in base communities, there is continual awareness of the limited nature of their influence. Their contribution may be distinctive and different but it is not in any way better or more significant. While not all of the biblical scholars in CEBI are organic intellectuals, they all work closely with organic intellectuals. In fact, most of CEBI's work involves the ongoing training of what they call facilitators or animators. In all aspects of the CEBI process the concerns of such committed intellectuals and facilitators are shaped primarily by the needs of the base.

In the third commitment the emphasis is as much on "the Bible" as it is on "socio-political transformation". In other words, the Bible is not merely a strategic tool for liberation (at least not for the ordinary people, nor for the vast majority of biblical scholars); the Bible is *the* source of "God's project", which is a project of liberation. Although there are a variety of modes of reading the Bible within CEBI, the predominant mode of reading is sociological. This emphasis arises out of the need for a critical consciousness among the poor and oppressed who are often trapped in a feudal and fatalistic culture of silence. The CEBI process of contextual Bible study works for a transfer of social analysis of the text to social analysis of the Brasilian context.

The CEBI Bible study process is transformative in two major respects. Bible study plays an important role in breaking the feudal and fatalistic religious culture of the poor and oppressed in Brasil. The CEBI process offers a new way of seeing reality from the perspective of God's project of liberation. Instead of being trapped in an unchangeable reality of oppression the Bible gives direction to and illuminates a dynamic reality of liberation. The poor and oppressed come to see themselves as active subjects and co-workers in God's project of liberation rather than as passive objects of fate.

The second major transformative role of contextual Bible study is that it gives the poor and oppressed analytical tools and so plays a role in developing a critical consciousness. This is particularly evident through the sociological mode of reading. This mode of reading offers *via its reconstructions* a grasp of historical and analytical concepts, tools, and skills. For example, through making available sociological and historical information people are given conceptual skills and frameworks which relate to time and space. Also, *via its method* this mode of reading offers social, economic, and political categories. For example, the most common sociological approach is the "Four Sides" approach of Gilberto Gorgulho. Here people are trained to pose four sets of questions to the text: economic, social, political, and ideological (including cultural). Reading the Bible from four sides creates categories of perception for text and life. As the people use this method of Bible reading there is some degree of transfer from text to Brasilian context. For example, a conflictual/class analysis of the biblical text leads to a conflictual/class analysis of Brasilian reality.

While CEBI's work has led to a liberative consciousness and praxis in many instances, this is not necessarily always the case. The developing of a transformative faith and a transformative critical consciousness in a society of socio-political and religious "silence" is no easy task. The task is no easier in South Africa.

The Institute for the
Study of the Bible in South Africa

The Institute for the Study of the Bible (ISB) is a South African attempt to develop an interface between biblical studies and ordinary readers of the Bible,[2] particularly the poor and oppressed. Given that the Bible has played and will continue to play a significant role in the life of Christians in South Africa *the primary aim of the ISB is to establish an interface between biblical studies and ordinary readers of the Bible in the church and community that will facilitate social transformation.* This interface has produced a number of related aims for the work of the ISB. These are to develop creative and contextual Bible study materials and processes; to set up a network of contextual Bible study groups throughout South Africa and Southern Africa; to train facilitators for contextual Bible study groups; to learn from and to reflect on the way in which the Bible is read by the poor and marginalized and through this to shape biblical and theological education and research; and to work for social transformation in South Africa.

The ISB is a project linked to the Department of Theological Studies at the University of Natal, Pietermaritzburg, and to a number of community and church groups and organizations throughout Southern Africa. Although the ISB only began work as such in 1990, the need for something like the ISB has a longer history.

The emergence of the ISB is rooted in two crucial assumptions. First, the readings of the Bible of the poor and oppressed in South Africa have a significant contribution to make to our understanding of the Bible and to what God is doing in South Africa. Second, the readings of socially committed biblical scholars have a significant contribution to make to our understanding of the Bible and to what God is doing in South Africa.

The process

Central to all the diverse work of the ISB (including a Community Faith and Life Bible Course in a peri-urban shack community, Bible studies in a Zulu-language educational supplement of a local newspaper, work with the Umtata Women's Group, a Pastoral Upgrading Programme with Concerned Evangelicals, workshops with mainline and African Independent Churches, and the teaching of biblical studies in the School of Theology) is the contextual Bible study process. This process is constituted by at least the following four commitments.[3]

(1) A commitment to read the Bible from the perspective of the South African context, particularly from the perspective of the organized poor and oppressed.

(2) A commitment to read the Bible in community with others.

(3) A commitment to read the Bible critically.

(4) A commitment to individual and social transformation through contextual Bible study.

As the discussion below will demonstrate, there are many similarities here with the contextual Bible study process of CEBI; the differences are an indication of differences in our contexts.

(1) A commitment to read the Bible from the perspective of the South African context, particularly from the perspective of the organized poor and oppressed

Contextual Bible study begins with the questions, needs, experiences, and resources of the poor and marginalized. While the ISB does play a role in facilitating this starting point, it is important that the community we are working with "owns" the project and that they are able "to talk back". Hence the use of the qualifier "organized".

We all bring our contexts with us to our readings of the Bible. This has always been the case, but it has not always been acknowledged. My context includes, for example, at least the following factors: I am a white, middle-class, Western/

African, male Christian. And I need to recognize that these and other similar factors shape my reading of the Bible. Contextual Bible study recognizes that we are all to some extent shaped by our contexts. Contextual Bible study also recognizes that our contexts influence our readings of the Bible. Again, this has always been the case, but it has not always been acknowledged. So instead of denying that we are shaped, for example, by our race, culture, gender, and class, and that these factors influence our readings of the Bible, a commitment of contextual Bible study is that we acknowledge and recognize the forces and factors that have formed us.

However, contextual Bible study is also more specific about context. We read the Bible in South Africa, and this must be acknowledged and recognized. Like any context, the South African context has affected us and our readings of the Bible. This is appropriate, but only if we acknowledge and recognize the influence our South African reality has on our readings of the Bible.

Acknowledging and recognizing the role our South African context has on our readings of the Bible is important because not only do we read the Bible in this context, but we should also want to read the Bible explicitly from and for the South African context. The Bible itself shows that particular people interact with God in particular contexts and that God speaks specifically to specific people in specific life situations.

But as we know, there are many different realities within the South African context, and many readings of the Bible from these differing realities. For example, the Bible has been read to support apartheid by some and to support the struggle for liberation by others, and the Bible continues to be used by some to maintain wealth and power and to struggle for justice and democracy by others. So we have to be even more specific about what we mean by "reading the Bible from and for the South African context".

Those who are committed to the contextual Bible study process have decided to choose to read the Bible from a particular perspective within the South African context, the perspective of the poor and marginalized (including women). The poor and marginalized are those who are socially, politically, economically, or culturally marginalised and exploited. We have made this choice because we believe God is particularly concerned for the poor and oppressed. Our readings of the Bible and our social anlaysis guide us in this choice. We also believe that justice, peace, reconstruction and development will only come in South Africa when the needs of the poor and oppressed are addressed.

Clearly such a commitment requires not only an acknowledgement and recognition of the effect of the South African context on ourselves and our readings of the Bible; it also requires an understanding and analysis of our South African context. We cannot hear either the concerns of the poor and marginalized or God's concern for them unless we are prepared to analyze our context. Initial questions like "Who are the poor and oppressed in South Africa?" and "Why are they poor and oppressed?" lead us to deeper and more complex questions. While these questions may be difficult both to ask and to answer we must be willing to probe and analyze every aspect of our South African context: the religious, the political, the economic, the social, and the cultural.

For those of us who are not from among the poor and marginalised this may seem a difficult commitment. However, if we are willing to acknowledge and recognize our own situation in South Africa and to analyze South African reality from the perspective of the poor and oppressed, and if we are willing to take the next commitment of the contextual Bible study process seriously, then we have already begun to share in the process of doing theology with ordinary people in our context.

(2) A commitment to read the Bible in community

This commitment stresses three aspects of "community consciousness". First, there is the importance of a communal reading of the Bible in which the categories and contributions of both trained and ordinary readers are important, even though they may be different. Second, a commitment to corporate readings of the Bible not only empowers ordinary readers, it also develops processes which facilitate the accountability of biblical studies and theological education to ordinary people. A third important element of community consciousness is the faith of the community. Faith and the struggle for liberation and life are one among the poor and oppressed.

The Western industrialised world's emphasis on the individual shapes most of us in South Africa, and so it is easy to lose a sense of community consciousness. In addition, those of us who have been theologically and biblically trained usually find it hard to genuinely hear and learn from ordinary people. We have to honestly believe that we can learn from the readings and theology of ordinary people. So for us reading the Bible with ordinary readers requires something of a conversion experience; we need to be converted to a sense of community consciousness—we need to be born from below.

Because of our training in theology and biblical studies we tend to read the Bible for ordinary people. We may give the impression that we are hearing the contributions of ordinary readers, but we are really concerned to tell them how they should read the Bible and what they should learn from it. The danger here is that we minimise and rationalise the contributions and experiences of ordinary people. Simply accepting the readings of ordinary people is also a temptation. Because we are sometimes aware of our privileged and powerful position (because of our skills and training) in the group, and because we are committed to reading the Bible in community, we sometimes tend to accept uncritically the readings of ordinary people. The danger here is that we idealize and romanticize the contributions of ordinary readers.

The contextual Bible study process, however, attempts to avoid these two dangers by reading the Bible *with* ordinary readers. What this means is that we as trained readers acknowledge and recognize the privilege and power our training gives us in the group. It also means that we must empower ordinary readers in the group to discover and then to acknowledge and recognize their own identity and the value and significance of their own categories, contributions, and experiences. This is particularly important when we are reading the Bible with people from poor and oppressed communities. Readers of the Bible from these communities have usually had their interpretations silenced and suppressed by the dominant interpretations. Some readers from these communities have even come to accept the dominant interpretations as their own. So if we are really going to read the Bible with ordinary readers we must work together to break the "culture of silence" and to recover the identity and experiences of the poor and oppressed. The poor and marginalised are not really silent, they just speak behind the backs of the dominant and so they are often not heard. Some of what they say is also shaped by centuries of colonization. It is only by talking with and to each other, recognizing the unequal power relations between us, that we can begin to construct transforming discourse.

It is only when both trained and ordinary readers are active "subjects" in the reading process that we really have a process of "reading with". In other words, for the contextual Bible study process to truly be a "reading with" both trained and ordinary readers must be active participants who are aware of who they are. For trained readers being active subjects means that we need not feel guilty about our theological and biblical training. We must feel free to share sensitively and creatively what we have learned from and about the Bible through our training. For ordinary readers being active subjects means that they must be able to speak with their own voice no matter how different this voice is from the dominant voices. This is not easy, because they are used to keeping their speaking hidden, and even then, much of what is spoken is not fully articulated. The next commitment offers resources to empower a speaking that is their own.

(3) A commitment to read the Bible critically

While the previous two commitments are self-evident to the communities we work with, this commitment is not initially articulated. But through a process of reflection on and analysis of the reading practices in their own contexts, most communities recognize the need for critical tools and categories, not only in social analysis, but also in reading the Bible. Poor and marginalized readers come to recognize that critical consciousness is just as important as community consciousness.

We are committed to reading the Bible critically for two reasons: because we are concerned that all readers recognize the ideological nature of the Bible and its interpretations, and because we are concerned that all readers develop critical skills and tools so that they are empowered to do their own critical readings of the Bible and its interpretations.

Commitments to reading the Bible from the perspective of the poor and oppressed and to reading the Bible in community with others require that the ideological nature of the Bible and its interpretations be investigated. This must be done because the Bible and its interpretations have often been used both to oppress ordinary people and to legitimate oppression of ordinary people. These two commitments also require that trained readers continue to read and appropriate the Bible. Some trained readers, when they realize how the Bible has been used to oppress black people and women, for example, decide to reject or abandon the Bible. We in the ISB, however, continue to read the Bible because the Bible is a significant resource and symbol for ordinary people and because it is important to stand in continuity with and to bear witness to the suppressed voices within the Bible and the neglected interpretations of the Bible.

The Bible is and will continue to be a significant resource for ordinary people in the church and community. If we do not find ways of reading the Bible which are transformative and liberating in our context then we are abandoning the Bible to those who use it to legitimate domination and oppression. We also must not abandon the memory of our foremothers and forefathers in the Bible who have struggled for the values of the community of God. Our struggle for justice and peace in South Africa is a part of their struggle. Their faithfulness to God's calling provides us with a "dangerous memory" which reminds, challenges, and empowers us. Instead of separating ourselves from the Bible and its interpretations we should continue to find critical and creative ways of reading it in and for our context.

Once we admit that the Bible is ideological there is the danger that we may become selective in our reading. In other words, we pick and choose what fits our perspective and ignore what does not. But this is not a critical reading of the Bible. If we read the Bible critically we can and should read any and every part of the Bible. But how do we do this?

In our work with communities we would suggest that there are at least three different ways or "modes" of reading the Bible critically. One way of reading the Bible critically is to read the Bible in its historical and sociological context. This "mode of reading" focuses on the historical and sociological context from which the text comes. It concentrates, for example, on the historical and sociological situation lying behind the gospels in order to understand the gospels and Jesus more fully. Another way of reading the Bible critically is to read it carefully and closely in its literary context. This mode of reading focuses on the different types of literature or writings in the Bible and the various relationships within the text. It focuses, for example, on what a "gospel" is and how and why Mark structures his gospel in the way that he does. The third way of reading the Bible critically is to read it in its thematic and symbolic context as a whole. This mode of reading focuses on the major themes and symbols in the Bible as a whole. It emphasises, for example, the central themes that run like a thread throughout the Bible.

These three critical modes of reading the Bible overlap and can be used together in the contextual Bible study process. But it is useful to differentiate between these critical forms of reading because we then become aware of a range of critical skills and concepts which are useful both in reading the Bible and in "reading" our context. Trained readers have been introduced to critical skills and concepts in their theological and biblical training. But while ordinary readers do have critical resources, they do not usually have a systematic understanding of the skills and concepts which constitute a critical reading of the Bible.

At this point it might be useful to state that what we mean by a critical approach to the Bible is that we ask questions in a systematic and structured way; it does not mean that we have a negative attitude towards the Bible. In fact, a critical reading of Bible attempts to minimise manipulation of the Bible by allowing the Bible to speak from its own contexts, including its historical and sociological contexts, its literary contexts, and its thematic/symbolic contexts. To be critical readers of the Bible means that we question and study the Bible rather than just accept and repeat what others have told us about the Bible. And such a critical approach to the Bible is not in opposition to the life of faith. Faith is, in fact, nourished and deepened as we seek to understand the relationship between our faith and our context.

So one of the commitments of the contextual Bible study process is that trained readers share their critical resources with ordinary readers, drawing wherever possible on the critical resources they as ordinary readers already have.

(4) A commitment to personal and social transformation through contextual Bible study

This fourth commitment is not merely a slogan but a real commitment to work for social transformation within those communities in South Africa where the Bible is a significant text. Participants see the contextual Bible study process as potentially transformative in a number of ways. Contextual Bible study plays an important role in breaking the "culture of silence" of the poor and oppressed, by enabling them to see reality from the perspective of God's project of liberation, to speak with their own voices, and to know themselves as active subjects and co-workers in God's project of liberation.

While a critical approach to the Bible and our South African context is something we must learn, there is already a remarkable willingness and ability on the part of ordinary readers to appropriate and apply the Bible to reality—to do theology. The Bible is already a resource for transformation for many readers. So this fourth commitment is usually an integral part of Bible study. However, within this readiness to read the Bible for transformation there are two areas of concern. In South Africa, and elsewhere, the Bible tends to be appropriated uncritically, and this can be dangerous. Apartheid theology is an example of the dangers of such appropriation of the Bible. So while the contextual Bible study process embraces the readiness of ordinary readers to appropriate and apply the Bible to the South African context it emphasises that this must be done critically.

Doing theology within the contextual Bible study process requires two steps. Reading the Bible critically is the first step in a critical appropriation and "reading" our context critically is the second step. A careful and systematic study of the Bible and a careful and systematic analysis of our con-

text enables us to appropriate the Bible more carefully because we are able to identify both the similarities and differences between the Bible and its contexts, on the one hand,
and ourselves and our contexts, on the other hand. Appropriation is perhaps the most important part of the contextual Bible study process, but it is a complex exercise which
requires both a community and a critical consciousness.

The second area of concern is that our readiness to read
the Bible for transformation should include both the personal and the social. In some contexts in South Africa, for
example in white churches and communities, Christians have
concentrated on individual transformation. But the contextual Bible study process is committed to both personal and
social transformation—to the transformation of all aspects
of social reality.

Facilitating the process

Contextual Bible study is a process and this process will
not just happen; it needs to be facilitated. The key to the
contextual Bible study process is facilitation. In a recent
workshop on contextual Bible study, participants agreed that
the five most important characteristics of a facilitator were
the following: the facilitator should use a method that encourages the whole group to participate; the facilitator should
manage conflict and make the group a safe place for member
contributions; the facilitator should train others to become
facilitators; the facilitator should clarify what is not clear
and should summarise the discussion; and the facilitator
should enable the group to become aware of and involved in
the needs of the community. A facilitator, then, is one who
helps the progress and empowerment of others, who makes
it easier for others to act, to contribute, and to acquire skills.

Anyone can be a facilitator, provided they are willing to
learn to be enablers and not dominators. Community consciousness and critical consciousness cannot develop in
authoritarian forms of Bible study. Solidarity and accountability can only develop where there is mutual respect and
trust and where there is a deep sense of community.

The process and the product in practice

It will be useful at this point to move from theory to practice. What does a contextual Bible study look like? I will briefly illustrate the contextual Bible study process and product as it took place in a series of Bible studies.

This series of Bible studies on Mark 10:17-22 with ordinary readers was a response to an earlier research project which Jonathan Draper and I conducted with a number of Anglican Bible study groups in the Pietermaritzburg area.[4] That research set out to understand how ordinary readers read the Bible. The Bible study on Mark 10:17-22 (see chapter seven) used by all of the participating groups was designed by us in such a way that a series of questions constantly returned the Bible study groups to the text. Other than this focus on a careful and close reading of the text the Bible study provided minimum input and maximum opportunity for the Bible study group to develop their own readings of Mark 10:17-22.

In our analysis of the reading product that emerged from the various groups, we noted that almost all the readers in that research, irrespective of their different contexts, understood Mark 10:17-22 as a story about individual sin.[5] In this story the sin was putting wealth/possessions before following Jesus. This was the sin of the man in the story (in the time of Jesus), and this was a potential sin for present day readers. The challenge to the wealthy man (then) and to the participants (now) was to make sure that wealth was not an idol, that possessions did not come between them and Jesus.

In one or two groups, significantly groups from poor and oppressed communities, there was some discussion of "structural sin". In other words, participants in some groups argued that the problem was not only one of individual sin but also one of structural or systemic sin. However, only one group pursued this reading with any persistence.[6] But it was this possible reading which provoked the series of Bible studies, particularly as "structural sin" was a key concept at that time in the struggle against apartheid.[7] I was interested, therefore, in exploring this possible reading of Mark 10:17-22. A series of workshops which I was invited to facilitate provided a useful opportunity to develop a contextual Bible study.

My commitment to a process of "speaking to/with" and to a participatory research methodology entailed that I acknowledge and foreground my own contribution to the process of "reading with". As I will describe in more detail below, my contribution to the reading process was limited to constantly encouraging and facilitating the ordinary readers to read the text carefully and closely. It was only in the final workshop of the research that I introduced "external" information, and I did this only when it was clear that a careful and close reading of the text with ordinary readers did generate a reading of Mark 10:17-22 which included both individual and structural sin.

In each workshop I carefully recorded the reading process and product. My detailed notes, and the notes of the "scribe" appointed by each workshop group, formed the basis of this reflection.

The Bible studies were conducted during seven workshops. Two of these workshops were held at the Federal Theological Seminary, Pietermaritzburg, one in 1990 and one in 1991, and included first year seminary students, 95% of whom were black. As the workshops took place early in the year, these students had not had very much biblical training. Another workshop was incorporated into a course in the Department of Theological Studies, the University of Natal, Pietermaritzburg, in 1990, and included Honours and Masters students, 60% of whom were black. Most of these students had had considerable theological training and some biblical training. Another workshop took place at the Anglican Students Federation Conference in 1991, and included a broad range of tertiary level students, 75% of whom were black. Some of these students had had some theological and biblical training, but the majority were students of other disciplines. Another workshop was the Theological Exchange Programme (TEP) National Workshop in 1991, which included ministers, facilitators, activists, and students, 85% of whom were black. Most of those attending the workshop did not have any formal biblical and theological training. The last workshop took place in Namibia and was a part of a larger workshop hosted by the Education and Documentation Centre for Eastern and Southern Africa (EDICESA). This workshop included a wide range of church officials, ministers, activists, and students, 95% of whom were black. Most of the participants had little formal training in theology and biblical studies.

All of the workshops brought together people from all over South Africa (as well as Southern and Eastern Africa in the case of the last). In each workshop women were present, but formed a small minority. A common feature of all workshops was that most of the participants were politically conscientized.

There was considerable continuity between workshops in that my own contribution had been shaped extensively by the previous workshop(s). In addition, I would also share the comments and questions of previous workshops with subsequent workshops. This enabled a form of dialogue to develop between successive workshops. In a sense, therefore, there was a "speaking with" through me with the participants who had shaped my speaking.

In each workshop Bible study a similar procedure was followed. We began with the experience of participants by considering what participants understood by contextual Bible study. Discussion and debate produced, in each case, a similar framework of commitments which constituted our understanding of contextual Bible study (see above).

Having analysed our experience and understanding of contextual Bible study, we then divided into smaller groups (of between 5-12 people) to do contextual Bible study. In each of the workshops we used the Bible study on Mark 10:17-22 outlined in chapter seven.

It is important to note that in all workshops, except the University one, the Bible studies were done as Bible studies or as training in methods of Bible study, and not as a research exercise. For each of the groups the Bible was a significant text, and Bible study a serious religious experience. Although the focus was on the way in which the Bible was read (the mode of reading) in each Bible study, groups also recorded and reported on the product of their reading.

In each case of my reading Mark 10:17-22 with ordinary readers I was acutely aware of the power dynamics implicit in my presence. My training gave me power in the context of Bible study. There were, of course, other locations of power in each Bible study group. Like Michel Foucault, I recognize that there are multifarious points of power.[8] The ordinary readers in the Bible study groups also had power, particularly those who came from communities of the poor and oppressed. They had power because they are the privileged voice of the poor and oppressed in the contextual Bible study process and in the process of "speaking to/with".

Recognizing these particular locations of power, I was especially concerned that ordinary readers did not simply defer to my reading/interpretation, that they did not offer the "expected" reading, and that they did not attach a predetermined interpretation onto the text. So I was determined to foreground my own contribution to the reading, and also to assist ordinary readers in *reading the text*. I therefore concentrated my contribution on certain aspects of the text, specifically the link between the commandments (v19) and the link between these commandments and the command to the man to sell all that he possesses and to give to the poor (v21). Because ordinary readers tend not to read the text carefully,[9] one of my roles as a facilitator was to focus their reading on the text. The Bible study questions provided a means of doing this.

When ordinary readers in these workshops read verse 19 carefully, prompted by the questions on the commandments, there was general agreement that these commandments were concerned with social relationships (in contrast to the omitted commandments which referred to the human-to-God relationship). Once ordinary readers realized this, they then began to explore *why* Jesus chose these commandments, and concluded that there was obviously something wrong in the area of the man's social relationships. This realization in turn led to considerable discussion and debate as the readers probed for a more precise understanding of the problems in the man's social relationships.

As ordinary readers began to explore and probe these questions, they were constantly driven *to reread the text*. For example, many readers went back to the questions concerning the challenge, and then back to the text, but this time with a more focused question. Verse 22, with its reference to "much property",[8] became a key verse in their attempt to understand this man's wealth. This response of ordinary readers to return to reread the text closely was a particularly exciting development because one of my contributions to "reading with" ordinary readers was to encourage a careful (and so a critical) reading of the text.

Their return to the text generated a certain amount of frustration, because they could not find out very much about the man's social relationships from the text. By drawing on their own South African experience some readers argued that the man probably obtained his "much property" through exploiting others. However, there were other ordinary readers who argued that this was not the only possible reading, and that this man could have worked hard for or inherited his "much property".[10]

Through most of this discussion and debate I attempted to facilitate discussion on as broad a basis as possible, encouraging all participants to share their views. But as I have already stated, my contribution was to pose specific questions which would return readers to the text. So when the ordinary readers themselves recognized the social and structural dimensions of "owning much property", I drew their reading to the relationship between the commandments (v 19), the command to the man to sell all he possessed and to give to the poor (v 21), and the statement that he owned much property (v 22). In other words, I constantly encouraged the ordinary readers to explore the internal relationships within the text.

Once again my contribution led to a return to the text. Those ordinary readers who had argued that the man had probably obtained his "much property" by exploiting others, based on their own South African experience, now found textual evidence to support this argument. Gradually others began to see this argument, and so a reading of Mark 10:17-22 which included a concern for social and structural sin began to emerge.

(In the last workshop Bible study organized by EDICESA in Namibia I also introduced "external" sociological resources for such a reading. Once ordinary readers had seen the possibility of such a reading, I then introduced extra-textual material, material which the ordinary readers did not have access to. In other words, I provided the participants with a sociological context against which to read the text.[11] My sociological sketch of first century Palestine included the sociology of the Jesus movement, the temple-state system, and other historical and sociological factors which interested the participants and which assisted their understanding of Mark 10:17-22.)[12]

In summary, my contribution to the process of reading the Bible with ordinary readers focused on facilitating a close reading of the text. (In one case I provided some sociological data.) With my contribution and their own considerable resources we came to a reading of Mark 10:17-22. Once again I must assert that my contributions were extensively shaped by successive readings of this text with ordinary readers. My contributions came from the interface between a concern for the text and communities of ordinary readers.

Along with many other ordinary readers, the participants in these workshops understood this text to be about individual sin, the sin of making wealth and possessions an idol, and of allowing wealth and possessions to come between people and God. But the ordinary readers who participated in the workshops also understood this text to be about social and structural sin.

In exploring the relationship between the commandments (v 19), the command to the man to sell all he possessed and to give to the poor (v 21), and the statement that he owned much property (v 22), we understood that the text (and Jesus)[13] made a connection between the socially orientated commandments, the wealth of the man, and the poor. We argued that Jesus chose these commandments because he knew that the man had gained his "much property" by exploiting the poor, whether the man himself had done so consciously or unconsciously. It was also argued that there might have been social structures which produced wealth for the man and poverty for the people, in the same way that the social system of apartheid empowered white South Africans to become wealthy and pushed black South Africans into poverty. So even if the man had worked hard for his property or had inherited his wealth, he was still part of sinful social structures.

Given this reading, the challenge of Jesus to the man (v 21) to sell all he possessed and to give to the poor made sense. The man could not follow Jesus until he had repented of, and made restitution for, his social and structual sin. As *The Road to Damascus* document argues, following Jesus requires structual repentance and conversion.

(My introduction of sociological background information in the EDICESA workshop contributed to this understanding. Recognizing that Jesus was from among the poor, and that the early Jesus movement consisted largely of the poor, made it even clearer why the man must first sell all he possessed and give to the poor. The man could not participate in a sinful system and participate in the Jesus movement. He had to make a choice.)

The commandments in verse 19 also took on a new meaning in the light of this reading. The man thought that he had kept the commandments, but he was thinking only on an individual level. While he himself might not have murdered anyone, or committed adultery, or stolen, or given false testimony, or defrauded, or dishonoured his parents, he was a part of and perpetuated a system that did all of these things. The ordinary readers in the workshops, most of whom were black, gave countless examples of how the apartheid system had resulted in murder, adultery, theft, legal injustice, unjust wages, and the destruction of black family life. For example, an inadequate health system for black people, impoverished "homelands" and townships, and biased and brutal security forces murdered black people everyday. The migrant labour system, pass laws, the group areas act, and single-sex hostels all generated adultery and destroyed family life. Forced removals, no minimum wage, and education for inferiority were forms of theft and fraud. The discriminatory legal system and the state controlled media constantly disseminated false and biased testimony.

(The ordinary readers in the Namibian workshop were fascinated by the sociological world of Palestine in the time of Jesus, and immediately saw South African parallels with the temple-state system, Roman occupation, ruling-class Jewish-Roman collaboration, the Sanhedrin, landowners, day-labourers, peasants, the position of women, etc. While I consistently cautioned against simple correspondences between "then" and "now",[14] this sociological perspective was clearly useful to the ordinary readers and provided a grounding for their reading of the text.)

The challenge of Mark 10:17-22 was clear to us. The man, and those who are like him today, must repent and make restitution before they/we could be reconciled to God. This text (and Jesus) seemed to say that there could be no reconciliation with God, and no membership in the community of Jesus, without repentance and restitution. So while we must be constantly alert to wealth as an idolaterous danger, we must also be constantly critical of our social location in sinful structures and systems.

Further reflections

Reading Mark 10:17-22 with ordinary readers has been a challenging and creative process. We have created a cumulative reading which is not found in any academic commentary nor among ordinary readers in the church and community. The key contribution of critical resources, in this case a close literary reading of the text, to the contextual Bible study process is that it enables ordinary readers themselves to articulate "the hidden transcript" and not only "the public transcript".[15] Critical tools and skills also provide ordinary readers with a means for articulating what is incipient and subjugated.[16] While the first response in many Bible study groups is often the "missionary response" or the dogmatically "correct" response, critical modes of reading enable ordinary people from poor and marginalized communities to begin to articulate readings and theologies that are incipient, and even perhaps elements of readings and theologies that are deliberately hidden from public view. The latter is clearly dangerous; what is hidden from the dominant is hidden for good reason, and can and should only be openly spoken in a context of trust and accountability. But within such a context, the intersection of community and critical resources enables the recognizing, recovering, and arousing of dangerous memories and subjugated knowledges, and of hidden transcripts.

The more systematic, critical, reading of the contextual Bible study process provides ordinary readers with the resources to situate the text both within its literary and linguistic context and within its historical and sociological context, and in so doing enables them and us to appropriate the text more critically. Situating the text in these ways prevents a simple correspondence between text and present context. And reading the Bible with ordinary readers encourages the trained reader to complete the hermeneutic cycle and risk appropriation, albeit a critical appropriation. We must not stay with "what it meant"; we must move on to risk asking "what it means", both for our community as well as for ourselves individually.

What is particularly exciting and challenging about reading the Bible with ordinary readers is that it is quite legitimate for ordinary readers and trained readers to emerge from the reading process with different elements of interest. The readings produced in this interface affect ordinary and trained readers differently, and this is not surprising because we come to the text from different places, and after the reading encounter return to our different places. Our subjectivities as trained and ordinary readers are differently constituted, and so the effect that the corporate reading has on our subjectivities will be different. However, and this is extremely important, we will have been partially constituted by each other's subjectivities.[17] And this should always be a constituent element of the contextual Bible study process: a desire to be partially constituted by those from other communities. For me, this means choosing to be partially constituted by working with poor and marginalized communities.

The interface between academic biblical studies and ordinary readers has produced readings, and I have given only one example from the work of the ISB,[18] which are profoundly challenging in our South African context. The present situation of transition in South Africa calls, I would suggest, for just such a creative and challenging reading of the Bible. The contextual Bible study process and the process of reading the Bible with ordinary readers offers us an interface in which to learn with each other.

Reading the Bible with ordinary readers is a creative and challenging process. From the perspective of liberation hermeneutics there is no choice. If we are serious about "an option for the poor and oppressed" then we must read the Bible with them. This is also true, of course, for all who are concerned to relate biblical studies to ordinary readers in the church and community.

Notes

Introduction

1. Tracy 1987:7.

2. The allusions here are to new metaphors which are emerging in contexts of struggle; see Richard 1983.

3. For a more detailed discussion of this concept see Nolan 1988:chapter 8. "In South Africa the yearning for liberation has been translated into action and we call it the *struggle*". "The struggle is the opposite of the [apartheid] system" (157).

   From the outset it must be recognized that important as social analysis is for theologies of liberation their analysis is still fragmentary (see for example Stanley Hauerwas' critique of Gutiérrez in Hauerwas 1986:74). The key concept of "the poor and oppressed" is still ambiguous, although there is consensus in liberation theologies that the distinctive characteristic of the poor is not economic statistics but "the underprivileged in the different power structures" (Frostin 1988:9 and 182-184). The understanding of "the poor" in this study is based on the comprehensive study of Wilson and Ramphele 1989. In addition, while there is usually agreement on liberation "from", there is often less agreement on liberation "for" and "to". Nevertheless, the issues discussed in this study are relevant to both phases of the liberation struggle.

4. The concept of "blackness" will be discussed in more detail in chapter four; but it is important to point out at this stage that "black" includes all those classified as "non-white" in apartheid legislation: africans, coloureds, and indians. "Black", as opposed to "non-white", is a positive description that defines people in their own terms, and not in terms of others.

5. Nolan 1988:157.

6. As will become clear in the study, liberation theology will be defined with methodology and not content as the distinguishing characteristic. The position advocated in this study is that the methodological identity expressed in the *epistemologica ruptura*, rather than geographical origin or progressive, political function is the distinguishing characteristic (Frostin 1988:11).

7. My particular focus will be on what Tracy calls the "hermeneutical-political" tradition within hermeneutics (see

especially Tracy 1985).

8. I am a white, western, male, South African whose life has been shaped by and impinges on each of these contexts. This study itself was produced in two settings: Britain and South Africa. I am committed to the struggle for liberation in South Africa.

9. Frostin 1988:1.

10. Frostin 1988:6.

11. This phrase is used extensively in Latin America, particularly with reference to Base Christian Communities.

12. If we are serious in our desire for an intercultural dialogue based on equality and mutuality, and a Western academic theology which has neglected the experience of the underprivileged ought to be, then the Western intellectual tradition must be seen as one voice among others, not as an absolute and infallible norm. "The present, unequal distribution of power within the system that comprises, among others, the First World and Africa makes it legitimate and even urgent to listen to the voices at the periphery of power, even when African theologies—arguably because of the uneven distribution of power and resources—have not been elaborated as systematically and academically as is common in the metropolis of power" (Frostin 1988:25-26).

13. Tracy 1987:114.

Chapter One

1. Barton 1984:200ff; McKnight 1985:2-3; and Abrams 1958:8-29.

2. Barton 1984:201. McKnight does not explicitly relate this schema to biblical criticism. While such a schema oversimplifies, there is some consensus on the broad shifts in interest.

3. See Lategan 1984.

4. Lategan 1984:3.

5. Old Testament criticism begins for Barton with the shift from (1), an emphasis on the historical events or theological ideas that lie behind or are communicated by the text, to (3), an emphasis on the author(s) and what the author(s) meant in the text.

6. Lategan 1984:3-4.

7. Barton 1984:202.

8. For a less serious discussion see Eagleton 1986. Eagleton too suggests that "one might very roughly periodise the history of modern literary theory in three stages: a preoccupation with the author (Romanticism and the nineteenth century); an exclusive concern with the text (New Criticism); and a marked shift of attention to the reader over recent years". He goes on to add that "The reader has always been the most underprivileged of this trio" (Eagleton 1989:119).

9. Lategan 1984:4.

10. Tracy 1987:12.

11. Theobald Kneifel argues that "Ever since the epochal event of the French Revolution, Europe has been permeated by a profound sense of *crisis*. Highlighted by events like the revolutions of 1848 and 1917 and by the industrial revolution and its consequences, marked by the horror of millions of dead in the two world wars, signalled by the massacres of Auschwitz, Hiroshima and Vietnam, this crisis was felt and interpreted by different thinkers, writers and artists in different ways". Nevertheless, "Most philosophers who have attempted a panoramic assessment of European thought over the last fifty years have referred to this thorough crisis in the West. Outstanding among these is perhaps K. Jaspers' *Die Geistige Situation der Zeit* (1931). 'If one wants to answer the question what [sic] today is still there, one has to say: the consciousness of *danger and loss as consciousness of a radical crisis*. There is only possibility, no secure possession or any guarantee. Any objectivity has become ambiguous; truth appears in what is inevita-

bly lost . . .' When 50 years later J. Habermas edits two volumes under the title *Stichworte Zur Geistigen Situation der Zeit*, thus referring explicitly to Jaspers' book, the sense of *crisis* is present throughout most of the contributions . . . When Walter Schulz begins his vast *Philosophie in der veränderten Welt* his first words are: 'The fact that our present time is a time of crisis (Umbruch) is generally known and recognised'" (Kneifel 1983:273-274).

12.   "In its classical formulation, the scientific method made a number of assumptions about the nature of the human observer and the world. Nature (the physical universe) was thought to be an accessible and objective external reality which could be studied by neutral investigators who would conduct experiments to gather data until they suggested some theory to account for what had been observed. After it had been formulated, the theory would be checked against the data for confirmation or falsification. Of course, as more facts were discovered, they might require modification of the theory, unless they were so puzzling as to require a new theoretical framework" (Herzog 1983:106).

13.   Herzog 1983:106.

14.   Tracy 1987:31.

15.   Tracy 1987:33. Russell Keat and John Urry outline three related claims which reflect the changing concerns and assumptions of more recent philosophers of science (Keat and Urry 1975). Firstly, there is the claim that many scientific statements are not to be seen as true or false descriptions of some external, independently existing "reality", but rather as creations or constructions of the scientist. This may develop into the more radical claim that, in some sense, the physical world of the scientist is created or constructed by scientific theories, and not described by them. In other words, theories are determinative of what is real, and when they change in a fundamental way, we are not faced with a different conception of the same world, but a different world (see particularly Feyerabend 1970 and 1975). Secondly, there is the claim that the kinds of considerations that are relevant in accepting or rejecting a scientific theory are somehow "subjective", in that they are essentially related to the scientist's practical interests, aesthetic or moral values, and so on. The source of this subjectivity may be seen as the individual scientist, or the scientific community. In either case, there is a denial of the existence or adequacy of rational, universally valid criteria and standards for the evaluation of scientific activity (see particularly Feyerabend 1970; 1975; Kuhn 1970; Duhem 1954; Hanson 1958; and Quine 1963). Thirdly, there is the view that the

truth or falsity of theories is "under-determined" by empirical data. Observation cannot provide an objective control for science; the idea that agreed facts can enable us to choose between theories is denied (see particularly Duhem 1954 and Quine 1963 for respectively weaker and stronger forms of this point). However, it must be made clear here that these three characteristics do not constitute a rejection of scientific practice, but an attempt to be more honest about that practice. What is rejected is "scientism" or "the ideology of objectivism" (see Wink 1973:7).

See also Bleich 1976:313ff. A.C. Outler detects that after two centuries of Enlightenment there is a "widespread sense of a great reversal, marked more by undertones of irony than of confidence" (Outler 1985:282).

16. Herzog 1983:108. Richard Rorty states that Michel Foucault's histories or "genealogies" made concrete and dramatic considerations which had been presented more schematically by Wittgensteinian philosophers of science such as Hanson, Toulmin, Kuhn, and Feyerabend. "Foucault's histories helped us to see the discontinuities, the sudden twists and turns" as against the prevailing view of science as rational and slowly progressing (Rorty:1981:5).

17. Cited in Herzog 1983:108.

18. Popper 1945:chapter 25. As the remarks of Popper suggest similar doubts concerning the objective observer (and the objective object) have been raised in the philosophy of history (see particularly Danto 1965; Huizinga 1936; Mink 1966; Mink 1978; Bann 1981; White 1975; and Levin 1967).

19. Herzog 1983:109-110.

20. West 1985:260.

21. West 1985:260.

22. West 1985:260. See "Two Dogmas of Empiricism" in Quine 1963:20-46 for his powerful and often persuasive arguments concerning his epistemological holism and methodological monism. For Quine's naturalism, particularly his conception of philosophy of as being continuous with science, see "Epistemology Naturalized" and "Natural Kinds" in Quine 1969.

23. West 1985:261. Goodman's postempiricist antireductionism is best seen in his classic essay "The Way the World Is" and in the essay "The Test of Simplicity" in Goodman 1972.

24. West 1985:261. Sellars' classic statement is Sellars 1956.

25. West 1985:261 and 271. For a more detailed discussion of American pragmatism see West 1989.

26. Rorty 1979:181. See also West 1985:261.

27. West 1985:261. See also Quine 1969:86-90.

28. West 1985:261.

29. West 1985:261-262 and West 1981:247. For a delightful romp through postmodern discourse via biology, psychology, history, philosophy, and literary theory see Hassan 1987. For his more detailed discussion of the traits of postmodernism see Hassan 1986.

30. West 1985:263.

31. Rorty 1982.

32. West 1981:247 and West 1985:264. West 1981 gives a detailed analysis of this and the other moves.

33. West 1981:259. See also West 1979.

34. West 1981:252.

35. West 1985:264 (see particularly Rorty 1979:182).

36. West 1981:259.

37. West recognizes that in addition to being a natural consequence of anti-realism, holism, conventionalism, and anti-foundationalism, this move is also "part of the general trend of modern analytic philosophy" in which notions such as the subject, self-consciousness, ego, and "I" are being questioned (West 1981:260).

38. West 1981:262-263. Here West cites Nietzsche *The Will to Power* in which he critiques Descartes: "'There is thinking: therefore there is something that thinks': this is the upshot of all Descartes' argumentation. But that means positing as 'true a priori' our belief in the concept of substance—that when there is thought there has to be something 'that thinks' is simply a formulation of our grammatical custom that adds a doer to every deed. In short, this is not merely the substantiation of a fact but a logical-metaphysical postulate" (263).

39. Dean 1986. Dean prefers to call them pragmatists rather than neo-pragmatists. He sees them as standing closer to William James and John Dewey, who are radically empirical and historicist, than to Charles Peirce and Josiah Royce, who are epistemological idealists (261).

40. Dean 1986:261.

41. Dean 1986:266.

42. Rorty 1982:xxxv. See also Dean 1986:268.

43. Dean 1986:269-270.

44. Lentricchia 1980:180.

45. Dean 1986:270. See also Lentricchia 1980:186.

46. Lentricchia 1980:177.

47. Dean 1986:271.

48. West 1985:265.

49. West 1985:265. For further discussion of this point see West 1988.

50. Dean 1986:266-267. The new historicists also accept that "history grows", a growth which they attribute "to the imaginative contribution of the historical interpreter". However, "the new historicists do not think that the imagination is supplied by something abiding within or beyond history. Rather, the imagination is supplied by the individual's own effort to perceive or to make sense of past history". They recognize that past history does determine the limits of that interpretation not only by providing what it is that will be interpreted but by setting limits for the act of interpretation itself. "In other words, no individual's interpretation is individual; it is what it is because the individual lives within and is profoundly affected by a historical community. Nevertheless, the constructive agent in history is the imaginative contribution of the historical interpreter" (267-268).

51. West 1981:263. "Quine describes himself as a 'relativist,' yet warns against associating him with the 'epistemological nihilism' of Kuhn. Goodman labels his position 'as a radical relativism under rigorous restraints, that eventuates in something akin to irrealism'. Rorty calls himself an 'historicist' and Kuhn admits to subscribing to a form of relativism" (265).

52. West 1981:265.

53. West 1985:267.

54. West 1985:269.

55. West 1982a:183.

56. West 1985:269. West argues that Rorty's thin historicism, while built on the work of Wittgenstein, Heidegger, Dewey, Peirce and James, betrays their more politically engaged views (271, and West 1982a:183).

57. West 1983:178-179.

58. West 1983:193.

59. West 1983:193. He continues, "To 'go beyond' the dead is either to surreptitiously recuperate previous 'contents' of life in new forms (Nietzsche), or to deceptively shrug off the weight of the dead whether by promoting cults of passive, nostalgic 'dwelling' (Heidegger) or by creative self-begetting and self-redescribing (Emerson, Bloom, Rorty)". He then outlines the Marxist contribution: "What is distinctive about the Marxist project is that it neither resurrects, attacks nor attempts to 'go beyond' metaphysical, epistemological, and ethical discourses. Rather it aims at transforming present practices—the remaining life—against the backdrop of previous discursive and political practices, against the 'dead' past" (193).

60. West 1983:194.

61. West 1983:190.

62. West 1985:270.

63. West 1985:270-271. He continues, "These marginal voices and peoples are excluded and oppressed not because they have a monopoly on truth which frightens the dominant culture—though there is much to learn from marginal peoples—but rather because the historical development of the structural societal mechanisms, such as class exploitation, state repression, patriarchy, and racism, reproduce and reinforce such marginality. Alienated intellectuals from marginal groups and subaltern classes often forget that their relative exclusion from the dominant conversation is a by-product of these mechanisms—not a personal conspiracy to silence their eager voices" (270-271).

64. West 1982a:185,note (see also Rorty 1981:6).

65. Dean 1986:267.

66. See Putnam 1981.

67. Bernstein 1983.

68. Dean 1986:272.

69. Dean 1986:272.

70. Dean 1986:273.

71. Lentricchia 1983:vii. See also Dean 1986:273.

72. Dean 1986:273.

73. Dean 1986:274. See also Lentricchia 1983:16-19.

   Having considered the new historicism of philosophers and literary critics Dean goes on to suggest that similar steps can be traced in the work of Jeffrey Stout and Cornel West in the area of theology.

Briefly, Jeffrey Stout's *The Flight from Authority* (Stout 1981)
"seeks to explain how it happened that in the modern West we
moved from the notion that moral theory depends on religious
theory to the notion that moral theory is autonomous, independent of religious theory" (Dean 1986:275). In groping
towards the way to a religiously founded ethic Stout rejects
both those positions that are so religiously traditional that they
are irrelevant to the current questions they seek to answer and
those positions that so collaborate with current points of view
that they lose any religious identity. Moving from the pragmatism of Willard Quine to what Stout calls "the new historicism"
of Ian Hacking, Thomas Kuhn, Alasdair MacIntyre, and
Richard Rorty, Stout concludes that the only possible answer
to the modernist's question is a postmodernist historicist
answer. He recognizes that moral theory by itself cannot
resolve the modern skeptical quest for certainty; it cannot offer
a certainty based on a neutral, foundationalist *scienta*. Rather,
moral theory must be founded on the probabilities of history,
specifically on one's private and cultural religious history as
seen from one's personal and communal location. The reasons
to which I appeal, says Stout, "are determined by my situation". Beyond that, to some more general, neutral, and non-
interpretive stance, one cannot go (Stout 1981:264; see also
Dean 1986:276).

74. Dean 1986:277. For a useful and accessible account of
     postmodern ways of speaking see Degenaar 1989.

75. Dean 1986:277-278. Dean's comments here, while accurate for
     some of the new historicists he has discussed, would not apply
     to them all.

76. Cited in Dean 1986:273.

77. Putnam 1981:216 (cited in Dean 1986:273).

78. Dean 1986:273.

79. West 1981:184 and West 1985:269.

80. West 1985:270.

81. West 1988:209.

82. West 1982.

83. West 1982:11.

84. West 1982:21.

85. These are words which Cornel West uses of the negative
     moment in Fredric Jameson's Marxist hermeneutics but which
     can also be applied to his own hermeneutic (see West
     1983:194). "Yet", he continues, "from a Marxist perspective,

Jameson's basis for a positive hermeneutics is utopian in the bad sense; for it is a utopianism which either rests upon no specifiable historical forces potentially capable of actualizing it or upon the notion that every conceivable historical force embodies it" (195). In other words, his major criticism of Jameson's positive hermeneutics is that it has "little or no political consequences", and is therefore "too theoretical" (196).

86.   West 1982:107. He recognizes the real differences between these groups but contends that "The primary aim of this encounter is to change the world, not each other's faith" (107).

87.   In roughly ascending order of progessivism: Stalinism, Leninism, Trotskyism, Gramscianism, Bernsteinianism, and Councilism (134-137). West seems to suggest that Gramscian Marxism offers the most adequate political and cultural analysis and practical procedure for the Afro-American situation (see the comments by Dean 1986:275).

88.   West 1982:146.

89.   Dean 1986:275.

90.   Dean 1986:275 (see West 1982:15).

91.   Tracy 1987:8.

92.   Tracy 1987:8. In focusing on the interpretation of texts he points out that "when literate cultures are in crisis, the crisis is most evident in the question of what they do with their exemplary written texts" (11).

93.   Tracy 1987:55.

94.   Tracy 1987:56.

95.   Tracy 1987:57.

96.   Tracy 1987:58. In a footnote he adds, "This is the reason why those thinkers (like Habermas) who defend some kind of transcendental analysis of communication make their case not on the basis of any transcendental philosophy of consciousness but on an analysis of discourse" (127,n.34).

97.   Tracy 1987:59. Later he adds, "The analysis of the plurality of language use by Wittgenstein and the interpretation of the plurality in every disclosure of language by Heidegger have now been joined by the analysis of Derrida on the plurality within language as an object of differential relations" (60).

98.   Tracy 1987:59.

99.   Tracy 1987:60. For a similar argument see Hoy 1982. David Hoy offers an incisive "sense-making reading" of Derrida. He argues that "Dissemination and hermeneutics need not be

contrasted so extremely. They are more plausibly seen not as irreconcilable theories of meaning, but as practical interpretive strategies, as facets of any good reading. So regarded, disseminative practice ensures that the text's complexity is not underestimated, while the hermeneutical sense-making activity keeps the dissemination from wandering off infinitely" (5). He also characterizes Derrida as "an anti-realist and post-empiricist who is less interested in advancing a positive doctrine than in debunking the metaphysical strains he finds not only in Plato but also in moderns like de Saussure and Lévi-Strauss" (5).

100. Tracy 1987:61.

101. Tracy 1987:61.

102. Tracy 1987:62. Tracy sees the following using this kind of discourse approach: Paul Ricoeur, Jaques Lacan, Michel Foucault, Frederic Jameson, Edward Said, and Julia Kristeva. He adds in a footnote: "The point, in sum, is not to claim the unity of a position but of a set of issues and a basically hermeneutical set of concerns that pervades the different methods and conclusions of those otherwise very different and sometimes mutually contradictory 'discourse analysts'" (129,n.44).

103. Tracy 1987:69.

104. Tracy 1987:69. He develops this more fully in 73-77. "Ideologies are unconscious but systematically functioning attitudes, values, and beliefs produced by and in the material conditions of all uses of language, all analyses of truth, and all claims to knowledge". "Ideologies are carried in and by the very language we use to know any reality at all. The critique of ideologies insists that all interpretations of every culture and every classic should include an analysis of the material conditions that underlie both its production and its reception"(77).

105. Tracy 1987:72. He develops this more fully in 96, 100-104,141,n.56.

106. Tracy 1987:106.

107. Tracy 1987:90.

108. Tracy 1987:77.

109. Tracy 1987:77,112.

110. Tracy 1987:79. Tracy here cites the work of Foucault in support of his argument. "What these analyses show is that every discourse bears within itself the anonymous and repressed actuality of highly particular arrangements of power and

knowledge. Every discourse, by operating under certain assumptions, necessarily excludes other assumptions. Above all,
our discourses exclude those others who might disrupt the
established hierarchies or challenge the prevailing hegemony of
power". "And yet the voices of the others multiply: the hysterics
and mystics speaking through Lacan; the mad and the crimi-
nals allowed to speak by Foucault; the primal peoples, once
misnamed the primitives, defended and interpreted by Eliade;
the dead whose story the victors still presume to tell; the
repressed suffering of peoples cheated of their own experience
by modern mass media; the poor, the oppressed, and the
marginalized—all those considered 'nonpersons' by the powerful but declared by the great prophets to be God's own privileged ones" (79).

111. Tracy 1987:79. Later he adds, "To interpret the religious
classics is to allow them to challenge what we presently consider possible. To interpret them is also to allow ourselves to
challenge them through every hermeneutic of critique, retrieval, and suspicion we posses" (84), which would included
historical-critical methods, social-scientific methods, semiotic
and structuralist methods, poststructuralist methods, and
hermeneutical discourse analysis (97-98).

112. Tracy 1987:79.

113. The exact nature of this solidarity will be analyzed in more
detail in chapter four.

Chapter Two

1. *The Kairos Document: A Theological Comment on the Political Crisis in South Africa* 1985:4. The Second Edition includes after "Church" the words "and all other faiths and religions" (4).

2. The implicit importance of the role of the Bible in the first edition of the *Kairos Document* is made more explicit in the second edition, from which this quotation comes. See *The Kairos Document: Challenge to the Church* 1986:17.

3. Some church leaders have made statements to this effect since the liberation movements were unbanned.

4. Smit 1990a and Smit 1990b.

5. See Kinghorn 1986.

6. Smit 1990a:17.

7. Smit 1990b:41.

   Here it is useful to distinguish between two uses of "ideology": critical and universalistic. In liberation theologies there is often a confusion between these different usages. The critical concept of ideology distinguishes between ideological and non-ideological ideas. The most well-known example of this position is Karl Marx. Ideology in Marx "is defined in terms of the practice of the dominant class and denotes illusory representations that hide social contradictions in the interests of the ruling class. This use of 'ideology' is no denial of the obvious fact that human thought generally is socially conditioned but it defines 'ideology' as a *particular* case of contextually induced distortion". The universalistic concept denies, implicitly or explicitly, such a distinction. Here ideology becomes virtually synonymous with "perspective". The argument, for example, of Karl Mannheim is that since human thought is socially determined it is impossible to distinguish between true and false ideologies (see Frostin 1988:164-165).

   While Smit clearly uses the term "ideology" in the former sense, the way in which the term is used by others will have to be discerned from the linguistic context. However, it is important to recognize that in the chapters which follow Allan Boesak and Itumeleng Mosala use the term differently, with Boesak adopting the former and Mosala the latter understanding.

8. In other words, in attempting to explain this shift Smit argues that this was not "only in reaction to socio-political use of the Bible, but also to dogmatic and ecclesial control" (Smit 1990b:41).

9.   Smit 1990b:43. Jonathan Draper makes a similar point in Draper 1991.

10. "At the 1987 Meeting of the NTSSA [New Testament Society of South Africa] on hermeneutics, for example, when the same pericope was read with a variety of different exegetical methods, it was remarkable, but symptomatic, to see that both historical readings and socio-ethical or ideological readings were almost completely absent" (Smit 1990b:42).

11. In South Africa theological faculties within universities fall into roughly four categories: Afrikaans speaking universities with theological faculties closely controlled by the Afrikaner churches; English speaking universities with theological faculties with ties to the "English" churches but with considerable autonomy; a predominantly Afrikaans correspondence university with a theological faculty with ties to mainly Afrikaner churches but with considerable autonomy; and "tribal" universities (creations of the "homeland" policy of the apartheid system) with theological faculties with ties to mainly Afrikaner churches but with varying degrees of autonomy. And while there is a great deal of uncertainty and potential for change after apartheid, the education system is yet to be comprehensively restructured.

12. Draper 1989:1. The critique of the "ideology of objectivism" in historical-criticism by Walter Wink and William Herzog is pertinent here; see especially Wink 1973; Herzog 1983; and Herzog 1974.

13. Wayne Meeks makes a similar point in Meeks 1986.

14. Herzog 1974:292.

15. Draper 1990:4.

16. See Smit's comments in note 10 above. For a more detailed discussion see chapters four and six; see also West 1992.

17. See Fowl 1990:389. For a similar, although more general position see Stout 1982:6; and Rorty 1985:13.

18. Fowl 1990:390. For further discussion on the politics of pluralism in literary studies see Rooney 1986:561-563; and Eagleton 1984.

19. Eagleton 1983:194. Catherine Belsey makes a similar point when she argues that the literary institution fiddles while Ronald Reagan destroys the world (Belsey 1983:17ff).

20. Eagleton 1983:196.

21. Eagleton 1983:195. He is then even more forthright: "It is not the fact that literary theory is political which is objectionable,

nor just the fact that its frequent obliviousness of this tends to mislead: what is really objectionable is the nature of its politics".

His own position is rather different. "I am countering the theories set out in this book not with a *literary* theory, but with a different kind of discourse . . . which would include the objects ('literature') with which these other theories deal, but which would transform them by setting them in a wider context". What would be specific to the kind of study he has in mind would be its concern for "the kind of *effects* which discourses produce, and how they produce them". He is here advocating two related strategies, first, that we read a text to see how its discourse is structured and organized, *and*, second, that we examine what kind of effects these forms and devices produce in particular readers in actual situations (205).

He is not interested in studying discourse "because it is there" but because of its *uses* (206-207). In this he sees himself closer to the liberal humanist than the structuralist, but with a crucial modification. He argues that the liberal humanist response is not weak because it believes that literature can be transformative but that "it is weak because it usually grossly overestimates this transformative power, considers it in isolation from any determining social context, and can formulate what it means by a 'better person' only in the most narrow and abstract of terms" (207).

What he is proposing, then, is "another way of conceiving what distinguishes one kind of discourse from another, which is neither ontological or methodological but *strategic*. This means asking first not *what* the object is or *how* we should approach it, but *why* we should want to engage with it in the first place". "It is not a matter of starting from certain theoretical or methodological problems: it is a matter of starting from what we want to *do*, and then seeing which methods and theories will best help us to achieve these ends. Deciding on your strategy will not pre-determine which methods and objects of study are most valuable. As far as the object of study goes, what you decide to examine depends very much on the practical situation" (210-211).

He concludes, "What you choose and reject theoretically, then, depends upon what you are practically trying to do. This has always been the case with literary criticism: it is simply that it is often very reluctant to realize the fact. In any academic study we select the objects and methods of procedure which we believe the most important, and our assessment of their importance is governed by frames of interest deeply rooted in our practical forms of social life" (211; Eagleton is deeply aware

of the implications that his views have for the literary critical
institution. "Men and woman do not live by culture alone, the
vast majority of them throughout history have been deprived of
the chance of living by it at all, and those few who are fortu-
nate enough to live by it now are able to do so because of the
labour of those who do not. Any cultural or critical theory
which does not begin from this single most important fact, and
hold it steadily in mind in its activities, is in my view unlikely
to be worth very much. There is no document of culture which
is not also a record of barbarism" (214-215)).

22. Smit 1990:42. This is even the case, as Smit demonstrates,
     with "progressive" scholars like W.S. Vorster. Smit presents a
     detailed discussion of the work of Vorster analyzing this ten-
     sion. For further examples of this tension in the work of
     Afrikaner biblical scholars see the following essays: Deist 1987;
     and De Villiers 1987.

     Nevertheless, as Smit has indicated, there are signs of more
     "engaged" readings of the Bible, and this is a sign of hope for
     the struggle. Here I must mention the work of my colleagues in
     the Department of Theological Studies at the University of
     Natal, Pietermaritzburg, Gunther Wittenberg and Jonathan
     Draper, whose biblical scholarship is committed to and at the
     service of the struggle.

23. For a similar observation concerning the American context see
     Belsey 1983:17.

24. Draper 1990:4. His use of "interesting readings" is based on my
     paper cited above.

25. Frostin 1988:17.

26. Mofokeng 1988:34.

     It will be noted that there is often a lack of consistency in the
     use of uppercase or lowercase in many of the works cited,
     along with a number of other typographical inconsistencies. It
     must be recognized, however, that black interpreters have often
     done their work under severe harassment. The South African
     government had until recently banned all liberation organiza-
     tions. Black interpreters too have experienced banning and
     harassment. "They represent, in the eyes of the State, the
     'religious arm' of the 'total onslaught' against South Africa, and
     therefore need to be combatted. The very first nationwide Black
     Theology seminar, held in April 1971, was disrupted by the
     police, and the book containing the papers there, *Essays in
     Black Theology*, was banned soon after publication. Since then
     numerous black theologians have been detained, accused of
     treason, and 'restricted' for varying periods of time" (Kritzinger
     1988:88).

27. Mofokeng 1988:34. Mofokeng also refers to this as the "well-known partnership between the gun and the Bible" (37).

28. Mofokeng 1988:34.

29. Mofokeng 1988:35.

30. Muzorewa 1985:24-25 (cited in Mofokeng 1988:35).

31. Gobi Mokoka refers to individual missionaries like J.T. van der Kemp, F. Pfanner, and C. Desmond as exceptions to the rule and who "to the best of their ability, did all they could to defend the rights of the indigenous peoples against violation by the settler regime"; cited in Kritzinger 1988:113.

32. I am indebted to James Cochrane for these comments. For more detailed discussion of the variety of missionary activity in South Africa see Du Plessis 1911.

33. Mokgethi Motlhabi recognizes that the missionary drive represented an "enlightening effort through education and other 'civilising' activities", but that it had managed in the process to distort African culture and to "make Africans ashamed of themselves and their heritage" (Motlhabi 1986:45 (cited in Kritzinger 1988:113)). For more detailed studies see Cochrane 1987, particularly chapter 2; Cuthbertson 1987; Majeke 1952:43-48, particularly the comments of Steve Biko. The "Introduction" of Nolan 1988, offers a more "popular" summary.

34. These are the words of Kalenga Matembele in Bühlman 1978:49.

35. Nolan 1988:2.

36. Nolan 1988:2.

37. Nolan 1988:2. For these and similar texts see Villa-Vicencio 1986.

38. It is important here to stress that the use of designation African Independent Churches is something of a generalization. In an important booklet, *Speaking for Ourselves*, a group of leaders of various AIC argue that a source of misunderstanding and distortion is "the academic tendency to generalise from particular cases. A limited number of Churches are studied and then broad generalisations are made about *all* the Churches who have now been categorised as African Independent Churches or Zionists or Ethiopians etc. The criteria for grouping us together and generalising about us are often external to our own beliefs and practices" (African Independent Churches 1985:5).

"Among ourselves we generally refer to our Churches as *Inkonzo zabantu* or *Dikereke tsa batho*. Literally this means the

'Churches of the People' although the people referred to are understood to be African or Black people. Again the Churches that have been classified as 'Zionist' or 'Apostolic' are frequently described by us as *Inkonzo zomoya* or *Dikereke tsa moya*, 'Churches of the Spirit' or 'Spiritual Churches'. Also we often speak of the 'mainline' Churches as *Amasonto omthetho abelungu* or *Dikereke tsa molao* which could be translated the 'Institutional Churches of the Whites'" (6).

In chapter seven I will discuss a particular church within the AIC in more detail.

39. Nolan 1988:2-3. See also De Gruchy 1979:41-46; and African Independent Churches 1985. See also chapter seven for discussion of a particular church within the AIC.

40. Nolan 1988:3.

41. Nolan 1988:3; and *Speaking for Ourselves* 1985:14.

42. Nolan 1988:3. An important example of a "prophetic" church within the AIC is the Ethiopian movement (see Kamphausen 1976). I am indebted to James Cochrane for this example. See also Kretschmar 1986:52-53.

43. The terms "public transcript" and "hidden transcript" are from the important work by James Scott (Scott 1990). I will discuss his perspective in more detail in chapter eight.

De Gruchy 1979:156. Allan Boesak contends that black theology is "as old as the attempts of white Christians to bring the gospel to blacks" (Boesak 1977:15).

44. Kretzschmar 1986:4-6.

45. Mosala 1989:1; and Nolan 1988:3-4. For more detailed discussions see De Gruchy 1979:149-168; Kretzschmar 1986:58-68; and Kritzinger 1988:57-91.

46. Mosala 1989:1. In a later more proleptic discussion of black theology Mosala writes that black theology is "an *insurgent* movement which is inextricably linked to the Black Consciousness philosophy whereby new black historical Subjects are created" (Mosala 1989b:1).

James Cochrane exposes the tenacious commitment to ideologies of domination of the apparently "progressive" English speaking churches (Cochrane 1987).

47. Mosala 1989:1-2.

48. Mosala 1989:2.

49. Mosala 1989:2.

50. Mosala 1989:2. The majority of black workers would belong to the AIC.

51. Mosala 1989:2-3.

52. Mosala 1989:3 (my emphasis).

53. Kritzinger 1988:91-92.

54. This concern for a *theoretically well-grounded* biblical hermeneutic of liberation is central to Mosala's work and will be discussed in more detail in chapters three and six.

55. Mosala 1989:3.

56. Mosala 1989:3. Mosala adds that Latin American liberation theology has failed just on this point, that is, in taking history and culture into account when identifying biblical hermeneutical factors. Specifically, Latin American liberation theology presupposes European history and culture and not the indigenous Latin American history and culture. It is for this reason that blacks and Indians are missing in the Latin American theology of liberation. "Similarly", argues Mosala, "Western social and political theologies have failed to become instruments of liberative praxis because they have been premised on the dominant and patriarchal class histories and cultures at the expense of the oppressed and women's histories and cultures. The rise of a feminist theology of liberation is an appropriate counter-response to this state of affairs" (3-4).

57. Mosala 1989:4.

58. Mosala 1989:4.

59. *The Kairos Document* 1986:17.

60. Bonganjalo Goba concurs, arguing that "The general hermeneutic that is reflected by the document can be described as a hermeneutic of suspicion" (Goba 1986a:64).

61. Elsewhere Mosala argues that the *The Kairos Document* reflects a "biblical hermeneutical bankruptcy" and "it surrenders the monopoly of biblical interpretation to the very theologies it is trying to castigate". He goes on to say, "A more hard-nosed, culturally and historically independent reading of the Bible by black people . . . is appropriate" (Mosala 1987a:23).

Chapter Three

1. Lategan 1984:4.

2. Thiselton 1980:11. Later, he adds, "Theologians who have been trained in the traditions of German philosophy find little problem in taking seriously the double-sided nature of historicality, or historical conditionedness, on the part of *both* the ancient text *and* the modern interpreter. However, a number of British and American scholars seem to view the problem as a merely theoretical one which is only of peripheral concern to the New Testament interpreter" (12). Perhaps the rise of "the new historicism" will have a similar effect on American and possibly British scholars that the work of Heidegger, Gadamer and Ricoeur have had on Continental scholars.

3. He argues that the historical-critical method "pretends to suspend evaluations, which is simply impossible, since research proceeds on the basis of questions asked and a ranked priority in their asking. But such judgements presuppose a system of values and an ontology of meanings which not only give weight to the questions asked but make it possible to ask them at all" (Wink 1973:7). Some reviewers have been hostile to Wink's positions, but this is largely because of his tendency to sometimes overstate his case and because of his polemical style. For Thiselton's comments on Wink see Thiselton 1980:86.

    For similar views to those of Wink see also the work of Rudolf Bultmann, Gerhard Ebeling, Ernst Fuchs, and Robert W. Funk.

4. The issue is not *whether* the historical-critical method has a necessary place, but what that place should be (Thiselton 1980:18-23).

5. These points are taken from Thiselton 1980:22.

6. Lategan 1984:6.

7. The work of Soares-Prabhu is cited by Harrington 1982:362-363. Lategan 1984 also uses Soares-Prabhu as an example, citing from Harrington's paper.

8. Cited in Harrington 1982:362. See also the excellent collection of Third World essays in Sugirtharajah 1991.

9. Lategan 1984:6. Lategan's reference to "'interest' theologies", even though he uses quotation marks, betrays perhaps the lurking assumption that there is a theology which is not an interest theology.

10. Another look at the diagrams at the beginning of chapter one supports this contention.

11. Frei 1974.

12. See particularly the excellent survey by Wilcoxen 1974.

13. Fackre 1983:342. Fackre also notes that "The feminist identification of and attack upon male hegemony in modes of discourse, religious and secular, made its influence felt on the reappreciation of the role of imagination" (342). See also Lategan 1984:5-6. Charles E. Winquist investigates a similar move, although using very different language, in Winquist 1986. For example, "Postmodern discourse will involve the recognition of wounds in and to rational argumentation. It will refuse to understand argument as a seamless fabric or linear progression" (x; see also 33-36).

14. Lategan 1984:6. For similar arguments, on which Lategan is here drawing, see the work of Hollenweger 1981. In the context of this discussion, as has already been indicated, this is also a protest at the separation between imagination and intellect, a separation strongly criticized in the 1960's by Thomas Altizer, the Frankfurt School, and more recently Jürgen Habermas, who extensively analyzes the limits of "rational-technicist" thinking (I am indebted to James Cochrane for this observation).

This proliferation of grassroots and base community Bible study is, of course, particularly prevalent in contexts of liberation (Sugirtharajah 1991).

15. Lategan 1984:4.

16. Gottwald 1985:308. In Malina 1983, Bruce Malina makes a similar observation when he suggests that "perhaps the historical-critical method is not historical or critical enough because it does not take the social sciences seriously enough. The move toward literary criticism only indicates how important an understanding of language is for biblical study. But this move is symptomatic rather than therapeutic. The thesis developed here is that without sharing a social system, people simply cannot communicate in language" (120). "In sum, it would appear that contemporary linguistics, reading theory, and communication theory all point to the central, crucial position of social systems for an understanding of meaning in texts" (128).

17. Lategan 1984:6.

18. Lategan 1984:7.

19. Lategan 1984:7.

20. Boesak 1984:149.

21. Boesak 1984:149.

22. Boesak 1984:149-150.

23. Boesak 1984:150.

24. Boesak 1984:150-151.

25. Boesak 1984:151.

26. Boesak 1984:151.

27. Boesak 1984:152.

28. Boesak 1984:152. Although he mentions South Africa for the first time here, his reading is pregnant with allusions to the South African context.

29. Boesak 1984:153.

30. Boesak 1984:154.

31. Boesak 1984:154.

32. Boesak 1984:155.

33. Boesak 1984:155.

34. Boesak 1984:155-156.

35. Boesak 1984:156.

36. Boesak 1984:157.

37. Boesak uses the phrase "text behind the text", but by it he means the presuppositions and interests behind *theologies* (Boesak 1977:84-85).

38. I use the phrase "in front of the text" to indicate a thematic or symbolic mode of reading. I will analyze this mode of reading in more detail in chapter six.

39. Boesak 1987.

40. This is clearly more of a consideration in the case of *Revelation* than it is in the case of the Cain and Abel story.

41. Boesak 1987:28-29.

42. Boesak makes a point of relating his sermon to the Dutch and European context, but his own South African context is clearly predominant. See also, for example, Boesak 1977 where Boesak argues that "theology must engage itself in the *black* experience, an experience shared by, and articulated in a community" (16). Later, he says the point is "not whether theology is determined by interests, but whether it is being determined by the interests of the poor and the oppressed, or by those of the oppressor" (85).

43. Boesak 1984:148.

44. I will return to this question in chapters five and six.

45. In his discussion of Cain's punishment Boesak makes the following aside: "In that day, after all, human beings were more primitive than we are" (150). Leaving aside the problems with the word "primitive", it is not clear what time period Boesak is referring to here. Does "in that day" refer to the time when the story was written or to the primeval setting?

   In his reading of Revelation he makes it clear that the text's situation of struggle refers to an actual situation of struggle, but the link with the South African situation of struggle is primarily through the text. In the Cain and Abel story Boesak does not make any reference to an "actual" historical situation.

46. Boesak 1984:148.

47. Mosala 1989:33-37.

48. Mosala 1989:35. Mosala bases this contention on Anthony Mansueto's argument that "existential or religious commitments to social revolution will not substitute for scientific analysis of the valence of a tradition in the class struggle" (Mansueto 1983:2).

49. Mosala 1989:35.

50. Mosala 1989:35-36.

51. Mosala 1989:36.

52. Mosala 1989:36.

53. Mosala 1989:37. As in most of Mosala's work, he devotes considerably more space to discussion of method than to discussion of the text. For further examples of Mosala's method at work on a text see Mosala 1989:chapters 4 and 6. While Mosala's biblical exegesis may not always be that careful and detailed, we should not allow this to prevent us hearing the very real and urgent challenges he is posing.

54. Mosala's choice of this particular sociological method is quite deliberate. Mosala offers a detailed critique of the ideological and political agendas accompanying the historical-critical methods and various sociological methods. "The essence of this objection is not that the sociological approaches employed by biblical scholars should not have had an ideological and political agenda. On the contrary, the plea is for an open acknowledgement of the class interests that are being represented and thus an acknowledgement of at least the social limitation of the methods" (Mosala 1986a:30).

55.   Mosala 1986:187.

56.   Mosala 1986:187.

57.   Mosala 1986:196-197.

58.   Mosala 1989:123-124.

59.   Mosala 1989:124. "This understanding is crucial to our cir-
      cumventing the empiricism that has bogged down the histori-
      cal-critical method for many years. The biblical texts, there-
      fore, do not represent an unproblematical record of historical
      events and struggles. On the contrary, they represent particu-
      lar *productions* of historical and social events and relations"
      (124).

60.   I have argued elsewhere that this is also the central link
      between Norman Gottwald's work and liberation struggles
      today (West 1987).

61.   As I indicated earlier, this is a dangerous time for the church.
      Now more than ever we need to nurture and resource the
      prophetic voice. The struggle between the forces of death and
      the God of life is still with us, and the church is still itself a
      site of struggle.

62.   Mosala 1989:32. The phrase "unstructural understanding" is
      also used by Gottwald. I discuss this crucial concern of both
      Mosala and Gottwald in more detail in chapter six.

63.   Mosala 1989:39.

64.   Mosala 1989:40. Mosala argues that "Biblical scholars have
      always been aware of the tendency in biblical literature for
      older traditions to be reused to address the needs of new
      situations", but that until recently they have not recognized
      the cultic-ideological origins of the texts of the Bible. In other
      words, "The issue that has not been faced squarely is what
      kind of additions [and whose] are they" (Mosala 1989:101-102;
      Mosala 1986:185-186, 195).

65.   Mosala 1989:33-34.

66.   Mosala 1989:30. Nothing, Mosala later adds, "could be more
      subversive to the struggle for liberation than enlisting the
      oppressors and exploiters as comrades in arms" (Mosala
      1989:33).

      I will be using the term "contextual" in a different way to
      Mosala. For Mosala black theology's failing is that it "is simply
      contextual theology, that is, white theology in black clothes"
      (Mosala 1989:22).

67.   Mosala 1989:32. Eagleton 1981:113.

68. Wittenberg 1987:16 (= Wittenberg 1988). See also Wittenberg 1989). Rowland and Corner offer other examples of Latin American readings of the Cain and Abel story (Rowland and Corner 1990:15ff).

69. Wittenberg 1987:14. Wittenberg agrees with Crüsemann and others that the "yahwistic" primeval history originally had no literary connection with the patriarchal narrative. "Gen. 2-11 is an independent literary work and has to be interpreted on its own". "If this is correct", he continues, "then we need to ask whether Brueggemann and others are right when they claim that the 'yahwistic' primeval history is 'an effort in royal theology'" (14). See Crüsemann 1978; and Brueggemann 1971.

70. Oded 1986; Gottwald 1980.

71. Wittenberg 1987:15.

72. Wittenberg 1987:16.

73. However, the different results they come to demonstrate that reading behind the text is no guarantee of agreement. Their different identifications of the ideology of the text lead to different sociological reconstructions and therefore different readings of the text. For Mosala Cain is the freeholding peasant, while for Wittenberg Cain represents the violence of the city state. For Mosala Abel represents the land interests of the royal and latifundiary classes while for Wittenberg Abel is the prototype of the Judean herdsman.

74. The emphasis is mine.

75. See the discussion in chapter six.

76. African Independent Churches 1985:26.

77. I will take up this question in chapter five.

78. Segundo 1985. In outlining the shift within Latin American theology between "two lines" of liberation theology, one essentially a middle class product and the other essentially the product of the "common people", Segundo notes that in the former "the *social sciences* are used in a way similar to the use theology made of philosophy in past centuries. The social sciences provide the theologian who wants to carry out a de-ideologizing task with valuable cognitive tools, but tools which . . . are beyond the grasp of the majority of people" (28). I discuss Segundo's analysis in more detail in chapter eight.

79. Draper and West 1989.

80. Mosala 1986:184. Unfortunately, Mosala does not elaborate on this. In chapter seven I will discuss some of Mosala's research among this sector.

81.   See Hoare and Smith 1971. See also West 1982:121.

82.   Mesters 1988 and Cardenal 1976. The former is an English translation, translated in South Africa, of Carlos Mesters' work. The illustrations, which form an integral part of the presentation, have been adapted for the South African context.

I will return to these considerations in chapters seven and eight.

83.   Dean 1986:261-281, 272. Here William Dean is putting forward the argument of Bernstein 1983; see also the discussion in chapter one.

84.   I discuss this question in chapters six, seven, and eight.

85.   I would be concerned to express this call in both socio-political and existential terms, along the lines drawn by Cornel West in his "Introduction" in West 1982.

This challenge will be discussed in more detail in chapter eight.

Chapter Four

1. Frostin 1988:1.

2. See for example the works of Schüssler Fiorenza discussed later in which she specifically refers to Kuhn's notion. For similar observations using different terminology see the following. José Míguez Bonino argues that Latin American liberation theolgians "will refuse to be subject to the academic theology of the West as a sort of *norma normans* to which all theology is accountable" (86); see Míguez Bonino 1975. Similarly, Desmond Tutu argues that "African and Black theology are a sharp critique of how theology has tended to be done mostly in the North Atlantic world" (Tutu 1975:59). In a later essay he states, "We who do liberation theology believe we are engaged in something too urgent to have to wait for the approbation of the West or of those who would blindly follow western standards of acceptability and play western games using western rules" (Tutu 1979:168 (cited in Frostin 1988:199,n.1).

3. Frostin 1988:1. Frostin is here thinking of Schüssler Fiorenza in particular. See Schüssler Fiorenza 1981:95-96; Schüssler Fiorenza 1983:xxi; and Schüssler Fiorenza 1984:48. Her discussion of Kuhn in each of these works is substantially the same. See also the detailed discussion and application of Kuhn's notion of paradigm in Cochrane 1988.

   Frostin notes that since there are conflicting interpretations of Kuhn's notion, "it must be clear that in liberation theology the phrase is used to underline the magnitude of the methodological shift and the difficulties of communication between proponents of the old and the new methodologies with out excluding the possibility of a 'common ground' of argumentation" (199,n.1).

4. Frostin 1988:1.

5. Frostin 1988:6-11.

6. It is this emphasis which shapes each of the others; see Frostin 1988:7-11.

7. I use the singular "issue" here because these are interdependent concerns.

8. Torres and Fabella1978:269 (cited in Frostin 1988:3).

9. Frostin 1988:3-4.

10. See Frostin 1988:4-6.

11. Gutiérrez 1974:ix (cited in Frostin 1988:201,n.24). See also Torres and Fabella 1978:259, 271; and Appiah-Kubi and Torres 1979:192.

12. Frostin 1988:6. See also Herzog 1974:400, who askes "What would happen if in the next fifty years the theological hermeneutic would be determined by the *poor Christ* and the poor with whom God in Christ is still battling for survival?"

13. Cited in Frostin 1988:6.

14. "The main issue between progressive Western theology and its interlocutors, has been whether God exists or not, while the central problem in Third World countries is not atheism but an idolatrous submission to systems of oppression" (Frostin 1988:7-8). See also Gutiérrez 1983:227; and Gutiérrez 1978:241.

15. Frostin 1988:4. See also his discussion of liberal theology (184-193). For a similar discussion see Fiorenza 1974.

16. Cited in Frostin 1988:201-202,n.29; quoted from Gibellini 1979:x. In his discussion of "Church and People" Johann Baptist Metz makes a related point. "Theology—including progressive, socially and politically committed theology—is above all experienced in libraries and conferences, where the opinions and counter-opinions of one's colleagues plays a much more prominent part than the religious life and history of suffering of the Christian people" (Metz 1980:137).

    Such a distinction would hold between Tracy's progressivist theology and liberation theologies. While Tracy is concerned "to hear the readings of the oppressed" (Tracy 1987:106), his primary interlocutors are the three "publics" of the society, church, and academy, not the poor and oppressed (see Tracy 1981:chapters 1-2). Tracy may, however, be moving on this question. In *Plurality and Ambiguity* he says that he "considers claims for the 'hermeneutical privilege' of the poor ambiguous: that they are the 'privileged ones' to God, yes; that they are the ones whose interpretations the rest of us most need to hear, yes (and a yes, which acknowledges the repression of those readings in past and present); that only those readings are 'privileged' to be heard by all, clearly and firmly no" (1987:141,n.56). "The option for the poor does translate, however, into the insistence that the readings of the op-pressed—however different and even uncivil by some tired standards of what can count as civil discourse—must be heard, and preferably heard first" (104).

    Smit 1990a also notes this move in Tracy's *Plurality and Ambiguity* (20).

17. Frostin 1988:6. For the reference to this important phrase, "the epistemologiocal privilege of the poor", see McAfee Brown 1978:61.

18. Frostin 1988:6. In the report from the first EATWOT conference Sergio Torres formulates this understanding as follows: "Herein lies the originality of this book and the emergent theology it represents. It proposes to develop scientifically a theology that speaks with the voice of the poor and the marginated in history" (Torres 1978:vii-xxiii, ix (cited in Frostin 1988:7)).

    Míguez Bonino discusses the phrase "the epistemological privilege of the poor" and insists that it does not imply that the poor are morally or spiritually superior but that they do see reality from a different perspective, which accounts for the emphasis on the *epistemological* contribution of the poor (Míguez Bonino 1983:43 (cited in Frostin 1988:202,n.32)).

19. I am not suggesting here that Frostin stops at "congnizance" while liberation theologians go on to embrace "commitment". I think the notion of "commitment" is implicit in his understanding of "cognizance". In responding to Schubert Ogden's critique of liberation theology, Frostin writes that in Ogden's critique of liberation theology, the commitment to "any and all human beings" is the main argument for rejecting a methodological option for the poor. Moreover, modernity is understood as an expression of "our common experience and knowledge". It follows, continues Frostin, that in Ogden's argumentation one is given to believe that the theology of liberation is committed to only a part of humanity, the poor and oppressed, while the theology of modernity is committed to "any and all human beings". Obviously, argues Frostin, two assumptions underly this argument: first, that there is no distinct Third World experience, and second, that modernity also represents the experience of the poor. Frostin goes on to argue that both these assumptions are denied by liberation theologians.

    However, Frostin does also go on to argue that in the view of liberation theologians "the option for the poor is not a partial as opposed to a universal option; rather, the self-affirmation of the poor is a necessary step on the way to an authentic universalism which does not discriminate against any group" (Frostin 1988:187).

20. Schüssler Fiorenza 1981:93; and Schüssler Fiorenza 1984:45.

21. Schüssler Fiorenza 1981:96; and Schüssler Fiorenza 1984:48.

22. Using insights from the sociology of knowledge and critical theory, Schüssler Fiorenza rejects the notion of a value-free, neutral, and detached scholarship. See also the discussion in chapter one. Frostin argues that "*all* theologies, also those with universal claims, actually are stamped by their contexts", consequently the analysis of context is of cental importance in this methodology (Frostin 1985:135). The importance of social

analysis in the new paradigm is discussed in more detail below.

Mosala makes a similar point when he argues that "all theology is contextual theology. The real question is not whether theology is contextual, but what is the socio-political context out of which a particular theology emerges and which it serves. Is it a theology of the *context of the oppressors* or is it a theology of the *context of the oppressed*? It is one or the other, and its agenda is determined by this context" (Mosala 1985:104).

23.   In discussing feminist theology specifically, Schüssler Fiorenza makes the perceptive point that "the feminist theologian challenges not only the supposedly neutral and objective stance of the academic theologian, but she also must qualify the definition of the advocacy stance of liberation theology as 'option for the oppressed.' Her involvement in liberation theology is not 'altruistic,' but it is based on the acknowledgment and analysis of her own oppression as a woman in sexist, cultural, and theological institutions. Having acknowledged the dimensions of her own oppression, she can no longer advocate the value-neutral, detached stance of the academician. In other words, feminist theologians' experience of oppression is different from those of Latin American theologians, for instance, who often do not belong to the poor, but have made the cause of the oppressed their own" (1981:92-93 and 1984:44).

24.   Schüssler Fiorenza 1983:xxi (my emphasis). For an earlier form of this argument see Schüssler Fiorenza 1981:95.

25.   Schüssler Fiorenza 1983:xxi.

26.   In her work as a feminist liberation theologian, Sharon Welch uses the language of accountability and solidarity (Welch 1990).

27.   See Frostin 1988:85. See also Chopp 1987). Her essay "concentrates on experience as a source and criterion for theology, though it is necessary to recognize . . . the Christian tradition as the other source and criterion in feminist theology" (241). "Indeed, feminist theologians sometimes argue that the *ulitmate* authority is theology's appropriateness, let alone credibility, to women's experience" (241). The main body of her essay expands on the nature of this experience.

28.   Cited in Frostin 1985:131. Frostin himself argues that "Objectivity . . . is not achieved by neutrality but denotes a state where no human experience is suppressed in the public discourse" (Frostin 1988:191).

In other, but related, terms John Rogerson argues that liberation theology accepts the Marxist critique of the notion of the

Verstandesmensch which underlies traditional critical academic studies. Liberation theology, he argues, "rejects the idea of a human reason which is exercised in isolation from economic and social conditions, and which is entirely interest free. Liberation theologians insist time and again that exegesis is fundamentally shaped by the social conditions in which it is practised, and that for them, the human race is a species in which a powerful minority enslaves the majority, thus calling forth the need to see God as the liberator of that majority from economic and social degradation" (Rogerson 1990:288).

29. As in other "contextual theologies" the context "is of theoretical relevance since it may clarify an intrinsic relationship between ideas that may otherwise appear as unconnected or contradictory to a student from a different context" (Frostin 1988:22).

    In what follows I am assuming some understanding of the South African situation. This is a fair assumption given the South Africa's "visibility" in recent years.

30. Sebidi 1986:20 (cited in Frostin 1988:86). For a similar observation see Kritzinger 1988:85.

31. Frostin 1988:86.

32. Frostin 1988:87.

33. Boesak 1977:26.

34. Goba 1986:67, who quotes Vilakazi (cited in Frostin 1988:224). See also the statement from the South African Council of Churches in 1968: "Until a man's [sic] racial identity is established, virtually no decision can be taken: but once established, it can be stated where he can live, whom he can marry, what work he can do, what education he can get, whose hospitality he can accept, where he can get medical treatment, where he can be buried . . . our racial identity is the final and all-important determining factor in the lives of men" (cited in Frostin 1988:224-225,n.12).

35. Frostin 1988:87. Adam Small argues that "It must be clear for anyone who knows the meaning of culture that blackness is for us a supremely cultural fact" (Small 1973).

36. Boesak 1984:24 (cited in Frostin 1988:87). Even though the term is used in slightly different ways by different black theologians, it is quite obvious that it always transcends the ethnic boundaries of apartheid legislation.

    Nevertheless, blackness is always *particular*. This emphasis is seen when Bonganjalo Goba discusses Tracy's "three principal sources of theology, (1) Christian texts, (2) common human experience and (3) language". However, Goba insists, "one modification I want to make in these categories, is that black theological reflection does not deal with common human experience, but particular experience of oppression" (Goba 1988:6).

37. Frostin 1988:87.

38. Welch 1990:137; see also 132ff.

39. Boesak 1977:139 (cited in Frostin 1988:225,n.14).

40. Cited in Kritzinger 1988:85. It should be noted that the black concept of experience differs substantially from the individual-istic concept of experience characteristic of the dominant western theologies (Frostin cites David Kelsey's conception of the individual subject here: "both as knower and as doer, a subject is autonomous, historical, and self-constituting" (101)). The black experience is a communal experience. Similarly, Gutiérrez argues that the notion of the individual conscious-ness as the starting point of cognition and action is character-istic of "the bourgeois mind", as opposed to the point of view of the oppressed (Gutiérrez 1978:228-231).

41. Moore 1973:ix (cited in Frostin 1988:87). Goba's emphasis is clear: "I want to suggest that as interpreters and witnesses of the biblical faith on the basis of our experience of oppression, we do not approach the Bible from a neutral point of view or as disinterested observers but rather with critical questions, presuppositions, and a particular way of seeing derived from a concrete experience", "our experience of oppression" (Goba 1988:6).

42. Mosala 1989:26.

43. Kritzinger 1988:87.

44. Boesak 1978:76 (cited in Kritzinger 1988:87).

45. Goba 1986:68 (cited in Kritzinger 1988:87). See also Moore 1973.

46. Mofokeng 1983:49 (cited in Kritzinger 1988:87).

47. Frostin 1988:94.

48. Cited in Frostin 1988:94-95.

49. Frostin 1988:99. The perceptions of the poor and the oppressed are clearly different from the perceptions of the oppressor. Obviously, such a juxtaposition of perceptions will have a relativistic tendency. However, this admission does not exclude that there is a truth claim in the black interpretation of the South African situation. Frostin's conception of truth here is fairly close to "what really happened", as his discussion of the

death of Steve Biko demonstrates (Frostin 1988:97ff). For other
conceptions of truth see the discussion in chapter one. Welch
offers another view when she argues that the truth claims
made in liberation theological discourse "are both verifiable
and transitory". She argues that the truth of such theological
discourse "is not measured by its 'coherence' or 'adequacy' but
by its efficacy in enhancing a particular process of liberation".
Such truth claims are, however, transitory in two ways. First,
they are true "for a specific situation, but the same formulation
may function oppressively or be ineffective in other situations".
Second, "a particular theological construction contains the
seeds of its eventual replacement". If a formulation is actually
liberating, it helps create a new situation in which different
problems and challenges will have to be addressed (Welch
1990:158; see also 156ff).

It is also important to note here the increasing emphasis in
black theology on social analysis. I will discuss this in more
detail later in the chapter.

50. Frostin is here thinking specifically of the work of Schubert
     Ogden. This choice is particularly apposite given Ogden's
     critique of liberation theology. See Ogden 1979; and Ogden
     1981.

51. Frostin 1988:101. In other words, Frostin supports, in broad
     terms, the analysis in the previous chapter of the interpretive
     frameworks of Boesak and Mosala. Frostin goes on to add that
     "It seems, however, that black theologians differ about the
     relationship between these two aspects of the subversive
     memory" (101). He is thinking here specifically of the differ-
     ences between Boesak and Mosala (see 164-166). In the follow-
     ing chapter I will pursue a more detailed analysis of these two
     aspects.

52. The first phrase is from Metz (Metz 1980) and the second from
     Foucault (cited in Welch 1990:149); for an incisive and creative
     discussion of Michel Fourcault's work within a feminist theol-
     ogy of liberation see Welch 1985. Metz says that the dangerous
     memory is "solidarity in memory with the dead and the con-
     quered" (184).

53. Mosala 1989:8-9.

54. Boesak 1977:1 (cited in Frostin 1988:88).

55. Frostin 1988:88. The phrase "alternative consciousness" is
     Boesak's.

56. Kritzinger 1988:91. Kritzinger mentions "the names of some
     black theologians merely as *representatives* of the different
     tendencies, not to suggest that they are the only ones following

that particular approach". Also, since the boundaries between these approaches are fluid, he does not "intend to convey the impression that they are rigid 'boxes'" (95).

57. Kritzinger 1988:91-92.

58. Kritzinger 1988:92.

59. Clearly these statements are in need of some elaboration, which will be the task of the following chapters. In support of his claim, Kritzinger quotes Boesak's declaration that "Nothing is more central to the Old Testament proclamation than the message of liberation . . . Just as in the Old Testament, the message of liberation forms the *cantus firmus* of the proclamation of the New Testament" (98,n.22). Kritzinger recognizes, however, that although Tutu has a similar perspective, he "acknowledges that there is a rich diversity of theologies in the Bible, and that Christians need to search for the biblical perspective that addresses their particular situation most directly" (98,n.22).

60. Kritzinger 1988:92.

61. Mofokeng 1988:37 (cited in Kritzinger 1988:92). Once again, there are issues here which will be taken up in subsequent chapters.

62. Mofokeng 1988:41 (cited in Kritzinger 1988:93).

63. Kritzinger 1988:93.

64. Kritzinger 1988:93.

65. Kritzinger 1988:93.

66. Cited in Kritzinger 1988:93.

67. Pityana 1973:63 (cited in Frostin 1988:89).

68. Mofokeng 1983:3 (cited in Kritzinger 1988:93 and Frostin 1988:225-226,n.27). Similarly, Mokgethi Motlhabi describes black theology as the theological aspect of black consciousness (Motlhabi 1973:76 (cited in Frostin 1988:226,n.27)).

Frostin comments that what these positions have in common is that "they interpret black theology as a theological expression of black consciousness, as different from a critical relationship" (226,n.27).

69. Frostin 1988:89.

70. Goba 1986:63, 61 (cited in Kritzinger 1988:93).

71. Goba 1986:69; see also Frostin 1988:226,n.28.

72. Kritzinger 1988:93.

73. De Gruchy 1979:155 (cited in Frostin 1988:91).

74. Frostin 1988:91 and Kritzinger 1988:93.

75. Mofokeng 1983:9 (cited in Frostin 1988:227,n.48 and Kritzinger 1988:93-94).

76. Motlhabi 1984:121 (cited in Kritzinger 1988:94).

77. Kritzinger 1988:94. Kritzinger is here quoting Goba and Mosala respectively.

78. Mofokeng 1983:122 (cited in Kritzinger 1988:94).

79. Goba 1986:63-65.

80. Goba 1986:69.

81. Mosala and Tlhagale 1986:viii.

82. Kritzinger 1988:94. Motlhabi, for example, believes "that Black Consciousness has served its purpose and that the time has come for all opponents of apartheid, Black and White, to join hands once more against the common foe" (Motlhabi 1984:276).

83. Frostin 1988:92.

84. See Frostin 1988:92. See also his more detailed discussion in 92-93.

85. Frostin 1988:92-93. Having said this, I do not want to minimize the important differences, differences which are more apparent now than they were a few years ago.

86. Kritzinger 1988:94.

87. Kritzinger 1988:94. Kritzinger notes that these theologians sometimes prefer the terms "people's theology", "critical theology", or "liberation theology" rather than "black theology".

88. Mosala and Tlhagale 1986:viii.

89. While black theology is not monolithic, as we have seen, and there are divergent emphases in its social analysis, the object of social analysis of black theology was and is the system of white domination in South Africa. Throughout the history of this system it has been given different labels, but it will be referred to here by its most common name, apartheid. Apartheid is, however, a complex phenomenon in which one may distinguish between different sub-ideologies, even though there is no accepted typology. Following Frostin and others, I will distinguish between four sub-ideologies, remembering that they do not form four different ideologies but "one structure or system" (Frostin 1988:230,n.6). See also Nolan 1988:69, where Nolan writes, "I am not particularly concerned about what we

call it as long as we realize that it is a total system that orders and controls every aspect of life, including the way Christianity is to be interpreted and how religion is to be practised". The four sub-ideologies are racism, capitalism, Afrikaner nationalism, and the ideology of the National Security State (Frostin 1988:105). Boesak mentions racism, nationalism, militarism, materialism, and national security ideology (Boesak 1984:83,158,163). *The Kairos Document* mentions three sub-ideologies: racism, capitalism, totalitarianism (cited in Frostin 1988:230,n.5). For a more detailed discussion see Frostin 1988:108-135. Clearly, the focus of social analysis is in the process of shifting as we move from apartheid to democracy.

While apartheid was undoubtedly a political and social problem, it was also a theological problem. So black theologians have analyzed apartheid in terms of four theological concepts: idolatry, heresy, sin, and blasphemy (Frostin 1988:105; see 105-108 for a more detailed discussion).

90.   He is also worried about the social analysis of Desmond Tutu, and even questions which side of the class struggle he stands (Mosala 1987:24-26). Mosala is clear where he stands, on the side of the black working class (see Mosala 1986:180). Also, while there is in black theology "a more or less distinct option for 'socialism' in the sense of a non-exploitative, egalitarian economic system and a distinct critique of the economics of 'greed' and 'competitive hatred'" (Frostin 1988:118), Mosala is clearer than most on what liberation is "to" (see especially Mosala 1989a; and Mosala 1986d). And this is where social analysis must now focus.

For a critique of the unstructural analysis of much political and liberation theology see Greeley 1974.

91.   Frostin 1988:93. See particularly Mosala 1985:105-109 where he outlines his historical-materialist sociological approach. For a more detailed discussion see Mosala 1986a; and Mosala 1985:103-111.

92.   Frostin 1988:94. See particularly Mosala 1989a; Mofokeng 1986; Kunnie 1986; Boesak 1977; Boesak 1984; and Webster1982. See also Frostin's discussion "Capitalism as the Root Cause of Apartheid", in Frostin 1988:116-121.

93.   Kritzinger 1988:86.

94.   See for example the work of Manas Buthelezi, particularly, Buthelezi 1973; Buthelezi 1973a; Buthelezi 1978; as well as Onwu 1985; Setiloane 1979; and the last chapter in Goba 1988.

95.   Cited in Frostin 1988:228,n.64. Frostin is here quoting from

the newspaper *The Sowetan*, April 9, 1985.

96. Mofokeng 1986:115 (cited in Frostin 1988:228,n.64).

97. Oosthuizen 1976.

98. Cited in Frostin 1988:228,n.64. Frostin notes here "some similarities to Metz's notion of *memoria* as a spiritual force in the struggle for justice".

99. Thetele 1979:151. Mosala too reflects on the ambivalence of the AIC but concludes that "The point must be made unequivocally . . . without creating the impression that all elements of African traditional culture and religion are progressive and relevant for contemporary society, that without a creative reappropriation of traditional African religions and societies both African and black theologies will build their houses on sand" (Mosala 1986c:99).

100. Frostin 1988:94.

101. Goba 1973:73 (cited in Frostin 1988:94).

102. Goba 1986:69. See also 66-68 for similar comments on black consciousness.

103. *ICT News* 1983 (cited in Frostin 1988:94).

104. Chikane and Tsele 1984:5 (cited in Frostin 1988:228,n.67). I take up this point in chapters seven and eight.

105. Chikane and Tsele 1984:4,141-142. See also the essays by Bernadette Mosala and Bonita Bennett in this Report. These essays are reprinted as: Mosala 1986; and Bennett 1986.

106. Frostin 1988:94. For detailed discussions of the debate see Tlhagale 1986; and Villa-Vicencio 1987.

    The violence in KwaZulu-Natal has added a new dimension to this debate. The question must be seriously posed as to whether or in what way Inkatha is a part of the struggle for liberation and life. Culture, politics, and violence are complex webs which are not easily analyzed. See the following for some analysis: Aitchison 1988; 1989; Aitchison 1989b; Aitchison 1989:58-61,72; Gultig and Hart 1990; Gwala [and Nzimande] 1988; Kentridge 1990; Leeb 1989; Mare and Hamilton 1988; Mare and Ncube 1989; Woods 1989. More recent studies are those of Truluck 1993 and Butler 1994.

107. For a more recent analysis of black theology which elaborates on many of the points I have made see Moore 1994.

108. Mosala 1989b:2.

Chapter Five

1. Barr 1980:52. In other words, there is a relationship of necessity between these propositions by virtue of the fact that the predicate of the statement is a result of analysis of the subject term (see Reese 1980:14,276-277).

2. In other words, Daly seeks to move from the reading of androcentric texts to the construction of a life-center that generates new cultural texts, traditions, and mythologies (see references below). Such a move rejects both biblical texts and biblical tradition (including a reconstruction of early Christian beginnings). For a detailed discussion of Daly's position see Schüssler Fiorenza 1983:21-26.

3. There is also debate concerning the *role* of tradition in theological argumentation. See for example Kelsey 1975; and Gifford 1986. For the relevance of this debate to the South African context see Loader 1987.

4. For illuminating discussions of this debate see: Tracy 1981; MacIntyre 1981; and Stout 1981.

5. Cady 1986:440.

6. Young 1990:20.

7. Cady 1986:442. In what follows I will draw on elements of Gadamer's hermeneutics that both Boesak and Mosala would assent to, leaving aside for the moment those elements where there would be contention.

8. Mark Brett makes the point that although this central metaphor of Gadamer's, the "fusion of horizons", is taken to be true for all understanding, "it is supposed to be especially applicable to the scholarly task of appropriating the past" (Brett 1988:242).

9. For an illuminating discussion of this unity see Hoy 1978.

10. Cited in Cady 1986:442-443.

11. Like Cady, I recognize that although "the differing aims and roles of the theologian and the judge rule out any exact appropriation of Dworkin's categories, there are, as Gadamer correctly notes, sufficient similarities between the areas to make such comparison worthwhile" (443).

    I also recognize that there are differing understandings of "past" in legal and biblical hermeneutics. However, once again there is enough overlap to provide illuminating discussion.

12. Cady 1986:443. In what follows I am following Cady's account of Dworkin's work. For a detailed bibliography see Cady's essay.

13. Cady 1986:444.

14. Cady 1986:444.

15. Cited in Cady 1986:445.

16. Cady 1986:446.

17. Cady 1986:446.

18. Cady 1986:447.

19. Cady 1986:447.

20. Cady 1986:447.

21. Cady 1986:448.

22. Cady 1986:448. In the initial stages of this discussion my use of the terms "past" and "biblical tradition" include both the text and the reconstructed situation behind the text. It is only when the logic of the discussion requires it that the text and the reconstructed situation behind the text are differentiated.

23. According to Cady, conventionalism "reflects a positivist conception of revelation as the disclosure of divine truths through religious authorities" (450).

24. Cady 1986:451.

25. Cited in Cady 1986:451.

26. Cady 1986:451. The feminist context "in front of the text" is a crucial factor in feminist hermeneutics, as we have already seen in the previous chapter and as will become even more apparent in the next chapter.

27. Cited in Cady 1986:451.

28. Ruether 1983:22. I discuss the work of Ruether in some detail here because of the similarities between her mode of reading and that of Boesak's.

29. Ruether 1983:12.

30. Ruether 1983:22. She also recognizes that both Testaments contain resources for "the religious sanctification of patriarchy" (22).

31. Ruether 1983:24.

32. Ruether 1983:24.

33. Ruether 1983:24. She makes it clear from the start "that feminism must not use the critical prophetic principles in Biblical religion to apologize for or cover up patriarchal ideology. Rather, the prophetic-liberating tradition can be appropriated by feminism only as normative principles of Biblical faith

which, in turn, criticize and reject patriarchal ideology. Patriarchal ideology thus loses its normative character. It is to be denounced, not cleaned up or explained away" (22-23).

34. Ruether 1983:24.

35 Ruether 1983:23.

36. Ruether 1983:18-19.

37. As I will argue in more detail below, Ruether's use of the term "content" is part of a larger semantic field of terms and must not be taken in isolation.

38. Ruether 1983:31.

39. "Feminist theology is not asserting unprecedented ideas; rather it is rediscovering the prophetic context and content of Biblical faith itself when it defines the prophetic-liberating tradition as norm" (31).

40. Ruether 1983:31.

41. Ruether 1983:31-32.

42. One again the term "principle" is part of a larger semantic field, including "content" which will be discussed in more detail below.

43. Ruether 1983:32.

44. Ruether 1983:32-33.

45. Cady 1986:452. See the discussion in chapter one.

46. Cady 1986:452,n.30.

47. Ruether 1983:18; cited also in Cady 1986:452,n.30.

48. Cady 1986:452,n.30. "That is, she writes as though the Bible is authoritative and hence must inevitably contain truths for all time" (452,n.30). Although Cady argues that the differences between instrumentalists and naturalists "do not revolve around the problem of authorities and how they operate in theological argumentation", (461) she continually makes asides in this direction.

49. Cady 1986:452,n.30.

50. Cady 1986:452-453.

51. Schüssler Fiorenza 1983:17.

52. Schüssler Fiorenza 1983:18.

53. Schüssler Fiorenza 1983:19. While this is not the place to answer Schüssler Fiorenza's critique of Ruether it should be noted that Ruether is not simply attempting to isolate pro-

phetic-liberating "essences" from the biblical patriarchal tradition. She argues that it "is important to see that the prophetic-liberating tradition is not and cannot be made into a static set of 'ideas.' Rather it is a plumb line of truth and untruth, justice and injustice that has to be constantly adapted to changing social contexts and circumstances" (27). Crucially, when "the religious spokepersons identify themselves as members of and advocates of the poor, then the critical-prophetic language maintains its cutting edge" (29). But "When the religious spokepersons see themselves primarily as stabilizing the existing social order and justifying its power structure, then prophetic language becomes deformed in the interests of the status quo. It becomes a language to sacralize dominant authorities and to preach revenge against former enemies" (29).

54.   Cady 1986:453.

55.   Cited in Cady 1986:453-454.

56.   Cady 1986:454.

57.   Cady 1986:454.

58.   Cady 1986:454. It is important to note here that Cady's use of terms "past" and "tradition" include the biblical text and extra-biblical sources. This will become clearer in my discussion below.

59.   Schüssler Fiorenza 1983:11. See also xix for similar arguments. This is Schüssler Fiorenza's paraphrase.

60.   Schüssler Fiorenza 1983:xix.

61.   Schüssler Fiorenza 1983:xvii-xix.

62.   Schüssler Fiorenza 1983:29.

63.   Schüssler Fiorenza 1983:32-33. See also below for further discussion in this area.

64.   It is not always clear what Ruether understands by her use of the terms "traditions", "patterns", "contents", "principles", "ideas", "imagery", "symbols", "paradigms", "themes". However, all these terms form a semantic field which obviously has its focus on the text.

65.   Ruether 1983:23 and Schüssler Fiorenza 1983:xxii.

66.   It may be more accurate to say that Ruether finds it primarily in front of the text. As I will argue in the next chapter, there is a difference between Phyllis Trible's literary reading of the text and Ruether's symbolic/thematic reading.

67.   It is here that I clarify the distinction between "past" and "text".

68.   Schüssler Fiorenza 1983:53. Schüssler Fiorenza argues that

we must "broaden the sources of information we use as a historical and theological basis for the reconstruction of early Christian beginnings and for formulating the meaning of the church" (56).

69. Schüssler Fiorenza 1983:52.

70. Schüssler Fiorenza 1983:56. "Although the canon preserves only remnants of the nonpatriarchal early Christian ethos, those remnants still allow us to recognize that the patriarchalization process is not inherent in Christian revelation and community but progressed slowly and with difficulty" (35-36).

71. Ruether 1983:33.

72. Ruether 1983:33-36.

73. Ruether 1983:34. It is at this point that Ruether goes on to investigate other sources for her feminist theology.

74. Ruether 1983:33. She refers explicitly to Schüssler Fiorenza 1983.

75. Ruether 1983:34.

76. Cady 1986:454. For Cady's discussion of this challenge to theology generally see 439-441.

77. Mosala 1986 and Mosala 1989:chapter 1.

78. Mosala 1986:177; Mosala 1989:15.

79. The work of James Cone played a significant role in the development of black theology in South Africa in the early 1970s. See Frostin 1988:89-90 for a detailed discussion of the nature of this role.

80. Mosala 1986:179; Mosala 1989:17. I do not think that labels such as "neo-orthodox" are very useful, but it is significant to note the similarity here with Schüssler Fiorenza who uses the same label to characterize the work of Ruether and others.

81. Mosala 1986:180-181; Mosala 1989:19; and see Boesak 1977:10.

82. Mosala 1989:16; Mosala 1986:178.

83. Mosala 1989:21; Mosala 1986:181.

84. Mosala 1986:196.

85. Mosala 1986:197.

86. Mosala 1986:196.

87. Mosala 1987:27-28. This chapter of his thesis is an expanded form of Mosala 1986.

88. Mosala 1986d:119.

89. Mosala 1986d:120.

90. Mosala 1986d:120.

91. Mosala 1986d:120.

92. Mofokeng's essay (Mofokeng 1988) clearly draws extensively on Mosala's work, although there is no explicit reference to it.

93. Mofokeng 1988:37.

94. Mofokeng 1988:37.

95. Mofokeng 1988:38.

96. Mofokeng 1988:37.

97. Mofokeng 1988:38.

98. Mofokeng 1988:40.

99. Mofokeng 1988:38.

100. Mofokeng 1988:38. Mofokeng also argues that there are texts which appear to be written to promote the cause of liberation (37).

101. Mofokeng 1988:39.

102. Frostin 1988:165. Another concept which Frostin mentions here and goes on to discuss is "ideology" (164-166).

103. Frostin 1988:164; see Mosala 1986:177-178.

104. Mosala 1989:17; Mosala 1986:178-179.

105. Boesak 1984:61; cited also in Frostin 1988:160.

106. Boesak 1977:12; cited in Frostin 1988:160. Boesak's concern is that Cone comes "perilously close to identifying" black power and the gospel (Boesak 1977:73). Boesak raises similar concerns against the black African-American theologian Albert Cleage and the black South African theologian Simon Maimela (Boesak 1977:120-121).

107. Boesak 1977:12.

108. Frostin 1988:164; see Boesak 1977:121. For a similar view see Goba 1988. Goba argues that "God's word authenticates its revolutionary foundation by proposing alternatives within the Christian community and the larger society different from the existing South African political situation". "The Word of God contained in scripture forces us to tell the truth and is itself the truth which seeks to unveil all the deceptions of our sinful society" (8). In the next paragraph he continues, "I am not here

interested in challenging biblical historical criticism nor for
that matter to encourage a black bibliolatry. I am also not
trying to make the Bible appeal to modern secular society . . .
As I have already indicated, I am interested in challenging the
black Christian community to evolve a biblical *hermeneutic*
arising out of our historical consciousness under the oppressive structures of Apartheid. As many observers have discovered, the interpretation of the Bible plays a very significant role
within the black community. There is a sense in which the
Bible has been and continues to be a source of strength in our
churches, a source which made us aware of the biblical distortions which were disseminated by the Western missionary
movement"(8). "The biblical witness of God's Word in both the
New and Old Testaments speaks to the historical struggle of
the oppressed. As the black Christian community, we have to
emphasize more than before that we need a black biblical
hermeneutic which addresses itself to the actual situation of
the oppressed" (8-9). In other words, "black biblical scholars
especially are called upon to pioneer a new approach to the
Bible, one informed by their experience of oppression".

He argues more generally that "the whole black Christian
community must once more discover the liberating Word of
God as contained in the scriptures in their actual participation
in the struggle for freedom" (9). He uses the phrase "Word of
God" in a consciously Barthian way here: "For Barth the Word
of God is synonymous with God's self revelation. The Word of
God confronts the human situation as a liberation Word of
Faith, as Barth writes: 'The Word of God is that word God
spoke, speaks and will speak in the midst of all men'" (9). Later
he is critical of aspects of this approach, particularly Barth's
radically Christocentric theology in which God is known only
through Jesus Christ as the Word of God which limits God's
revelation "to Christ and the Bible, denying any revelation of
God through nature, human reason, or experience" (37). The
last is clearly the crucial factor of his hermeneutic. He concludes this chapter with a summary which includes: "We need
a theological hermeneutic informed by the scripture and our
experience and geared to active involvement in the liberation
process" (17).

109. Boesak 1977:144.

110. For a detailed discussion of Boesak's notion of "the wholeness
of life" see Frostin 1988: chapter 5.

111. I am not minimizing the significant differences within this
position. "Naturalist" is not here being used to conjure up an
illusory unity. I have been careful and specific about the
differences between interpreters. However, Cady's taxonomy is
a useful heuristic tool for investigating the important concepts

of continuity and solidarity. This becomes clearer in the discussion that follows.

112. See Cady 1986:455-458.

113. Cady 1986:458.

114. Cady 1986:459. The emphasis is mine.

115. Gadamer 1982:244. For an illuminating discussion of these aspects of Gadamer's work, particularly as they apply to the work of Brevard Childs, see Brett 1988:236-260.

116. Brett argues that while Gadamer clearly endorses the necessity of criticism in preventing naive and premature appropriations of tradition, yet "his main argument seems to be that *criticism itself is determined by tradition*, and in this sense it has its own limitations and finitude" (Brett 1988:240).

117. Tracy 1981:100 (cited in Cady 1986:460). See also Moltmann 1968.

118. Cady 1986:460.

119. Cady 1986:460.

120. See in particular Daly 1973; Daly 1975; Daly 1978; Daly 1984; and Christ 1979. See also Schüssler Fiorenza's discussion of these works in Schüssler Fiorenza 1983:18-36.

121. Cady 1986:460-461.

122. Cady sums up their position as follows: "Insofar as the political, social, and religious realms remain patriarchal, women must modify these realities and reclaim the center, rather than locate "salvation" at the periphery of patriarchy, where Daly's sisterhood lies" (461,n.50).

123. Schüssler Fiorenza 1983:xix. For an eloquent defence of the Bible as a source of power see Flesseman-van Leer 1975. She concludes, "I have learned from my *praxis* that the Bible can break through preconceived and traditional ideas and that it can be a source of power, giving people a basic trust and the freedom to speak out against the *status quo*. That is the reason why you did not succeed in convincing me that I do not meet in the Bible a word 'from the other side'" (242).

124. Ruether 1983:18.

125. Schüssler Fiorenza 1983:xix.

126. Schüssler Fiorenza 1983:xix-xx.

127. See particularly Metz 1980.

128. Schüssler Fiorenza 1983:31.

129. See also Welch 1990:chapters 6,7, and 8 for a similar position.

130. Mofokeng 1988:41.

131. Mosala 1989b:4,12. Mosala emphasizes the disclosive power of the Bible by arguing that "the roots of socialist politics and society are strongly established in the progressive traditions of the Bible" (4).

132. Frostin 1988:101. The concept of "contrast experience" forms a crucial part of Frostin's analysis of black theology in general and Boesak's theology in particular (see 94-103,151-176).

133. It should be obvious that this three category typology or continuum is a heuristic and analytical resource. Feminist biblical hermeneutics has other useful typologies. For example, Ruether offers a similar typology when she discusses the degrees of crisis in a tradition. The first level of crisis, more aptly called reform, involves the continual exegesis of the Bible and tradition in order to articulate more adequate formulations for the present. The second level of crisis, representing a more radical break, occurs when a tradition is considered more ambiguous in its effects; the perceived distortion in a tradition leads to a focus on the founder, earliest community, or revelatory paradigms which are still deemed authentic. The third and last level of crisis, constituting the most radical crisis, is experienced when no dimension of the tradition is considered retrievable, a judgement which necessitates the move to alternate traditions or to the creation of totally new ones (Ruether 1983:16-18; see also Cady 1986:461-462). For a similar typology see also Sakenfeld 1985.

     The particular power of Cady's analysis lies in her use of legal hermeneutics, at Gadamer's suggestion, to explore the role of the past in feminist hermeneutics.

134. Cady 1986:461.

135. Cady 1986:461. Later she adds, "In my judgment, Dworkin's methodological analysis is most useful in helping to reorient our focus—away from the inflammatory and misleading problem of authority to the real substantive judgments which divide us" (461). In other words, Cady's analysis is an explication of the notion of "authority".

136. See for example Loader 1987.

137. Frostin 1988:17 notes that the Bible is "the basic source of African theology". See Young 1990:chapter 4 for a useful discussion of the distinction between the Christian tradition as "source" and the Christian tradition as "norm" in feminist theology.

138. I will return to the importance of the ordinary reader in chapters seven and eight.

139. As I mentioned in chapter four, another significant difference between Boesak and Mosala is their respective understandings of the nature of this struggle within the biblical text.

Chapter Six

1. Stout 1982:2. I am particularly indebted to an essay by Stephen Fowl in which he develops various aspects of Stout's argument and relates them to biblical studies; see Fowl 1990.

2. Stout 1982:5.

3. Stout 1982:6.

4. See Fowl 1990:385.

5. Richard Rorty makes a similar proposal in Rorty 1985. See also Mailloux 1985.

6. Fowl 1990:385.

7. See also Fowl 1990:380.

8. The first level of possible disagreement is in terms of how we formulate our interpretive interests. For example, interpreters may claim that their interest is in an authors intention. For some this would mean a focus on the communicative aims explicit or implicit in the text. For others, however, the author's intention might be construed in terms of his or her motives for writing the text. In this latter case the author's explicit or implicit description of his or her intentions need not be taken at face value (see for example Mosala 1986b; and Mosala 1989:chapters 6 and 7). This brief example shows that "once we have eliminated talk of meanings we will still have disagreements about how we formulate our particular interpretive interests. As with the explication of meaning, the more precision we inject into this discussion the more interests we are bound to end up with. We will also be better able to evaluate the results of any particular reading once we are clear about what the reading is actually trying to achieve" (Fowl 1990:386).

   Fowl argues that a second level of possible disagreement might be found in terms of interpretive practice. Given a particular and clearly defined interest, we may still have disagreements about the reading strategies or methods employed in researching that interest. For example, interpreters may share an interest in the sociological reconstruction of pre-monarchic Israel, but they may disagree about what is to count as evidence and how we are to read that evidence. Some would adopt a structural-functionalist approach while others would adopt a historical-materialist approach. Unlike debates about meaning, or disagreements on the formulation of interpretive interests, explication will be of no use to us here. "Once we have agreed that we are talking about the same thing, we have reached the point of genuine disagreement. Unfortunately, there is no single method for resolving these disputes" (386-387). At this point we either cease to dialogue with one another or we search for some means of resolving our disagreements.

Fowl goes on to suggest a possible means of resolving such disagreements. He suggests we might "rely on rhetorical argumentation, the ability to narrate an account that makes comprehensive sense of the recognized evidence while at the same time accounting for the strengths and weaknesses of alternative views" (387). Fowl is here following the criteria proposed by Alasdair MacIntyre for resolving epistemological crises in science (see MacIntrye 1977:455).

9. Fowl 1990:388. I have discussed this important notion of the "embeddedness" of the interpreter within an interpretive community in chapters one and four.

10. See Fowl 1990:389. Stout 1982:6ff and Rorty 1985:13ff also make this point. See also my discussion in chapters one and two.

11. Fowl 1990:389.

12. See Fowl 1990:388. Some of these issues have been raised in the discussion in chapter two.

13. Fowl uses the term "social responsibility" but implies what I have made explicit in adding the term "universal"; see 391.

14. This is the sort of position Virginia Held argues for (see Held 1983). See also the replies by Richard Rorty and Alasdair MacIntryre in the same volume.

15. See Fowl 1990:393ff for further discussion of this point.

16. Fowl 1990:396. He argues that "This refusal is fundamentally rooted in the recognition that the dream of moral philosophy since the Enlightenment—to establish ethical reasoning on ahistorical universal truths of reason to which all rational people would be responsible—is an illusion". See also MacIntyre 1984, especially chapters 4, 5, and 6.

17. See my discussion in chapter four. This is a crucial argument in the South African and other contexts of liberation. Latin American liberation theologians advance such a critique as a crucial difference between their work and that of "European" political theologies. See for example Segundo 1977, particularly chapters 1 and 3.

18. Fowl 1990:396.

19. Mosala 1989:4.

20. Mosala 1987:16. See chapter two, note 7 for some discussion on Mosala's use of the term "ideology".

21. Cited from the work of Anthony Mansueto in Mosala 1989:34; Mosala 1987:17.

22. Mosala 1989:30; Mosala 1987:18.

23. Assmann 1976:104 (cited in Mosala 1989:31 and Mosala 1987:19).

24. Gottwald 1985:9-10 (cited in Mosala 1989:31-32 and Mosala 1987:19-20).

    In discussing the work of Norman Gottwald, Burke Long recognizes that Gottwald "wants to do nothing less than change the way biblical scholars think" (Long 1982:254).

25. Gottwald 1980:703. He then devotes considerable space to developing this point (see particularly 703-706).

26. Gottwald 1980:705-706.

27. Mosala 1989:32; Mosala 1987:20. The phrase "unstructural understanding" is taken from Gottwald.

28. Mosala 1989:24.

29. Mosala 1989:8-9.

30. Mosala 1989:9.

31. Mosala 1989b:3. As I have argued earlier, although Mosala is here critiquing Boesak's mode of reading he is not calling into question Boesak's commitment to the community of struggle. "The problem is basically one of contradiction. It has to do with the difficult area of the interface between personal existential commitments and structural-ideological locations as well as frameworks of political activity. It is not enough to be existentially committed to the struggles of the oppressed and exploited people. One must also effect a theoretical break with the assumptions and perspectives of the dominant discourse of a stratified society" (Mosala 1989:39; Mosala 1987:26). However, in discussing the work of Desmond Tutu, Mosala does argue that "the real difficulty in criticizing Tutu's biblical hermeneutics . . . is one's assumption that he shares an ideological uneasiness about ruling class values. This assumption is based on his speaking liberation as the goal of this theology. It is, however, sometimes difficult to maintain that assumption" in the face of some of his assertions (Mosala 1989:38-39; Mosala 1987:25).

32. Cited in Mosala 1989:32; Mosala 1987:21. See also Mosala 1989b:4.

33. Here Mosala is focusing on a structural analysis of the Bible rather than of South African society; his concern for the latter

is dealt with in more detail in chapter four.

34. Mosala 1989:32; Mosala 1987:21. Mokogethi Motlhabi makes a similar point but not with respect to the biblical text: "In trying to achieve relevance for this message they [liberation theologies] are faced with two primary tasks. The first is polemical, condemning traditional and current Western theology for being abstract, evasive and, for the large part, irrelevant in speaking about the Word of God and applying it to the concrete human situation. The second task is constructive, trying to redirect theology to its proper goal of addressing, without apology or abstraction, the situation in question—that of the people at whom the Word of God is aimed" (Motlhabi 1987:1-2).

35. Mosala 1989b:4.

36. Mosala 1989:41; Mosala 1987:28.

37. Mosala 1987:15; Mosala 1989:27-28. Gottwald observes that sociological criticism "has definitely converged with an un- masking and demystifying project that casts what Paul Ricoeur has called 'an ideological suspicion' over biblical texts" (Gottwald 1983a:146).

38. Mosala 1989b:3. Gottwald argues that "what later generations remember about an earlier society is often very misleading as testimony for a faithful reconstruction of that society" (Gottwald 1980:597).

39. Mosala argues that "Biblical scholars have always been aware of the tendency in biblical literature to use older traditions to address the needs of new situations", but that until recently they have not recognized the cultic-ideological origins of the texts of the Bible. In other words, "The issue that has not been faced squarely is what kind of additions [and whose] are they" (Mosala 1986:185-186,195; Mosala 1989:101). B.W. Anderson attempts to come to grips with this issue but for him the crucial question is "If these major theological traditions are infected with ideological interests, so much so that Scripture cannot be 'de-ideologized', . . . how can the Bible be the me- dium of the Word of the God who transcends all ideologies and who cannot be domesticated in human word-worlds?" (Anderson 1985:300).

40. Mosala 1989b:3-4; Mosala 1989:41-42; see also Mosala 1987:28-29. Mosala is here drawing on the work of Hall 1973.

41. Mosala 1989b:4. Schüssler Fiorenza makes a similar point when she argues that "The failure to bring a critical evaluation to bear upon the biblical texts and upon the process of inter- pretation within Scripture and tradition is one of the reasons why the use of the Bible by liberation theologians often comes

close to·'proof texting'". Later she adds, "a critical hermeneutic must be applied to *all* biblical texts and their historical contexts" (Schüssler Fiorenza 1981:101-102,108).

42. Mosala 1989:32; Mosala 1987:20. Tracy too recognizes this. In Tracy 1981:1-3, he notes that "the particular form of 'correlation' [between the tradition and contemporary situation] that liberation and political theologies take will ordinarily prove to be a form not of liberal identity nor one of the several forms of analogy or similarity but rather one of sheer confrontation" (2). "The confrontations will be demanded by both the retrieval of the prophetic tradition's stand for the oppressed and by the suspicions released by the prophetic ideology-critique embedded in that retrieval" (3).

43. Mosala 1987:15.

44. We will return to this crucial point in chapter eight.

45. Mosala goes on to argue that the need for such a framework "can be seen from the use of even a semiological approach to texts". I mention this here because it relates to my discussion of Croatto's mode of reading later in the chapter. Describing how a semiological approach underscores the urgency of *materialist readings* Michael Clevenot argues that "the reading that is interested only in the meaning is idealist, believing in the innocence and transparency of the text. The exchange is governed here by the general equivalent—just as on the economic level, fascinated by the signifier 'gold', workers are unable to see the real process of production; and just as on the political level, fascinated and intimidated by power and its signifiers such as king and Caesar, the subjects find the established order natural. So on the ideological level, fascinated by a 'god' or the 'truth' and by the false evidence of the signified (the meaning of the text), people read with the eyes of faith and 'good sense'" (Clevenot 1985:67 (cited in Mosala 1989:41)).

46. Mosala is adamant that black theology's "hermeneutics of liberation must be equally applied to black history and culture. Not to do so will amount to a mere nostalgic romanticism on the part of black theologians" (Mosala 1989b:4).

47. In Schüssler Fiorenza 1981, Schüssler Fiorenza levels a similar critique at Latin American liberation theologies, particularly the work of Segundo.

48. Schüssler Fiorenza 1983:19.

49. Schüssler Fiorenza 1983:21. For an illuminating discussion of Schüssler Fiorenza's concern here, see Cornel West's review of Schüssler Fiorenza 1983 in West 1988:250-256.

50. Schüssler Fiorenza 1983:20.

51. Trible 1978:8. Trible is here quoting from Hazelton 1972; and Hazelton 1975.

52. See Trible 1978:27,n.40, for further discussion.

53. Schüssler Fiorenza 1983:20.

54. Schüssler Fiorenza 1983:21. Note once again the use of such phrases as "reconstruction" and "rehabilitation" (21). Schüssler Fiorenza's naturalist commitment is clear.

55. Schüssler Fiorenza 1983:28.

56. Schüssler Fiorenza 1983:27. In words reminiscent of Mofokeng, Schüssler Fiorenza 1981 insists that "The Bible is not a 'neutral' book, but it is a political weapon against women's struggle for liberation. This is so because the Bible bears the imprint of men who never saw or talked with God" (103). It is not just that the Bible has been misunderstood! (105).

57. Schüssler Fiorenza 1983:28-29.

58. Schüssler Fiorenza 1983:29.

59. Schüssler Fiorenza 1983:29.

60. Schüssler Fiorenza 1983:43-48.

61. Schüssler Fiorenza 1983:49-53. This includes the "active elimination of women from the biblical text" (51).

62. Schüssler Fiorenza 1983:53-56. In other words, "the canon is a record of the 'historical winners'" (55).

63. Schüssler Fiorenza 1983:34-35.

64. Schüssler Fiorenza 1983:41. I will argue below that this is precisely what Trible does, she reads the silences of androcentric texts.

65. Schüssler Fiorenza 1983:35-36. Schüssler Fiorenza demonstrates what she asserts here in chapters 2-8. Like Trible she uses the term "remnant".

66. Schüssler Fiorenza 1983:68-92. Of course they differ in a number of respects in their choice of models. This is not surprising given the paucity of concern with feminist issues in the historical-materialist model.

67. Schüssler Fiorenza 1983:91. Schüssler Fiorenza elaborates on these models in 84-92.

68. Schüssler Fiorenza 1983:29.

69. Schüssler Fiorenza 1983:29-30. "What is therefore necessary is not just a feminist analysis of biblical texts but also a

metacritique of the androcentric frameworks adopted by biblical scholarship without any critical reflection on their systemic presuppositions and implications" (42).

70. Schüssler Fiorenza 1983:30-31. Later she adds, "I would therefore suggest that the revelatory canon for theological evaluation of biblical androcentric traditions and their subsequent interpretations cannot be derived from the Bible itself but can only be formulated in and through women's struggle for liberation from all patriarchal oppression. It cannot be universal but must be specific since it is extrapolated from a particular experience of oppression and liberation. The 'advocacy stance for the oppressed' must be sustained at the point of feminist critical evaluation of biblical texts and traditions and their authority claims. The personally and politically reflected experience of oppression and liberation must become the criterion of appropriateness for biblical interpretation and evaluation of biblical authority claims" (32).

71. Schüssler Fiorenza 1983:35. See West 1988:253-256 for an illuminating analysis of this ambiguity in Schüssler Fiorenza.

72. Schüssler Fiorenza 1983:21. Later she adds that Ruether, Trible, and others argue "that the Bible is not totally androcentric but also contains some absolute ethical principles and feminist liberating traditions" (27).

73. Schüssler Fiorenza 1983:27.

74. It should be clear from the discussion that Schüssler Fiorenza is not committed to historical cultural materialism in the same way that Mosala and Gottwald are, and hence her understanding of "structural" would be somewhat different. This is quite understandable in terms of her feminist rather than class commitments.

75. Boesak's mode of reading incorporates aspects of Trible's and Croatto's (see below) modes of reading.

76. Trible 1984:3.

77. Trible 1984:3.

78. Trible 1978:1. This metaphor is also central in Trible 1984.

79. Trible 1978:1.

80. Trible 1978:4. Trible is here drawing on the work of J.A. Sanders.

81. Trible 1978:4-5.

82. Trible 1978:5. She adds that "this clue is a process of understanding rather than a method of control" (5).

83. Trible 1978:5. Or, "conversely, they view present interests in light of the Bible" (5).

84. Trible 1978:7.

85. Trible 1978:7-8.

86. Trible 1978:7.

87. Trible 1978:8.

88. Trible 1978:24,n.10.

89. Trible 1978:8. Trible distinguishes her approach from structuralism. "Throughout this study I am concerned with the surface structures of literary compositions and not with the deep structures" (26,n.37).

90. Trible 1978:8.

91. Trible 1978:27,n.41.

92. Trible 1978:8-9. The "extrinsic factors" are "essential in the total exegetical enterprise, but in literary analysis they are supporting rather than primary concerns" (Trible 1984:6,n.11).

93. Trible 1978:8. Trible goes on to clarify a number of aspects of her literary approach (8-12). She includes here a discussion of the relationship between form and content, the delimiting of the text, plot, motif, stylistic devices, the typical and unique, genre, and related issues. In "The Foreword" she also mentions the interdisciplinary influence of psychoanalysis, existentialism, philosophical hermeneutics, structuralism, and Zen Buddhism on her study (xvi).

94. Trible 1984:3-4.

95. Trible 1978:11.

96. Trible 1978:200. More specifically, in *God and the Rhetoric of Sexuality* she takes up Genesis 1:27 as the "first scriptural clue for the subject of God and the rhetoric of sexuality" (Trible 1978:12). The metaphor of "the image of God male and female" then becomes a guide to her search for and recovery of the feminist struggle in the Bible. In *Texts of Terror* she tells sad stories, tales of terror, which by enabling insight might inspire repentance. "In other words, sad stories may yield new beginnings" (Trible 1984:2).

97. Trible 1984:3-4.

98. Trible 1978:23.

99. Trible 1978:23,n.5.

100. Trible 1978:202.

101. Trible 1978:202.

102. See Trible 1978:11.

103. Trible 1973:49.

104. Trible 1978:202 (my emphasis).

105. Trible 1973:31 and 35.

106. Trible 1973:48.

107. Trible 1973:48.

108. Trible 1978:202. Her work in Trible 1984 in fact highlights the oppressive, male-dominated, character of the Bible.

109. Trible 1978:xvi. Her readings *demonstrate* this last point. For a similar argument by another feminist interpreter who also adopts a rhetorical/literary reading see Anderson 1987.

110. See Trible 1978:5, where she discusses interactions between the Bible and black experience. "When set in a context of the poor and the powerless, the Bible critiques every culture of injustice to proclaim the good news of liberation" (5).

111. Trible 1978:202.

112. Trible 1978:xvi.

113. Trible deconstructs biblical texts in much the same way that Jacques Derrida deconstructs Claude Lévi-Strauss's texts (Derrida 1988).

    For a mode of reading similar to Trible's, although with a closely argued theoretical grounding, see the work of Mieke Bal, especially the "Introduction" to Bal 1989; Bal 1988; and Bal 1985.

114. Jobling 1987:3. The following are useful treatments of deconstruction: Belsey 1980, especially chapters 5-6; Eagleton 1983, especially chapters 4, 5, and Conclusion; and Culler 1982.

115. Jobling 1987:3. Jobling gives the example of the western system of rationality which has had to exclude various kinds of discourse, myth, dream, etc., in order to establish itself (3).

    Significantly, Jobling goes on to argue that "text" and "textuality" are "privileged concepts in deconstruction". "Deconstruction is a possibility and a necessity because language itself is deconstructive—it exposes as illusory the determinacy of meaning upon which systems erect themselves—and it is in texts, with their open linguistic play, that this character of language is best displayed" (4).

116. Jobling 1987:3-4.

117. Jobling 1987:4.

118. Jobling 1987:4.

119. See the detailed discussion in chapter one. In fact, I would argue that it is only a commitment to a context of struggle which rescues deconstruction from its usual ahistorical and apolitical appropriation, evident particularly in North America. For a similar observation see Jobling 1987:6-8, where he draws primarily on French rather than North American deconstruction.

120. Jobling is thinking here specifically of feminism.

121. Jobling 1987:4.

122. In proposing a cooperation, albeit problematic, between liberation (including feminist) theology and deconstructive practice, Jobling asks, "What else are liberation movements doing, at the level of theory, than deconstructing a tradition of oppression, unpacking its logic to show that it is finally based upon nothing other than the monopolization of power?" (4).

123. Trible 1978:xvi.

124. This is particular apparent in Trible 1984 where at the end of each recovered story of terror she calls for repentance and challenges the reader to a new beginning.

125. See Gottwald 1983:199.

126. In the "Editor's Foreword" to Trible 1984 Walter Brueggemann argues that Trible's work "makes clear how much the regnant methods, for all their claims of 'objectivity', have indeed served the ideological ends of 'the ruling class'. What now surfaces is the history, consciousness, and cry of the victim, who in each case is shown to be a character of worth and dignity in the narrative. Heretofore, each has been regarded as simply an incidental prop for a drama about other matters. So Trible's 'close reading' helps us notice. The presumed prop turns out to be a character of genuine interest, warranting our attention. And we are left to ask why our methods have reduced such characters, so that they have been lost to the story" (x).

127. I think, too, that there is also a difference between Mosala and Gottwald in their use of this term. Gottwald's major study, *The Tribes of Yahweh*, can be divided into two related yet distinct parts. In the first part his goal is "to assemble the most reliable information about *the rise of Israel* as determined by recognized methods of biblical science, including literary criticism, form criticism, tradition history, and history of religion" (Gottwald

1980:xxii). He then applies the methods of the social sciences to this body of data and theory developed within biblical science "in order to delineate and to conceptualize *early Israel as a total social system*" (xxii). Having established what early Israel looked like as a total social system he goes on in the second part to focus on the relationship between Israel's religion and other elements of the social structure (xxii-xxiii). This second part is the focal part for Gottwald's discussion of the relationship between his sociological reconstruction and liberation struggles today (see particularly 594-707). Although Mosala does share this interest with Gottwald (see Mosala 1986c:94) his focus, however, is more on the social system as a whole.

128. Gottwald 1985:11-12 where he refers specifically to the work of Schüssler Fiorenza as "the most sophisticated engagement with biblical materials of any work among liberation theologians".

129. It must be said here that not all behind the text modes of reading foreground method to quite the same extent as Mosala, Schüssler Fiorenza, and Gottwald. For example, Carol Meyers supplements her incisive and creative behind the text work with the literary work of Trible (Meyers 1988:chapters 4 and 5).

130. Croatto 1978:vi.

131. Croatto 1987:dedication page.

132. Croatto 1987:5; and Croatto 1983.

133. Croatto 1987:5.

134. Croatto 1987:ix-x.

135. Croatto 1987:69.

136. My interest is in Croatto's "theory of reading" rather than in his use of Ricoeur and Gadamer. Croatto's debt to Ricoeur and Gadamer, however, is apparent on every page of his work, although he rarely cites them directly.

137. Croatto 1978:3.

138. Croatto 1983:142; Croatto 1987:13. Croatto places his "theory of reading" within the field of semiotics.

139. Croatto 1983:143; Croatto 1987:15-16.

140. Croatto 1987:15; Croatto 1983:143. Croatto is not talking about "deliberate polysemy" here.

141. Croatto 1987:14; Croatto 1983:143.

142. Croatto 1987:16; Croatto 1983:143. Croatto uses this term

"text" in a broad sense to include oral texts as well as written texts.

143. Croatto 1987:16; Croatto 1983:144.

144. Croatto 1987:16.

145. "Authors (if we are speaking of writing) 'die' in the very act of coding their message".

146. The "cultural and historical context is no longer the same; current addressees receiving the message have another 'world' of interests, concerns, culture, and so on". Croatto 1987:16-17; Croatto 1983:144.

147. Croatto 1987:25.

148. Croatto 1987:18.

149. Croatto 1987:21; Croatto 1983:145.

150. Croatto 1983:146. "To 're-read' the biblical message from our perspective is the only way to explore its reservoir-of-meaning . . . What allows us to 'enter' into the meaning of the text is the present event; from then on, even though we begin by approaching the biblical text, we are already 'pre-understanding' it from the perspective of our existential situation, which for us Latin Americans is well known" (Croatto 1978:82).

See also the discussions of Gary Comstock and William Placher on these aspects of Ricoeur's and Frei's work in Comstock 1986; and Placher 1987.

151. Croatto 1987:36; Croatto 1983:150.

152. "An event becomes significant for some reason, something in the context in which it takes place, something that gives it what we might call its 'historical effect'—its influence on the practices of a particular human group" (Croatto 1987:37).

153. Croatto 1987:37; Croatto 1983:150. The points made in these paragraphs are central to Croatto's understanding of the interpretation process. For detailed support of his arguments from the philosophy of history see Danto 1965.

154. Croatto 1987:38.

155. Croatto 1987:42. For an illuminating account of this process at work in the Writings see Morgan 1990.

156. Croatto 1987:42-43.

157. Croatto 1987:43; Croatto 1983:153.

158. Croatto 1987:47.

159. Croatto 1987:49.

160. Croatto 1987:51. James Cone too argues that "The Exodus was the decisive event in Israel's history, because through it Yahweh revealed himself as the Savior of an oppressed people" (Cone 1974:423).

161. Croatto 1987:52.

162. Croatto 1987:53.

163. Croatto 1987:53; Croatto 1983:154.

164. Croatto 1987:57-58.

165. Croatto 1978:79.

166. Croatto 1987:62-63.

167. Croatto 1987:72.

168. Croatto 1987:76-77.

169. Croatto 1987:74.

170. Croatto 1987:74,76.

171. Croatto 1987:77.

172. Croatto 1987:79. The concept of "the signs of the times" is an important one in all theologies of liberation. See Nolan 1988:19-22 for a discussion of this concept in the South African context.

173. Croatto 1987:40. The readers context and praxis is a crucial strand of Croatto's mode of reading. He recognizes too that the biblical text and events are read both to motivate a liberation process and to legitimate its repression. This is because the readings are made from within different practices. "No interpretation is innocent, flawlessly objective. An interpreted event is never objective. This does not imply that the *reading* is subjective. There must be *something* in the event that permits the derivation of such-and-such an interpretation. What is decisive is the *praxis* that generates the reading. The concepts of objectivity and subjectivity are of singularly little utility in the analysis of what occurs in the hermeneutic act" (Croatto 1987:40). "In other words, *what* really generates the rereading of the Bible, and gives it its orientation, are successive practices" (Croatto 1987:65).

174. Croatto 1987:68-69; Croatto 1983:159.

175. Croatto 1987:69-70; see also 64-65. So this actualizing is not simply an "updating", it is a re-creating of the message of the Bible (Croatto 1987:70).

176. It should be pointed out here that in the final analysis each of these interpreters draws on symbols or themes when it comes

to appropriation, irrespective of whether what is being appropriated is appropriated behind the text, in the text, or in front of the text. See for example the passages cited from Gottwald above. See also Eagleton 1984:123, where Eagleton says that the role of the contemporary critic is to reconnect the symbolic to the political.

177. Croatto 1987:26.

178. Croatto 1987:30.

179. Croatto 1987:37.

180. Croatto 1987:39. For a similar argument see Sheppard 1982. Hayden White states explicitly that "a specifically *historical* inquiry is born less of the necessity to establish *that* certain events occurred than of the desire to determine what certain events might *mean* for a given group, society, or culture's conception of its present tasks and future prospects" (White 1986:487).

181. Croatto 1987:67.

182. Croatto 1987:71.

183. Croatto 1987:45.

184. In other words, historical-critical (and sociological) results depend on *who* is doing the reconstructing, and for *whom.*

185. Croatto 1987:7-8. This would not be fair to Gottwald, Schüssler Fiorenza, and Mosala, but would be true of "mainstream" historical-critical approaches. See my chapters one and two for similar critiques of historical-critical approaches.

Here and in other aspects of his mode of reading Croatto shares many of James Sanders' concerns (see particularly Sanders 1984). However, see Brett's comments in note 220 below.

186. Croatto 1987:80.

187. Croatto 1987:9.

188. Croatto 1987:80.

189. Croatto 1987:9.

190. Croatto 1987:8-9. Croatto's use of the phrase "a theology of oppressed peoples" here takes on special significance in what follows.

191. In the context of this paper it may be useful to briefly outline a feminist in front of the text reading. What I have called an in front of the text reading is outlined and advocated by the feminist biblical scholar Sandra Schneiders (Schneiders 1989).

In this essay Schneiders is attempting to answer the crucial feminist question: how can a text which is not just accidentally but intrinsically oppressive of women open a world of liberating possibilities to the very people whose oppression it has legitimated? (Schneiders 1989:3-4). In indicating the directions for an answer she draws on the work of Hans-Georg Gadamer and Paul Ricoeur.

Briefly, she begins with an understanding of "the text as a mediation of meaning which takes place as event in the reader". The text is, in other words, a "dynamic medium" rather than a static object (Schneiders 1989:5). Implicit in this understanding is some sense of continuity between the past event and the present (Schneiders 1989:6). Schneiders finds this connection in Ricoeur's work on the productive function of distanciation in interpretation (Schneiders 1989:6).

Schneiders uses Ricoeur rather than Gadamer here because of the criticism that Gadamer's approach to the text "involves an uncritical surrender of the reader to the ideological distortions in the text" (Schneiders 1989:7). "According to Ricoeur, by inscription the vividness of dialogical discourse does not fade into the pale traces of writing requiring the interpreter to revive the text by a new kind of dialogue as Gadamer seems to suggest, but rather the discourse is enriched by a surplus of meaning which makes it susceptible of endless and diverse interpretation. Herein we might find the possibility of not only multiple valid interpretations but of the text's exploding the very world out of which it came and whose prejudices and errors it ineluctably expresses". On this hypothesis, Schneiders argues, it might be possible for the biblical text "to subvert the patriarchal world which produced it and whose biases it expresses and promotes" (Schneiders 1989:7).

According to Ricoeur's theory of distanciation the fixing of discourse by writing works three crucial changes which facilitate this liberating of the text. First, the discourse is sheltered from destruction by the permanence and stability of the written word. Second, the text attains a relative semantic autonomy in relation to the author's intentions. And third, the text transcends its own psycho-sociological conditions of production. It can therefore, argues Schneider, "be decontextualized and recontextualized by successive readings" (Schneiders 1989:7).

Most importantly for her mode of reading, distanciation allows a text "to create a world which it projects ahead of itself". "This projected world, this possible reality, which Ricoeur calls the world of the text, is not limited by the actual reality of the writer's historical world even though it is in some sense derived therefrom. The text projects reality, not under the modality of what is, but under the modality of what can be. What the reader does by interpreting the text is to discern that projected world, and to respond to the invitation to inhabit it, to be according to its structures and dynamics" (Schneiders 1989:7). This world in front of the text, a world which is proposed by the text as a real possibility for the reader, "is what Ricoeur calls the 'world of the text' and what Gadamer calls the 'matter of the text'. Both maintain that this is the real referent of the text, the truth claim of the text, what the text finally says about reality, what the text is actually about" (Schneiders 1989:8).

Appropriation, then, "is actually a kind of deconstitution of the self and reconstitution of the self according to the coordinates of the world of the text". Interpretation, in other words, "is a hermeneutics of transformation" (Schneiders 1989:8).

In answering the question posed by feminist ideology criticism of whether and how an oppressive text can function liberatively, such a mode of reading offers possibilities. We must recognize that the world of the biblical text, and much of the world behind the text, out of which it came, and which largely determined the attitudes and behaviours of its writers, was a patriarchal world (Schneiders 1989:8). But the world projected by the text, the world in front of the text which is the real referent of the text, is the world of struggle for liberation (Schneiders 1989:8; I am here reading Schneiders with a more general focus than the specifically New Testament focus of her essay. In doing this I remain faithful to the thrust of her argument). This is the world structured by God's project of liberation, "in which life issues from death, and by the eschatological hope of liberation for all in the the boundless shalom of the reign of God" (Schneiders 1989:8).

A critical dimension is retained, however, in that "the text itself can generate an effective history which is constitutive of the effective historical consciousness of subsequent readers" (Schneiders 1989:8). This hermeneutics of transformation, the remaking of generations of God's people through an entrance into the world of the text, creates an effective history, a tradition of struggle, through which the text is drawn forward from its past into our present (Schneiders 1989:8).

The biblical text, then, can be seen as a "symbolic structure" by which the interpreter accepts the invitation to enter into and inhabit the world of God's liberation. "The text thus creates . . . [people] who will draw the text itself forward out of an oppressive historical determinism through an effective history of struggle for liberation into a future of eschatological shalom" (Schneiders 1989:9).

Appropriately "the oppressiveness in the text remains both as a witness to that from which we have been saved and as a challenge to action on behalf of justice". The hermeneutic of transformation emerging from such a reading in front of the text enables an engagement with the text "which is neither surrender to nor mastery of the text. It is, rather, an ongoing engagement of the text in the process of liberation, a liberation of ourselves but also of the text from the ideology of patriarchy" (Schneiders 1989:9).

See also Schneiders 1991 for a fuller discussion of these and other aspects of her hermeneutic approach.

192. Croatto 1987:51.

193. Croatto 1987:43.

194. Croatto 1987:54.

195. Croatto 1987:55.

196. Croatto 1987:55.

197. Croatto 1987:56-57.

198. Croatto 1987:57.

199. Croatto 1987:57-58. Sanders detects five tendencies in the canonical biblical literature's adaption of various traditions. One of these is that "God betrays a divine bias for the weak and dispossessed" (Sanders 1984:48-51).

200. Croatto 1987:58.

201. Croatto 1987:51; see note 221 below.

202. Croatto 1987:58-59.

203. Croatto 1987:82.

204. Croatto 1987:60.

205. Croatto 1987:72.

206. Croatto 1987:51.

207. Croatto 1987:62. For a similar position, although from a different point of view, see Clines 1978.

208. Croatto 1987:64.

209. Croatto 1987:63.

210. Croatto 1987:50.

211. Croatto 1987:65.

212. Croatto 1987:64.

213. Croatto 1987:50.

214. Croatto 1987:157.

215. Croatto 1987:155.

216. Gottwald 1985b:314,315. Here Gottwald is responding primarily to the canonical approach of Brevard Childs.

217. Brett 1988:254. Here and in what follows I am indebted to the incisive analysis of Brett 1988 in which Mark Brett analyzes Gottwald's critique of Childs. See also Brett 1991.

218. Gottwald 1985b:321.

219. Brett 1988:255.

220. In this respect Croatto is more honest than others who advocate some form of canonical approach. See Brett's analysis of Childs and Sanders (Brett 1988:255-260). Morgan 1990 also does not adequately address the ideological question.

221. Croatto 1987:51; earlier he makes the point that "the selection of sacred texts was made, let us make no mistake, in conformity with political, and not only religious, criteria" (44).

222. See Brett 1988:260. Commenting on my work here, Brett suggests that "Croatto's emphasis on the 'hermeneutic distance' of texts from original events might be read as an answer to Mosala's thesis that 'oppressive texts cannot be totally tamed' (see above). Croatto seems to be following the Gadamer/Popper line that texts often become abstracted from their original social settings, and this is a good thing since the text can thereby be liberated from narrow social prejudices or ideological struggles". This is certainly the argument of Sandra Schneiders (see note 191 above). Brett continues, "It is certainly the case that ideological struggles behind the text have to be *reconstructed*, and as is evident from Schüssler Fiorenza, Gottwald, and Mosala these reconstructions can be extremely hypothetical. All historical work is hypothetical, of course, but some hypotheses are based on a lot of evidence, and some read more like pure inventions to suit a theory. If an ideological struggle behind the biblical text is—in the view of the distanciation of writing—so difficult to reconstruct, one might be forgiven for not assenting to Mosala's thesis that oppressive texts cannot be tamed" (personal correspondence).

223. Croatto 1987:58-59.

224. This emphasis will be discussed more fully in chapters seven and eight.

225. See for example Croatto's rejection of "concordism", an uncriti-

cal seeking of correspondences between real-life situations and occurrences related in the Bible (Croatto 1987:6-7). For similar rejections see Boff 1987:137-146; and Chikane 1985:49.

For some illuminating discussion of *how* appropriation ought to take place see Boff 1987:146-150; Nolan 1988:7-30; and Segundo 1986. For an illuminating discussion of how appropriation takes place in Latin American liberation readings of Paul see Long 1990.

226. Schüssler Fiorenza 1981:108.

227. This demonstration is important. The danger is that the socio-scientific modes of reading may slide into a form of scientism. There are hints of this danger in the work of Mosala, Schüssler Fiorenza, and Gottwald. For example, Mosala states that "If black theology is to become an effective weapon in the struggle to critique and transform present realities, it needs to employ analytical concepts that can get to the bottom of *real* events, relationships, structures, and so forth" (Mosala 1989:4; my emphasis). The framework offered by chapter one provides a necessary caution here, particularly the remarks of Cornel West concerning a revised distinction between the "literary" and the "scientific".

228. I will argue in the next chapter that this concern is implicit in the other interpreters discussed.

229. See chapter four.

230. Gottwald 1985:5. See also Gottwald 1985b:321. This is also argued in Gottwald 1985a.

Chapter Seven

1. See Lategan 1984:4.

2. Lategan and Rousseau 1988:392.

3. See for example, Lategan and Rousseau 1988; and Smit 1989.

4. The use of the plural in what follows is deliberate. This research forms part of a wider research project conducted by J.A. Draper and myself. The preliminary research findings have been published in Draper and West 1989.

5. As different population groups were required to live in different "group areas" according to the Group Areas Act, parishes tend to reflect the divisions of the apartheid system.

6. We would like to express our appreciation to John Aitchison, Deputy Director of the Centre for Adult Education at the University of Natal, Pietermaritzburg, for his valuable assistance in the construction of this questionnaire.

7. The dynamics of the group made a statistical approach inappropriate.

8. It should also be pointed out that these are only preliminary observations. The research is still continuing and we hope to publish a more detailed analysis later.

9. The racial classifications used in this paper reflect the official population group to which people have been assigned. We reject the structures which have so classified people.

10. For further analysis of the conflict in Natal see note 106 in chapter four.

11. We were particularly concerned to work with, rather than on, the groups in a form of participatory research.

12. Barr 1983:46.

13. As I have mentioned in chapter five, there are some black theologians who would wish to raise the question of whether the church ought to have this readiness. However, in the groups participating in this research we were unable to detect this perspective.

14. This seems to be a concern of Dirk Smit's (see Smit 1988:473-474).

15. Group 13 had never had a Bible study of this nature. See our comments below.

16. We are using the term "canonical" here a little loosely, but in a way that is related to the concerns of Brevard Childs' canonical

approach. See for example, Childs 1979.

17. Cited by Smit 1989:464.

18. See Smit 1989:464.

19. At the 1988 New Testament Society of South Africa Congress which explored a number of different readings of a certain text, no one offered any form of canonical reading (see Smit 1989). See also the discussion in chapter six.

20. I will return to this latter point in chapter eight and in the Afterword.

21. Because similar Bible study groups in Brasil do not appear to have the same difficulty, and because they are largely Catholic, suggests that the predominantly Protestant environment in South Africa may be a significant factor here. I discuss the Bible movement in Brasil in the Afterword.

22. This research forms part of the work of the Institute for the Study of the Bible (ISB). See the Afterword at the end of this study for an outline of the work of the ISB.

23. Some of the characteristics of participatory research are: (1) that the focus of the research emerges from the needs and experience of communities of the poor and oppressed; (2) that it rejects the possibility of doing value-neutral research in favour of dialectical notions of rationality and truth, and it therefore moves reflexively between theory and practice; (3) that it uses the interpretive categories of the participant practitioners as a basis for the discourse from within which the practitioners develop their own theorizing; (4) that it provides a means by which distorted self understandings of the participants may be overcome by analyzing the socio-economic forces that shape these understandings; (5) that by linking theory to practice (action to reflection) reflexively, it offers transformative strategies which may overcome institutional and societal obstacles to democratic and free practices; and (6) that it is motivated by an emancipatory concern, and therefore the process is just as important as the product (Luckett 1990). For further discussion of participatory or action research see Cohen 1982; Carr and Kemmis 1986; Grundy 1987; Morphet 1983); and Philpott 1993.

24. Cochrane 1991.

25. Cochrane 1991:181. "Many will learn to understand their faith only through an encounter with the Bible, whether via preaching and teaching, or in personal and group reflection. Very few, proportionally, will read the kinds of papers produced for this Conference, even if these papers were to be greatly simplified and produced in accessible language and format" (181-182).

26. Cochrane 1991:182.

27. Cochrane 1991:182.

28. Cochrane 1991:182. See also the similar comments of Nolan 1991 discussed in chapter eight.

29. ICT Church and Labour Research Group 1991.

30. ICT Church and Labour Research Group 1991:272.

31. ICT Church and Labour Research Group 1991:272.

32. The responses were collated from group workshops and so reflect group rather than individual responses.

33. ICT Church and Labour Research Group 1991:272. Collated examples of the "master/slave" view responses are as follows: to obey the employer, master and servant to respect each other mutually; the verse in the Bible says leaders must treat their workers well and workers must obey their leaders; Bible advocates fairness and fair treatment; teaches not to steal from your employer; encourages workers to be diligent, "Thou shall eat the sweat of your brow"; confidence in your job; provides physical health; builds up honesty; makes you a light among unbelievers.

34. ICT Church and Labour Research Group 1991:273. Collated examples (not available in the published report) of the "personalistic individualistic ethic" responses are as follows: Bible does give guidelines but it depends on how it is interpreted; it says many things about the workers' daily life, gives directions for the solving of social problems, encourages work ethic, makes a worker think holy; helps us to persevere in a difficult situation, gives spiritual nourishment; it is important because when one arrives back from work it relieves you; it is encouraging to our daily lives, comforting morally and spiritually; makes us aware of our own responsibility.

35. ICT Church and Labour Research Group 1991:273.

36. ICT Church and Labour Research Group 1991:273. It must be noted that the respondents do not have English as a first language. Collated examples (not available in the published report) of the "prophetic focus on justice" responses are as follows: people should be treated equally because they are created in the image of God; people should be treated justly and the Christian should oppose injustice; in the first pages of Genesis it is said that we must toil for our survival, either manually or intellectually. This distinguishes the human being from other creatures; the Bible emphasizes the workers' rights, not to be exploited, oppressed, dehumanized, killed, harassed, evicted; it speaks in favour of the exploited and oppressed

masses, eg. Jesus was on the side of the poor. If Jesus were to come to SA he would be on the side of the workers, the oppressed and exploited; Moses liberated the Israelites from Egypt; Christ came for the down trodden (workers); there are many verses for workers, eg. the eye of the needle, against the rich; in the first chapters the Bible speaks about Israelites, who are workers; in the last chapters Paul teaches workers to respect their employers and employers their employees; it says, the priests themselves take heavy things directed it to the labourers and they carry easy things, like today with employers and employees; the Bible is a sacred document whereby the workers could express their feelings, e.g. Jesus himself is from a working class family; the worker must be paid according to the agreement of the worker and employer. Employers must not decide for the worker what to earn.

37. Collated examples (not available in the published report) of responses from this group are as follows: does not mean anything; workers are not aware of Bible's relevancy.

38. ICT Church and Labour Research Group 1991:273-274.

39. Stevens 1985:25-26. The YCW was founded by the Roman Catholic Church but any young worker is allowed to join. The YCW does not have a particularly strong relationship with the rest of the Roman Catholic Church. Most of the YCW members are skeptical of the church which they see as not being based in the "real world". Young workers are encouraged to discover their own faith in the light of the Bible, which is seen as a history of struggle (28).

40. Young Christian Workers 1987:16. Once again it must be noted that I am quoting from documents which are often produced under harassment and which reflect the English of English second language speakers. I have emended some typographical/spelling errors.

41. This testimony is found again and again among young black workers. See the numerous examples in Dumortier 1983.

42. Young Christian Workers 1988:11.

43. For this and other examples see Young Christian Workers 1989.

44. Young Christian Workers (undated).

45. Young Christian Workers 1987:A.

46. Young Christian Workers 1987:B. The texts which are most commonly used are the following: Moses' call to lead the liberation of Israel; texts on harassment; texts on difficulty in organizing; texts on strengthening your brothers; texts on fear;

and texts on the involvement of the apostles (Young Workers 1988:12).

47. I have no full transcripts of their readings of the Bible and so work from summaries produced by the participants. Another qualification to "actual readings of the Bible" is that in many of the workshops discussion is based on a "retelling" of a biblical story. For example, a fascinating discussion takes place around a retelling of the Moses story and the retelling of Simon Peter's "story" (see Young Christian Workers 1984:43-67). Here the story is "retold" with the inclusion of relevant background material.

48. Young Christian Workers 1986:5. Similarly with other texts. In discussing Moses and Simon Peter they ask: "What have been the steps in Moses' life and commitment?"; "What have been his discoveries, his improvements?"; "What choices did he have to make?"; "What helped him?" These questions are then followed by these: "What do we discover?"; "How does the story of Moses resemble our own story?"; "What new light do we discover about our mission in the YCW?"; "What questions would we like to share in general assembly?"; and "What is the use of reading the Bible in the YCW?" (Young Christian Workers 1984:63,67).

49. Young Christian Workers 1986:6.

50. Young Christian Workers 1986:6.

51. Young Christian Workers 1986:6.

52. Young Christian Workers 1986:6.

53. "The YCW helps us to find that the bible is the story of the liberation of oppressed people. We have to read it in this line" (Young Christian Workers 1984:46). The thematic selection of biblical texts and the availability of selected historical and sociological data clearly facilitates such a reading of the Bible. More importantly, however, the young workers do read the Bible as the story of liberation. In other words, the conviction of the YCW that the Bible is a story of liberation and their commitment to this conviction is strengthened by their reading of the Bible where the "theme of the good news of the liberation of the poor, proclaimed throughout the Gospel, can also be found as a powerful undercurrent pushing its way through every page of Israel's history" (Dumortier 1983:88).

54. "The task of the YCW is to challenge the Church and the priests about the way they are interpreting the Bible from the sky" (Young Christian Workers 1984:46). The young workers are committed to reading the Bible from and for their own context, and so want to challenge readings of the Bible which are not contextual.

55.   "We have to know how the Bible was written, in which situations and to whom" (Young Christian Workers 1984:56). It is not clear whether this need is something that workers themselves perceive. In situations where such background is not provided there appears to be no difficulty in reading the text (see for example the reading of Matthew 13 above). However, as I have already mentioned, general historical and sociological background information is often provided along with the text for workers, so the YCW offers a fairly structured reading environment for workers.

56.   "It is important to read the Bible together, and to compare it with our life and our actions" (Young Christian Workers 1984:46). These two aspects, reading the Bible corporately and reading in from and for their own context, are crucial to their mode of reading.

57.   Young Christian Workers 1984:47.

58.   Young Christian Workers 1984:46.

59.   See chapter two for details.

60.   Mosala 1989c.

61.   Mosala 1989c:7. "They make no effort to recruit whites and neither are whites naturally attracted to these churches except as exotic objects of anthropological enquiry" (7).

62.   Mosala 1989c:8. "In this aspect of their life they reflect their character as *anti-colonial cultural* movements. The represent a cultural subversion of official and 'normal' christianity and its structures and procedures" (8).

63.   Mosala 1989c:8. "They arise initially out of the industrial urban gutters of capitalist civilisation and naturally extend into the rural hinterlands through the agency of migrant workers" where they "fill the gap *ideologically* that has been created *materially* by the absence of a significant labour component of the rural household economy, the migrant worker himself". A related point is that the prominent role played by women bishops in these churches "must be correlated with the key role they play as heads of households in the rural economy from which their men have been dislodged, at least while they are physically strong. Of course later they will be dumped back in these areas to become welfare burdens of among others religious organisations such as the AICs" (8).

64.   Mosala 1989c:2.

65.   Mosala 1989c:14.

66.   Mosala uses a cultural studies paradigm from a historical materialist perspective to define the notion of "sub-culture" "as

a heuristic tool for understanding the specific character of the AICs as a distinctive cultural practice within the wider cultural network of working class discourses". In terms of this paradigm, then, the question which Mosala's study seeks to answer is, "how does this subculture's relation to black working class parents affect the adherents' appropriation of the Bible and how does its articulation with dominant [white] culture shape its use of the biblical text. At any rate, is there a distinctively sub-cultural appropriation of the Bible?" (4). See also 2-5.

67. Mosala 1989c:14.

68. African Independent Churches 1985:26.

69. This research was undertaken in the black township of Manguang in Bloemfontein. This area was chosen because of Mosala's familiarity with the social and material topography of the area. The method of research comprised interviews through the use of questionnaires. The research was confined to two different congregations of the same African Independent Church. In the one congregation individual members were interviewed. These happened either when the members attended their individual healing sessions with the Healer or at separate agreed times. In the other congregation services were attended with the permission of the minister. The purpose here was to listen to sermons, hymns, and any other activity that involved the use of the Bible or biblical texts (Mosala 1989c:5-6).

70. Mosala 1989c:1.

71. Mosala 1989c:15. This view is generally accepted.

72. Mosala 1989c:16-17. "In Kantian terms, involvement with the Bible is analytic in being a Christian" (Barr 1980:52).

73. Mosala 1989c:16. Mosala critiques his own research because "The assumption of this study and the way in which its hypotheses were constructed presupposed a literate community" (16).

74. Mosala 1989c:16. Many of the preachers would be semi-literate.

75. Mosala 1989c:16.

76. Mosala 1989c:17.

77. Mosala 1989c:17.

78. Mosala 1989c:18. In the some of the AIC there are relatively few barriers against women.

79. Mosala 1989c:19.

80. Mosala 1989c:17.

81. Mosala 1989c:17,19.

82. Mosala also notes that often the more "difficult" the text the greater its appeal.

83. Mosala 1989c:16. Just what ordinary readers understand by the "authority" or "inspiration" of the Bible requires further research.

84. As Mosala had quite specific goals in his study he does not elaborate on this "hermeneutics of mystification", but clearly it requires further analysis. I found a similar focus in Bible groups in the north of Brasil. See my discussion of the Bible movement in Brasil in the Afterword.

85. Mosala 1989c:19.

86. Mosala 1986:184. For similar comments see Mofokeng 1988:40-41.

87. See also the Afterword.

Chapter Eight

1.   It may be useful here to include James Cochrane's summary of these two modes of reading, based as it is on my analysis. "What Boesak does with the story is to read it for its historical meaning then, in order to derive from the story an understanding which produces meaning now. The text is seen to have more than one relevant historical context, and its polysemy is plumbed for what it says in this historical context. Critical treatments of the text only supplement this goal, and may even be temporarily discarded if the logic of the story suggests meaning perhaps not intended by the original author. The key hermeneutic measure of meaning (and therefore of the truth of the text) is the community within which Boesak locates himself, the particular community of struggle. There is a prior commitment to read the text from within this community of struggle, and the text is interpreted in terms of an analogy of struggle located in the story itself.

   Mosala's strategy is quite different, and it is developed in direct response to Boesak's reading. His approach is opposed to a reading of the text in its final form, for he believes that this final form is the deposit of a tradition primarily recorded by a particular strata in society.

   His scholarly work leads him to judge this strata as the dominant elite of the time, whose voice overrides and suppresses the voice of the dominated or the oppressed. This latter voice is present in the text only in the traces of its suppression, and the task for the biblical scholar must be to uncover these suppressed traces while simultaneously revealing the ideological nature of the final form. The pay-off in approaching the text in this way of critical theory is to introduce the reader to an analogous way of critically reading contemporary existence—in short, to conscientize the reader to oppression whether it appears in the form of an authoritative text or in the form of an authoritarian action" (Cochrane 1989:29).

2.   Cochrane 1989:30. Cochrane is here reflecting on the challenges of Boesak's and Mosala's work as represented in my analysis (particularly chapter three).

3.   Cochrane 1989:30. Cochrane may be right here, but the role of story in ordinary readers' reading of the Bible certainly requires further research. While Ronald Grimes would agree with Cochrane that storytelling is akin to ritual enactment, he offers a salutary critique of some of the common assumptions among narrative theologians. Like Cochrane, Grimes focuses on the relations between narrative and ritual, or, more broadly, language and action (Grimes 1986). See also Lauritzen 1987.

4.   Cochrane 1989:30.

5.   See Mosala 1987:20.

6.   Segundo 1985:22.

7.   Segundo 1985:28.

8.   Segundo 1985:23.

9.   Segundo 1985:23.

10. Segundo 1985:23.

11. Segundo 1985:24.

12. Segundo 1985:24 (my emphasis). In this respect Segundo shares the same concerns as Mosala. See also Parrat 1984.

13. Segundo 1985:24.

14. Segundo 1985:24. In his discussion of "Church and People" Metz discusses a similar tension. He argues that "Theology—including progressive, socially and politically committed theology—is above all experienced in libraries and conferences, where the opinions and counter-opinions of one's colleagues plays a much more prominent part than the religious life and history of suffering of the Christian people" (Metz 1980:137). He goes on to discuss paradigms of a church of the people with particular reference to those minority movements "which, according to Francis and Dominic, brought the Gospel *non equester sed pedester* to the people, in other words, at their own level, often had the effect of a salutary shock on the greater Church or a dangerous memory, reminding the Church that the process by which the people were to become subjects in the Church had not been forgotten.

     Characteristically, these movements were often lacking in theology. They did not see the Bible primarily as a book for exegetes, but mainly as a popular book or a mystical biography of the people, in which a divine interpretation of their sufferings and hope could be found" (145-146). "They sensed that the Church would survive the persecution of the powerful and the scorn of the clever men more easily than the doubts of the little and impotent people" (146).

     This leads him into a discussion of the theologian's task as being "always ready to help the people themselves to speak", to have "a maieutic function with regard to the people" (148). However, "There is a false attempt to bridge the gap between theology and the people which characterizes modern theology regarded as the theoretical exponent of a middle-class religion: it is the attempt of bridging that gap by means of pure sociology. This mistake is made by all élitist views. Sociology is, after all, as far removed from the history of the life and suffering of the people as theology. And to transform theology into a form of sociology cannot make up for the loss of the people and society in theology. To change theology into sociology is to assume that the experiences of the people themselves and not simply data about attitude are expressed in sociology. It is therefore hardly surprising, if this is borne in mind, that more can be learnt about sociological theories (originally formulated by others) than about the history of the life and suffering of the people in many branches of modern progressive and critical theology" (149). But, "As against this, there is also a simple, romantically regressive transfiguration of the 'people' which ultimately achieves nothing but a defamation of the achievement of critical theology" (150). "The critical interest of this theology, however, must always be governed by the conviction that the symbols, stories and collective memories of the people in the Church are absolutely necessary to any theology that wishes to avoid losing all foundation" (150). He insists, however, that "This concern is in no way an expression of a theological movement back to a pre-critical attitude" (150).

15. Nolan 1976.

16. Nolan 1991:161. Later Nolan emphasizes the point that a theology of work in South Africa should serve the interests of workers and should nourish and strengthen the faith and commitment of workers (164).

17. Nolan 1991:165.

18. Nolan 1991:165. Of course, the nature of the skills one makes available plays a role in shaping the theology.

   See also Pixley 1983. In outlining the role of the biblical scholar George Pixley argues that "As biblical scholars, we must respond to this power off the Holy Spirit using the minds of unlettered Bible readers. In my opinion, a response which is faithful to our special calling must be twofold: first, we must bear witness to the presence of God in unsuspected ways. And second, we must put the tools of our trade at the disposal of the Holy Spirit to deepen and protect the insights which He has revealed without our help to a believing people who put their lives on the line in the confidence that God is a God of salvation" (159). He then argues that a simple reading of the gospel by the poor "calls out for a socio-ecomomic analysis which we as biblical scholars must provide in order that those issues relevant to our situation be retained and those made outdated by modern progress and oppression be discarded or adapted" (159).

   For a useful overview of different roles of the intellectual in

Latin American liberation theology see Miguez Bonino 1975, particularly chapter eight.

19. Nolan 1991:165.

20. "This will often mean working in groups instead of working alone at our desks, developing an oral theology instead of a book theology, collecting opinions and expressions of faith that we cannot fully identify with and sacrificing any personal prestige associated with the fact that what we write are our original ideas" (165).

    Tracy too is wary of what he calls "unconscious elitism", a view that "only a learned elite can read these texts properly" (Tracy 1987:104).

21. Nolan 1991:165-166. Workers on the whole do not have the time or the leisure to indulge in such pursuits as constructing a theology of work; they are too busy surviving. So if workers are to construct their own theology of work it would have to be done when and where workers do have the time and over a long period of time (165-166).

22. Workers would, of course, only be prepared to take up such a task if it was in their interests. Nolan argues that here the professional theologian might have to take the initiative, but only to get the process started, in order to give workers some initial indication of what use a theology of work might have. "What will have to be shown is that a theology of work might be useful not only for theology or for the Church but also and much more importantly, for the worker and for his and her struggles" (166).

23. Nolan 1991:168.

24. See especially Welch 1990 and the work of Michel Foucault, particularly Foucault 1980.

25. Giroux 1985:xii.

26. Giroux 1985:xviii.

27. Giroux 1985:xix.

28. Scott 1990:85-90.

29. Scott 1990:xii.

30. Scott 1990:2.

31. Scott 1990:13.

32. Scott 1990:xii.

33. Scott 1990:198.

34. Scott 1990:90.

35. Scott 1990:90.

36. Scott 1990:91.

37. Scott 1990:96.

38. Scott 1990:92.

39. Scott 1990:93.

40. Scott 1990:101.

41. Scott 1990:102-103.

42. Giroux 1985:xx.

43. Mosala would argue, as I have indicated, that many black theologians have also to some extent internalized their own oppression in their use of the dominant hermeneutical epistemology for which truth is not historical, cultural, or economic (Mosala 1989:19).

44. Giroux 1985:xx-xxi.

45. Giroux 1985:xxiii. For similar arguments see Bal 1989:15-16.

46. Giroux 1985:xxiii. Frostin makes a similar point when he argues that "when oppressed people live in silence, they use the words of their oppressors to describe their experience of oppression. Only within the praxis of liberation and in dialogue with what Antonio Gramsci called 'organic intellectuals' is it possible for the poor to break this silence and create their own language" (Frostin 1988:10). For a detailed account of this phenomenon see Memmi 1965.

47. Giroux 1985:xxiii.

48. Welch 1985:44; see also Foucault 1977:209.

49. Spivak 1988; Arnott 1991. Spivak uses the preposition "to", but I prefer the preposition "with".

50. Arnott 1991:125.

51. Arnott 1991:125.

52. Spivak 1988:297; Arnott 1991:125.

53. Arnott 1991:125.

54. Arnott 1991:127.

55. In an important work Matthew Lamb refers to this relationship as "an ongoing dialogue and mutual learning process with the poor, oppressed, exploited races, classes, and sexes within histories and societies" (Lamb 1982:87).

For a more general discussion of the role of the intellectual see Rorty 1983; Held 1983; and MacIntyre 1983.

56.   Segundo too sees similarities between his two theologies. While recognizing that they are based on different presuppositions, that they have different strategies, and that their methods are not easily compatible, he also recognizes that as attempts to liberate and to empower the same people through the same Christian faith, they share much in common (Segundo 1985:2).

57.   This is true not only for the struggle *against* apartheid but also for the struggle *for* a non-racial, democratic, and just South Africa.

58.   "Final Communiqué", in Appiah-Kubi and Torres 1979:192,197 (cited in Frostin 1988:17). See also Cone 1986.

59.   Particularly if *vox victimarum vox Dei*—the cries of the victims are the voice of God (Lamb 1982:1).

60.   Gutiérrez 1975:24.

In taking up this concern Victor Makhetha offers an illuminating discussion of what he calls "an Africanist interpretation of the Bible", which "employs tools that are indigenous to Africa (specifically South Africa)" and is therefore "understandable even to the most illiterate African" (Makhetha 1989:1).

61.   Welch 1990:151. Welch presents a creative and powerful exploration of such a commitment from her perspective as a white middle-class woman.

62.   A contextual theology should remain critical and prophetic with regard to its own situational experience.

The phrase "solidarity with victims" is taken from Lamb's excellent work by that title (see Lamb 1982).

I recognize that this challenge will take different forms in different contexts. Rogerson 1990 and Rowland and Corner 1990 offer some insights into the nature of this challenge for British and European biblical studies.

At the very least, the challenge of the new paradigm is not a matter of propositions or ideas but a question of a new methodology where awareness of the suppressed voices of humankind is of crucial importance (Frostin 1988:190). Just as Western theology has "become a subconscious part" of theologizing in the Third World so too liberation theologies need to become a part of theologizing in the West (Mbiti 1976:16-17).

63.   *The Road to Damascus* 1989. This document was prepared by Third World Christians from South Africa, Namibia, South Korea, Philippines, El Salvador, Nicaragua, and Guatemala.

Afterword

1. Much of the discussion of CEBI arises from a research trip to Brasil. Rowland and Corner 1990 also reflect on what can be learned from the Brasilian context.

2. I use the term "reader" in the phrase "ordinary reader" to allude to the shift in hermeneutics towards the reader outlined in chapter one (Abrams 1958:8-29; Barton 1984:201-207; Lategan 1984:3-4; McKnight 1985:2-3; Eagleton 1989:119). However, my use of the term "reader" is metaphoric in that it includes the many who are illiterate, but who listen to, discuss, and retell the Bible. The term "ordinary" is used in a general and a specific sense. The general usuage includes all readers who read the Bible pre-critically. I also use the term "ordinary" to designate a particular sector of pre-critical readers, those readers who are poor and oppressed (including, of course, women). In the latter sense the term "ordinary" is similar to the terms "the people" or "the masses" as they are popularly used. Because I am working within a liberation paradigm the particular usuage usually takes precedence over the general.

3. In this presentation of the four commitments I am using language that is closer to the English usage of groups we work with (see West 1993).

4. Draper and West 1989.

5. Draper and West 1989:42-43.

6. Draper and West 1989:43.

7. Nolan 1988; *The Kairos Document* 1986.

8. Foucault 1980; see also Welch 1985.

9. Draper and West 1989:41,45.

10. No one translation was used during these Bible studies. Participants used various translations. I am using the New American Standard translation here and below.

11. My sociological sketch was based substantially on the work of Horsley 1989; Waetjen 1989; Wengst 1987; and Nolan 1986.

12. I include some preliminary commentary on this aspect of the Bible studies below, in brackets, because it was not a component of the other workshops.

13. Ordinary readers did not distinguish between "the text" and "Jesus". The ideological perspective of this particular text was not the concern of these Bible studies, although some partici-

pants did raise the question when referring to the synoptic parallels (see also Draper and West 1989:41).

14. Draper 1992:67; Nolan 1988:7-30; Boff 1987:132-153.

15. Scott 1990.

16. Cochrane 1994; Foucault 1980; Welch 1985.

17. West 1993a; Welch 1990.

18. See West 1994 and West 1995 for further examples; see also *Challenge* magazine for many examples of contextual Bible studies and "peoples' theology" produced by the ISB.

Bibliography

Abrams, M.H. (1958) *The Mirror and the Lamp: Romantic Theory and the Critical Tradition*, W.W. Norton, New York.

Aitchison, J.J.W. (1988) "Numbering the Dead: Patterns in the Midlands Violence", Centre for Adult Education, University of Natal, Pietermaritzburg.

Aitchison, J.J.W. (1989) "The Civil War in Natal", in Moss, G. and I. Obery (eds) (1989) *South African Review 5*, Ravan, Johannesburg, pp.457-473.

Aitchison, J.J.W. (1989) "The Pietermaritzburg Conflict: Experience and Analysis", Centre for Adult Education, University of Natal, Pietermaritzburg. Aitchison, J.J.W. (1989) "Natal's Wastelands: The Unofficial War Goes On", in *Indicator South Africa*, 7, pp.58-61, and 72.

African Independent Churches (1985), *Speaking for Ourselves*, Institute for Contextual Theology, Braamfontein.

Anderson, B.W. (1985) "Biblical Theology and Sociological Interpretation", in *Theology Today*, 42, pp.292-306.

Anderson, J.C. (1987) "Mary's Difference: Gender and Patriarchy in the Birth Narrative", in *The Journal of Religion*, 67, pp.183-202.

Appiah-Kubi, K. and Torres, E. (eds) (1979) *African Theology En Route, Papers from the Pan-African Conference of Third World Theologians, December 17-23, 1977, Accra, Ghana*, Orbis, New York.

Arnott, J. (1991) "French Feminism in a South African Frame?: Gayatri Spivak and the Problem of 'Representation' in South African Feminism", in *Pretexts*, 3, pp.118-128.

Assmann, H. (1976) *Theology for a Nomad Church*, Orbis, New York.

Bal, M. (1985) *Narratology: Introduction to the Theory of Narrative*, University of Toronto Press, Toronto.

Bal, M. (1988) *Death and Dissymmetry: The Politics of Coherence in the Book of Judges*, University of Chicago Press, Chicago.

Bal, M. (ed) (1989) *Anti-Covenant: Counter-Reading Womens' Lives in the Hebrew Bible*, The Almond Press, Sheffield.

Bann, S. (1981) "Towards a Critical Historiography: Recent Work in Philosophy of History", in *Philosophy*, 56, pp.365-385.

Barr, J. (1980) *Explorations in Theology 7: The Scope and Authority of the Bible*, SCM, London.

Barr, J. (1983) *Holy Scripture, Canon, Authority, Criticism*, Clarendon.

Barton, J. (1984) *Reading the Old Testament: Method in Biblical Study*, Darton, Longman and Todd, London.

Belsey, C. (1980) *Critical Practice*, Methuen, London.

Belsey, C. (1983) "Literature, History, Politics", in *Literature and History*, 9, pp.17-29.

Bennett, B. (1986) "A Critique of the Role of Women in the Church", in Mosala, I.J. and B. Tlhagale (eds) (1986) *The Unquestionable Right To Be Free*, Skotaville, Johannesburg, pp.169-174.

Bernstein, R. (1983) *Beyond Objectivism and Relativism: Science, Hermeneutics, and Praxis*, University of Pennsylvania Press, Philadelphia.

Bleich, D. (1976) "The Subjective Paradigm in Science, Psychology, and Criticism", in *New Literary History*, 7, p.313-325.

Boesak, A.A. (1977) *Farewell to Innocence: A Socio-Ethical Study on Black Theology and Power*, Orbis, Maryknoll.

Boesak, A.A. (1978) "Coming In Out of the Wilderness", in Torres, S. and V. Fabella (1978) *The Emergent Gospel: Theology from the Underside of History*, Orbis, New York, pp.76-95.

Boesak, A.A. (1984) *Black and Reformed: Apartheid, Liberation and the Calvinist Tradition*, Skotaville, Johannesburg.

Boesak, A.A. (1987) *Comfort and Protest: Reflections on the Apocalypse of John of Patmos*, The Westminster Press, Philadelphia.

Boff, C. (1987) *Theology and Praxis*, Orbis, Maryknoll, pp.137-146.

Brett, M.G. (1988) *The Canonical Approach to Old Testament Study*, Unpublished PhD Thesis, Sheffield University, Sheffield.

Brett, M.G. (1991) *Biblical Criticism in Crisis?: The Impact of the Canonical Approach on Old Testament Studies*, Cambridge University Press, Cambridge.

Brueggemann, W. (1971) "Kingship and Chaos: A Study in Tenth Century Theology", in *Catholic Biblical Quarterly*, 33, pp.317-332.

Bühlman, W. (1978) *The Missions on Trial: Addis Ababa 1980*, St Paul Publications, Slough.

Buthelezi, M. (1973) "African Theology and Black Theology: A Search for a Theological Method", in Becken, H-J. (ed) (1973) *Relevant Theology for Africa*, Lutheran Publishing House, Durban, pp.18-24.

Buthelezi, M. (1973a) "An African Theology or a Black Theology", in Moore, B. (1973) *Black Theology: The South African Voice*, C. Hurst and Company, pp.29-35.

Buthelezi, M. (1978) "Towards Indigenous Theology in South Africa", in Torres, S. and V. Fabella (1978) *The Emergent Gospel: Theology from the Underside of History*, Orbis, New York, pp.56-75.

Butler, M. (1994) *Natal, Violence and the Elections*, Centre for Adult Education, University of Natal, Pietermaritzburg.

Cady, L.E. (1986) "Hermeneutics and Tradition: The Role of the Past in Jurisprudence and Theology", in *Harvard Theological Review*, 79, pp.439-463.

Cardenal, E. (1976) *The Gospel in Solentiname*, Orbis Books, New York.

Carr, W. and S. Kemmis (1986) *Becoming Critical*, Falmer Press, Barcombe.

Chikane, F. (1985) "The Incarnation in the Life of the People of South Africa", in *Journal of Theology for Southern Africa*, 51, pp.37-50.

Chikane, F. and M. Tsele (1984) "Foreword", in *Black Theology and Black Struggle*, Conference Report, 10-14 September 1984, Cape Town, Institute for Contextual Theology, Braamfontein.

Childs, B.S. (1979) *Introduction to the Old Testament as Scripture*, Fortress, Philadelphia.

Chopp, R. (1987) "Feminism's Theological Pragmatics: A Social Naturalism of Women's Experience", in *The Journal of Religion*, 67, pp.239-256.

Christ, C.P. (1979) "Why Women Need the Goddess: Phenomenological, Psychological, and Political Reflections", in Christ, C.P. and J. Plaskow (1979) (eds) *Womenspirit Rising: A Feminist Reader in Religion*, Harper and Row, San Francisco.

Clevenot, M. (1985) *Materialist Approaches to the Bible*, Orbis, New York.

Clines, D.J.A. (1978) *The Theme of the Pentateuch*, JSOT Press, Sheffield.

Cochrane, J.R. (1987) *Servants of Power: The Role of English-Speaking Churches 1903-1930*, Ravan, Braamfontein.

Cochrane, J.R. (1988) "Changing the Context of Theological Education", Unpublished Paper, Federal Theological Seminary, Pietermaritzburg.

Cochrane, J.R. (1989) "Struggle and the Christian Story: The Exploitation of Truth as a Challenge to Tradition", Unpublished Paper, Cambridge University, Cambridge.

Cochrane, J.R. (1991) "Already, But Not Yet: Programmatic Notes for a Theology of Work", in Cochrane, J.R. and G.O. West (eds) (1991) *The Threefold Cord: Theology, Work and Labour*, Cluster Publications, Pietermaritzburg, pp.177-189.

Cochrane, J.R. (1994) "Conversation or Collaboration?: Base Christian Communities and the Dialogue of Faith", in *Scriptura*, forthcoming.

Cohen, Y. (1982) "Some Critical Reflections on Participatory Research", in *Convergence*, 15, pp.77-80.

Comstock, G. (1986) "Truth or Meaning: Ricoeur versus Frei on Biblical Narrative", in *The Journal of Religion*, 66, pp.117-140.

Cone, J.H. (1974) "Biblical Revelation and Social Existence", in *Interpretation*, 28, pp.422-440.

Cone, J.H. (1986) "Christian Theology and Scipture as the Expression of God's Liberating Activity for the Poor", in Cone, J.H. (1986) *Speaking the Truth: Ecumenism, Liberation, and Black Theology*, Eerdmans, Grand Rapids, pp.4-16.

Croatto, J.S. (1978) *Exodus: A Hermeneutic of Freedom*, Orbis, New York.

Croatto, J.S. (1983) "Biblical Hermeneutics in Theologies of Liberation", in Fabella, V. and S. Torres (eds) (1983) *Irruption of the Third World: Challenge to Theology*, Orbis, New York, pp.140-141.

Croatto, J.S. (1987) *Biblical Hermeneutics: Toward a Theory of Reading as the Production of Meaning*, Orbis, New York.

Crüsemann, F. (1978) "Die Eigenstaendigkeit der Urgeschichte. Ein Beitrag zur Diskussion um den 'Jahwisten'", in Jeremias, J. and L. Perlitt (eds) (1978) *Die Botschaft und die Boten Festschrift fuer Hans Walter Wolff zum 70 Geburtstag*, Neukirchener Verlag, Neukirchen-Vluyn, pp.11-30.

Culler, J. (1982) *On Deconstruction: Theory and Criticism After Structuralism*, Cornell University Press, Ithaca.

Cuthbertson, G. (1987) "The English-Speaking Churches and Colonialism", in Villa-Vicencio, C. (ed) (1987) *Theology and Violence: The South African Debate*, Skotaville, Johannesburg.

Daly, M. (1973) *Beyond God the Father: Toward a Philosophy of Women's Liberation*, Beacon, Boston.

Daly, M. (1975) *The Church and the Second Sex: With a New Feminist Postchristian Introduction by the Author*, Harper and Row, New York.

Daly, M. (1978) *Gyn/Ecology: The Metaethics of Radical Feminism*, Beacon, Boston.

Daly, M. (1984) *Pure Lust: Elemental Feminist Theology*, Beacon, Boston.

Danto, A. (1965) *Analytical Philosophy of History*, Cambridge University Press, Cambridge.

Dean, W. (1986) "The Challenge of the New Historicism", in *The Journal of Religion*, 66, pp.261-281.

Degenaar, J. (1989) "Writing as a Revolutionary Activity", in Breitenbach, R. (ed) (1989) *Transitions: A Collection of Lectures:*

Standard Bank Arts Festival Winter School, 1820 Foundation, Grahamstown, pp.7-13.

De Gruchy, J.W. (1979) *The Church Struggle in South Africa,* David Philip, Cape Town.

Deist, F. (1987) "How Does a Marxist Read the Bible?", in De Villiers, P.G.R. (ed) (1987) *Liberation Theology and the Bible,* University of South Africa, Pretoria, pp.15-30.

Derrida, J. (1988) "Structure, Sign and Play in the Discourse of the Human Sciences", in Lodge, D. (1988) (ed) *Modern Criticism and Theory: A Reader,* Longman, London.

De Villiers, P.G.R. (1987) "The Gospel and the Poor. Let Us Read Luke 4", in De Villiers, P.G.R. (ed) (1987) *Liberation Theology and the Bible,* University of South Africa, Pretoria, pp.45-76.

Draper, J.A. (1991) "'For the Kingdom Is Inside of You and It Is Outside of You': Contextual Exegesis in South Africa", in Hartin, P.J. and J.H. Petzer (1991) (eds) *Text and Interpretation: New Approaches in the Criticism of the New Testament,* E.J. Brill, Leiden.

Draper, J.A. and G.O. West (1989) "Anglicans and Scripture in South Africa", in England, F. and T.J.M. Paterson (eds) (1989) *Bounty in Bondage,* Ravan, Johannesburg, pp.30-52.

Duhem, P. (1954) *The Aim and Structure of Physical Theory,* Princeton University Press, Princeton.

Dumortier, J.M. (1983) *Many in This City Are My People: Young Christian Workers,* YCW, Durban.

Du Plessis, J.H. (1911) *A History of Christian Missions in SA,* C. Struik, Cape Town.

Eagleton, T. (1981) *Walter Benjamin, or Towards a Revolutionary Criticism,* Verso, London.

Eagleton, T. (1983) *Literary Theory: An Introduction,* Basil Blackwell, Oxford.

Eagleton, T. (1984) *The Function of Criticism: From The Spectator to Post-Structuralism,* Verso, London.

Eagleton, T. (1986) "The Revolt of the Reader", in Eagleton, T. (1986) *Against the Grain: Essays 1975-1985,* Verso, London.

Eagleton, T. (1989) "Reception Theory", in Barry, P. (ed) (1989) *Issues in Contemporary Critical Theory,* Macmillan, London, pp.119-127.

Ellsworth, E. (1989) "Why Doesn't This Feel Empowering?: Working through the Repressive Myths of Critical Pedagogy", in *Harvard Educational Review,* 59, pp.297-324.

Fackre, G. (1983) "Narrative Theology. An Overview", in *Interpretation*, 37, pp.340-352.

Feyerabend, P. (1970) "Against Method: Outline of an Anarchistic Theory of Knowledge" in Radner, M. and S. Winokur (ed) (1970) *Minnesota Studies in the Philosophy of Science*, 4, University of Minnesota Press.

Feyerabend, P. (1975) *Against Method: An Outline of an Anarchistic Theory of Knowledge*, NLB.

Fiorenza, F.P. (1974) "Latin American Liberation Theology", in *Interpretation*, 28, pp.441-457.

Flesseman-van Leer, E. (1975) "Dear Christopher, ...", in Hooker, M. and Hickling, C. (eds) (1975) *What About the New Testament: Essays in Honour of Christopher Evans*, SCM, pp.234-242.

Foucault, M. (1977) *Language, Counter-memory, Practice: Selected Essays and Interviews*, Cornell University Press, Ithaca.

Foucault, M. (1980) *Power/Knowledge: Selected Writings and Other Interviews 1972-1977*, Pantheon, New York.

Fowl, S. (1990) "The Ethics of Interpretation or What's Left Over After the Elimination of Meaning", in Clines, D.J.A., S. Fowl, and S.E. Porter (eds) (1990) *The Bible in Three Dimensions*, Sheffield Academic Press, Sheffield.

Frei, H. (1974) *The Eclipse of Biblical Narrative: A Study in Eighteenth and Nineteenth Century Hermeneutics*, Yale University Press, New Haven and London.

Frostin, P. (1985) "The Hermeneutics of the Poor—The Epistemological 'Break' in Third World Theologies", in *Studia Theologica* 39, pp.127-150.

Frostin, P. (1988) *Liberation Theology in Tanzania and South Africa: A First World Interpretation*, Lund University Press, Lund.

Gibellini, R. (1979) (ed) *Frontiers of Theology in Latin America*, Orbis, New York.

Gifford, P. (1986) "The Sola Scriptura Ideal: The Almost Normative Status of a Purely Contingent Theological Tradition", in *Journal of Theology for Southern Africa*, 57, pp.43-56.

Giroux, H.A. (1985) "Introduction", in Freire, P. (1985) *The Politics of Education*, Macmillan, London, pp.xi-xxv.

Goba, B. (1973) "Corporate Personality: Ancient Israel and Africa", in Moore, B. (1973) *Black Theology: The South African Voice*, C. Hurst and Company.

Goba, B. (1986) "The Black Consciousness Movement: Its Impact on Black Theology", in Mosala, I.J. and B. Tlhagale (eds) (1986) *The Unquestionable Right To Be Free*, Skotaville, Johannesburg, pp.57-69.

Goba, B. (1986a) "The Use of Scripture in the Kairos Document: A Biblical Ethical Perspective", in *The Journal of Theology for Southern Africa*, 56, pp.61-65.

Goba, B. (1988) *An Agenda for Black Theology: Hermeneutics for Social Change*, Skotaville, Johannesburg.

Goodman, N. (1972) *Problems and Projects*, Bobbs-Merrill, New York.

Goodman, N. (1979) *Ways of Worldmaking*, Hackett Publishing Co., Indianapolis.

Gottwald, N.K. (1980) *The Tribes of Yahweh: A Sociology of the Religion of Liberated Israel, 1250-1050 B.C.E.*, SCM, London.

Gottwald, N.K. (1983) "The Theological Task After *The Tribes of Yahweh*", in Gottwald, N.K. (ed) (1983) *The Bible and Liberation*, Orbis, New York.

Gottwald, N.K. (1983a) "Sociological Method in Biblical Research and Contemporary Peace Studies", in *American Baptist Quarterly*, 2, pp.142-156.

Gottwald, N.K. (1985) "Socio-Historical Precision in the Biblical Grounding of Liberation Theologies", Unpublished Paper, San Francisco.

Gottwald, N.K. (1985a) *The Hebrew Bible: A Socio-Literary Introduction*, Fortress, Philadelphia.

Gottwald, N.K. (1985b) "Social Matrix and Canonical Shape", in *Theology Today*, 42, pp.307-321.

Greeley, A.M (1974) "Theological Table-Talk: Politics and Political Theologians", in *Theology Today*, 30, pp.391-397.

Grimes, R.L. (1986) "Of Words the Speaker, of Deeds the Doer", in *The Journal of Religion*, 66, pp.1-17.

Grundy, S. (1987) *Curriculum: Product or Praxis*, Falmer Press, Barcombe.

Gultig, J. and M. Hart (1990) "'The World is Full of Blood': Youth, Schooling and Conflict in Pietermaritzburg, 1987-1989", in *Perspectives in Education*, 11, pp.1-19.

Gutiérrez, G. (1974) *A Theology of Liberation: History, Politics and Salvation*, SCM, London.

Gutiérrez, G. (1975) "Liberation Praxis and Christian Faith", in Gibellini, R. (ed) (1975) *Frontiers of Theology in Latin America*, SCM, London, pp.24-24.

Gutiérrez, G. (1978) "Two Theological Perspectives: Liberation Theology and Progressivist Theology", in Torres, S. and V. Fabella (1978) *The Emergent Gospel: Theology from the Underside of History*, Orbis, New York. pp.227-255.

Gutiérrez, G. (1983) "Finding Our Way to Talk About God", in Fabella, V. and S. Torres (eds) (1983) *Irruption of the Third World: Challenge to Theology*, Orbis, New York.

Gwala, N. [and B. Nzimande] (1988) "Class Alliances in the Struggle Against Inkatha", in *South African Labour Bulletin*, 13.

Hall, S. (1973) *Encoding and Decoding in the Television Discourse*, Centre for Contemporary Cultural Studies, Birmingham.

Hanson, N.R. (1958) *Patterns of Discovery*, Cambridge University Press, Cambridge.

Harrington, D.J. (1982) "Some New Voices in New Testament Interpretation", in *Anglican Theological Review*, 64, pp.362-370.

Hassan, I. (1986) "Pluralism in Postmodern Perspective", *Critical Inquiry*, 12, pp.503-520.

Hassan, I. (1987) "Making Sense: The Trails of Postmodern Discourse", in *New Literary History*, 18, pp.437-459.

Hauerwas, S. (1986) "Some Theological Reflections on Gutiérrez's Use of 'Liberation' as a Theological Concept", in *Modern Theology*, 3, pp.67-76.

Hazelton, R. (1972) "Transcendence and Creativity", The Russell Lecture, Tufts University.

Hazelton, R. (1975) *Ascending Flame, Descending Dove*, Westminster Press, Philadelphia.

Held, V. (1983) "The Independence of Intellectuals", in *The Journal of Philosophy*, 80, pp.572-582.

Herzog, W.R. (1974) "Liberation Hermeneutic as Ideology Critique?", in *Interpretation*, 28, pp.387-403.

Herzog, W.R. (1983) "Interpretation as Discovery and Creation: Sociological Dimensions of Biblical Hermeneutics", in *American Baptist Quarterly*, 2, pp.105-118.

Hoare, Q. and Smith, G.N. (eds) (1971) *Selections from the Prison Notebooks of Antonio Gramsci*, Lawrence and Wishart, London.

Hollenweger, W.J. (1981) "The Other Exegesis", in *Horizons in Biblical Theology*, 3, pp.155-179.

Hoy, D.C. (1978) *The Critical Circle: Literature, History, and Philosophical Hermeneutics*, University of California Press, Berkeley.

Hoy, D.C. (1982) "Deciding Derrida", in *London Review of Books*, 4, 3, pp.3-5.

Huizinga, J. (1936) "A Definition of the Concept of History", in Klibansky, R. and H.J. Paton (ed) (1936) *Philosophy and History*, Claredon Press, pp.1-10.

ICT News (1983) 3.

ICT News (1990) 8.

ICT Church and Labour Project Research Group (1991) "Workers, the

Church and the Alienation of Religious Life", in Cochrane, J.R. and G.O. West (eds) (1991) *The Threefold Cord: Theology, Work and Labour*, Cluster Publications, Pietermaritzburg, pp.253-275.

Jobling, D. (1987) "Introduction", Unpublished Paper, Sheffield University, Sheffield.

Kamphausen, E. (1976) *Anfänge der Kirchlichen Unabhängigkeitsbewegung in Südafrika: Gesichte und Theologie der Äthiopischen Bewegung, 1872-1912*, Peter Lang, Frankfurt.

Keat, R. and J. Urry (1975) *Social Theory as Science*, Routledge and Kegan Paul.

Kelsey, D.H. (1975) *The Uses of Scripture in Recent Theology*, SCM, London.

Kentridge, M. (1990) *An Unofficial War*, David Philip, Cape Town.

Kinghorn, J. (ed) (1986) *Die NGK en Apartheid*, Macmillan, Johannesburg.

Kneifel, T. (1983) *Epoch and Horizon: On Two Basic Concepts for a Hermeneutic Phenomenology of History. Martin Heidegger in Dialogue with Wilhelm Dilthey and Edmund Husserl*, Unpublished PhD Thesis, University of Natal, Durban.

Kretschmar, L. (1986) *The Voice of Black Theology in South Africa*, Ravan, Johannesburg.

Kritzinger, J.N.J. (1988) *Black Theology—Challenge to Mission*, Unpublished PhD Thesis, University of South Africa, Pretoria.

Kuhn, T.S. (1970) *The Structure of Scientific Revolutions*, 2nd Edition, University of Chicago Press, Chicago.

Kunnie, J. (1986) "Christianity, Black Theology and Liberating Faith", in Mosala, I.J. and B. Tlhagale (eds) (1986) *The Unquestionable Right To Be Free*, Skotaville, Johannesburg, pp.153-168.

Lamb, M.L. (1982) *Solidarity with Victims: Toward a Theology of Social Transformation*, Crossroad, New York.

Lategan, B.C. (1984) "Current Issues in the Hermeneutical Debate", in *Neotestamentica*, 18, pp.1-17.

Lategan, B.C. and J. Rousseau (1988) "Reading Luke 12:35-48: An Empirical Study", in *Neotestamentica*, 22, pp.391-413.

Lauritzen, P. (1987) "Is "Narrative" Really a Panacea? The Use of "Narrative" in the Work of Metz and Hauerwas", in *The Journal of Religion*, 67, pp.322-339.

Leeb, W. (1989) "Death, Devastation and Destruction: Refugees in Natal", Centre for Adult Education, University of Natal, Pietermaritzburg (Paper presented at the Special Committee against Apartheid: International Seminar on Women and Children Refugess in Southern Africa and Namibia, Harare, 16-19 January 1989).

Lentricchia, F. (1980) *After the New Criticism*, University of Chicago Press, Chicago.

Lentricchia, F. (1983) *Criticism and Social Change*, University of Chicago Press, Chicago.

Levin, D. (1967) *In Defense of Historical Literature*, Hill and Wang.

Loader, J. (1987) "Exodus, Liberation Theology and Theological Argument", in *Journal of Theology for Southern Africa*, 59, pp.3-18.

Long, B.O. (1982) "The Social World of Ancient Israel", in *Interpretation*, 36, pp.243-255.

Long, T.M.S. (1990) *Reading Paul in the South African Context of Struggle for Liberation: Some Insights from Latin American Liberation Theology*, Unpublished MA Thesis, University of Natal, Pietermaritzburg.

Lorde, A. (1984) *Sister Outsider*, The Crossing Press, New York.

Luckett, S. (1990) "Contextualisation of Theological Research and Education: The Promise of Collective Participatory Methods", Unpublished Paper, University of Natal, Pietermaritzburg.

MacIntrye, A. (1977) "Epistemological Crises, Dramatic Narrative and the Philosophy of Science", in *The Monist*, 60.

MacIntyre, A. (1981) *After Virtue*, University of Notre Dame Press, Notre Dame.

MacIntyre, A. (1983) "Moral Arguments and Social Contexts", in *The Journal of Philosophy*, 80, pp.590-591.

MacIntyre, A. (1984) *After Virtue*, 2nd Edition, University of Notre Dame Press, Notre Dame.

Mailloux, S. (1985) "Rhetorical Hermeneutics", in *Critical Inquiry*, 11, pp.620-641.

Majeke, N. (1952) *The Role of Missionaries in Conquest*, Society of Young Africa, Johannesburg.

Makhetha, V. (1989) "An Africanist Interpretation of the Bible", Unpublished Paper, University of Natal, Pietermaritzburg.

Malina, B.J. (1983) "Why Interpret the Bible with the Social Sciences", in *American Baptist Quarterly*, 2, pp.119-133.

Mansueto, A. (1983) "From Historical Criticism to Historical Materialism: Towards a Materialist Reading of Scripture", Unpublished Paper, Graduate Theological Union, Berkeley.

Mare, G. and G. Hamilton (1988) "Policing 'liberation politics'", Unpublished Paper, University of Natal, Pietermaritzburg.

Mare, G. and M. Ncube (1989) "Inkatha: Marching from Natal to Pretoria", in Moss, G. and I. Obery (eds) (1989) *South African Review 5*, Ravan, Johannesburg, pp.474-490.

Mbiti, J.S. (1976) "Theological Impotence and the Universality of the Church", in Anderson, G.H. and T.F. Stransky (eds) (1976) *Third World Theologies*, Paulist Press, New York, p.16-17.

McAfee Brown, R. (1978) *Theology in a New Key: Responding to Liberation Themes*, Westminster, Philadelphia.

McKnight, E.V. (1985) *The Bible and the Reader: An Introduction to Literary Criticism*, Fortress Press, Philadelphia.

Meeks, W.A. (1986) "A Hermeneutics of Social Embodiment", in *Harvard Theological Review*, 79, pp.176-186.

Memmi, A. (1965) *The Colonizer and the Colonized*, Souvenir Press, London.

Mesters, C. (1988) *God's Project*, The Theology Exchange Programme, Cape Town.

Metz, J.B. (1980) *Faith in History and Society: Toward a Practical Fundamental Theology*, Burns and Oates, London.

Meyers, C. (1988) *Discovering Eve: Ancient Israelite Women in Context*, Oxford University Press, Oxford.

Míguez Bonino, J. (1975) *Doing Theology in a Revolutionary Situation*, Fortress, Philadelphia.

Míguez Bonino, J. (1983) *Toward a Christian Political Ethics*, SCM, London.

Mink, L. (1966) "The Autonomy of Historical Understanding", in Dray, W.H. (ed) (1966) *Philosophical Analysis and History*, Greenwood Press, pp.160-192.

Mink, L. (1978) "Narrative Form as a Cognitive Instrument", in Canary, R.H. and H. Kozicki (ed) *Literary Form and Historical Understanding*, University of Wisconsin, pp.129-149.

Mofokeng, T.A. (1986) "The Evolution of the Black Struggle and the Role of Black Theology", in Mosala, I.J. and B. Tlhagale (eds) (1986) *The Unquestionable Right To Be Free*, Skotaville, Johannesburg, pp.113-128.

Mofokeng, T.A. (1983) *The Crucified Among the Crossbearers: Towards a Black Christology*, J.H. Kok, Kampen.

Mofokeng, T.A. (1988) "Black Christians, the Bible and Liberation", in *The Journal of Black Theology*, 2, pp.34-42.

Moltmann, J. (1968) "Toward a Political Hermeneutics of the Gospel", in *Union Seminary Quarterly Review*, 23, pp.303-323.

Moore, B. (1973) "Preface", in Moore, B. (1973) *Black Theology: The South African Voice*, C. Hurst and Company.

Moore, B. (1973) "What is Black Theology?", in Moore, B. (1973) *Black Theology: The South African Voice*, C. Hurst and Company, pp.1-10.

Moore, B. (1994) "Black Theology in South Africa Today", in *Bulletin for Contextual Theology in Southern Africa and Africa*, 1, pp.7-19.

Morgan, D.F. (1990) *Between Text and Community: The "Writings" in Canonical Interpretation*, Fortress, Minneapolis.

Morphet, A.R. (1983) "Seminar on Research Methods: Action-Research", in Steinberg, M.B. and S.E. Philcox (1983) *Research Methods for Higher Degrees*, University of Cape Town, Cape Town, pp.93-101.

Mosala, B. (1986) "Black Theology and the Struggle of the Black Woman in Southern Africa", in Mosala, I.J. and B. Tlhagale (eds) (1986) *The Unquestionable Right To Be Free*, Skotaville, Johannesburg, pp.129-133.

Mosala, I.J. (1985) "African Independent Churches: A Study in Socio-Theological Protest", in Villa-Vicencio, C. and J.W. De Gruchy (eds) (1985) *Resistance and Hope: South African Essays in Honour of Beyers Naudé*, David Philips, Cape Town, pp.103-111.

Mosala, I.J. (1986) "The Use of the Bible in Black Theology", in Mosala, I.J. and B. Tlhagale (eds) (1986) *The Unquestionable Right To Be Free*, Skotaville, Johannesburg, pp.175-199.

Mosala, I.J. (1986a) "Social Scientific Approaches to the Bible: One Step Forward, Two Steps Backward", in *Journal of Theology for Southern Africa*, 55, pp.15-30.

Mosala, I.J. (1986b) "Black Theology Versus the Social Morality of Settler Colonialism: Hermeneutical Reflections on Luke 1 and 2", in *Journal of Black Theology*, 1, pp.26-42.

Mosala, I.J. (1986c) "The Relevance of African Independent Churches and Their Challenge to Black Theology", in Mosala, I.J. and B. Tlhagale (eds) (1986) *The Unquestionable Right To Be Free*, Skotaville, Johannesburg, pp.91-100.

Mosala, I.J. (1986d) "Ethics of the Economic Principles: Church and Secular Investments", in Tlhagale, B. and I.J. Mosala (eds) (1986) *Hammering Swords into Ploughshares: Essays in Honour of Archbishop Mpilo Desmond Tutu*, Skottaville, Johannesburg, pp.119-129.

Mosala, I.J. (1987) *Biblical Hermeneutics and Black Theology in South Africa*, PhD Thesis, University of Cape Town.

Mosala, I.J. (1987a) "The Meaning of Reconciliation" in *The Journal of Theology for Southern Africa*, pp.19-25.

Mosala, I.J. (1989) *Biblical Hermeneutics and Black Theology in South Africa*, Eerdmans, Grand Rapids.

Mosala, I.J. (1989a) "Christianity and Socialism: Appropriating Moses and Jesus for National Liberation in Azania", Unpublished Paper, Pietermaritzburg.

Mosala, I.J. (1989b) "Black Theology", Unpublished Paper, Cape Town.

Mosala, I.J. (1989c) "Race, Class and Gender as Hermeneutical Factors in the African Independent Churches' Appropriation of the Bible", Unpublished Report for the Human Sciences Research Council, Pretoria.

Motlhabi, M. (1973) "Black Theology: A Personal View", in Moore, B. (1973) *Black Theology: The South African Voice*, C. Hurst and Company.

Motlhabi, M. (1984) *The Theory and Practice of Black Resistance to Apartheid: A Social-Ethical Analysis*, Skotaville, Johannesburg.

Motlhabi, M. (1986) "The Historic Origins of Black Theology", in Mosala, I.J. and B. Tlhagale (eds) *The Unquestionable Right To Be Free*, Skotaville, Johannesburg, pp.37-56.

Motlhabi, M. (1987) "Liberation Theology: An Introduction", in de Villiers, P.G.R. (ed) (1987) *Liberation Theology and the Bible*, University of South Africa, Pretoria, pp.1-14.

Muzorewa, G.H. (1985) *The Origins and Development of African Theology*, Orbis, New York.

Nolan, A. (1976) *Jesus Before Christianity: The Gospel of Liberation*, David Philip, Cape Town.

Nolan, A. (1988) *God in South Africa: The Challenge of the Gospel*, David Philip, Cape Town.

Nolan, A. (1991) "A Worker's Theology", in Cochrane, J.R. and G.O. West (eds) (1991) *The Threefold Cord: Theology, Work and Labour*, Cluster Publications, Pietermaritzburg, pp. 160-176.

Obed, B. (1986) "The Table of Nations (Genesis 10): A Socio-Cultural Approach", *Zeitschrift für die alttestamentliche Wissenschaft*, 98, pp.14-31.

Ogden, S. (1979) *Faith and Freedom: Toward a Theology of Liberation*, Christian Journals, Belfast.

Ogden, S. (1981) "The Concept of a Theology of Liberation: Must a Christian Theology Today Be So Conceived?", in Mahan, B. and L.D. Richesin (eds) (1981) *The Challenge of Liberation Theology: A First World Response*, Orbis, New York.

Onwu, N. (1985) "The Hermeneutical Model: The Dilemma of the African Theologian", in *Africa Theological Journal*, 14, pp.145-160.

Oosthuizen, G.C. (1976) "Black Theology in the History of Africa", in *University of Durban-Westville Journal*, 2 (no pagination).

Outler, A.C. (1985) "Towards a Postliberal Hermeneutics", in *Theology Today*, 42, pp.281-291.

Parrat, J. (1984) "African Theology and Biblical Hermeneutics", in *Africa Theological Journal*, 13, pp.88-94.

Philpott, Graham (1993) *Jesus is Tricky and God is Undemocratic: The Kin-dom of God in Amawoti*, Cluster Publications, Pietermaritzburg.

Pityana, N. (1973) "What Is Black Consciousness?", in Moore, B. (1973) *Black Theology: The South African Voice*, C. Hurst and Company.

Pixley, G. (1983) "The Poor Evangelize Biblical Scholarship", in *American Baptist Quarterly*, 2, pp.157-167.

Placher, W.C. (1987) "Paul Ricoeur and Postliberal Theology: A Conflict of Interpretations?", in *Modern Theology*, 4, pp.35-52.

Popper, K. (1945) *The Open Society and Its Enemies*, vol. II.

Putnam, H. (1981) *Reason, Truth and History*, Cambridge University Press, Cambridge.

Quine, W.V. (1963) "Two Dogmas of Empiricism" in Quine, W.V. (1963) *From a Logical Point of View*, Harper and Row, New York.

Quine, W.V. (1969) *Ontological Relativity and Other Essays*, Columbia University Press, New York.

Reese, W.L. (1980) *Dictionary of Philosophy and Religion: Eastern and Western Thought*, Humanities Press, Atlantic Highlands.

Richard, P. (1983) *The Idols of Death and the God of Life: A Theology*, Orbis, Maryknoll.

Rogerson, J.W. (1990) "What Does it Mean to Be Human?': The Central Question of Old Testament Theology?", in Clines, D.J.A., S. Fowl, and S.E. Porter (eds) (1990) *The Bible in Three Dimensions*, Sheffield Academic Press, Sheffield.

Rooney, E. (1986) "Who's Left Out? A Rose by Any Other Name Is Still Red; Or, The Politics of Pluralism", in *Critical Inquiry*, 12, pp.550-563.

Rorty, R. (1979) *Philosophy and the Mirror of Nature*, Princeton University Press, Princeton.

Rorty, R. (1981) "Beyond Nietzsche and Marx", in *London Review of Books*, 19 February-4 March, pp.5-6.

Rorty, R. (1982) "The World Well Lost", in Rorty, R. (1982) *Consequences of Pragmatism (Essays: 1972-1980)*, University of Minnesota Press, Minneapolis, pp.3-18.

Rorty, R. (1983) "Postmodernist Bourgeois Liberalism", in *The Journal of Philosophy*, 80, pp.583-589.

Rorty, R. (1985) "Texts and Lumps", in *New Literary History*, 17, pp.1-16.

Rowland, C. and M. Corner (1990) *Liberating Exegesis: The Challenge of Liberation Theology to Biblical Studies*, SPCK, London.

Ruether, R.R. (1983) *Sexism and God-Talk: Towards a Feminist Theology*, SCM, London.

Sakenfeld, K.D. (1985) "Feminist Uses of Biblical Materials", in Russell, L. (ed) (1985) *Feminist Interpretation of Biblical Literature*, Blackwell, London, pp.55-64.

Sanders, J.A. (1984) *Canon and Community: A Guide to Canonical Criticism*, Fortress.

Schneiders, S.M. (1989) "Feminist Ideology Criticism and Biblical Hermeneutics", in *Biblical Theology Bulletin*, 19, pp.3-10.

Schneiders, S.M. (1991) *The Revelatory Text: Interpreting the New Testament as Sacred Scripture*, Harper Collins, San Francisco.

Schüssler Fiorenza, E. (1981) "Toward a Feminist Biblical Hermeneutics: Biblical Interpretation and Liberation Theology", in Mahan, B. and L.D. Richesin (eds) (1981) *The Challenge of Liberation Theology: A First World Response*, Orbis, New York, pp.91-112.

Schüssler Fiorenza, E. (1983) *In Memory of Her: A Feminist Theological Reconstruction of Christian Origins*, SCM, London.

Schüssler Fiorenza, E. (1984) *Bread Not Stone: The Challenge of Feminist Biblical Interpretation*, Beacon, Boston.

Scott, J.C. (1990) *Domination and the Arts of Resistance: Hidden Transcripts*, Yale University Press, New Haven and London.

Sebidi, L. (1986) "The Dynamics of the Black Struggle and Its Implications for Black Theology", in Mosala, I.J. and B. Tlhagale (eds) (1986) *The Unquestionable Right To Be Free*, Skotaville, Johannesburg, pp.1-36.

Segundo, J.L. (1977) *The Liberation of Theology*, Gill and Macmillan, Dublin.

Segundo, J.L. (1985) "The Shift Within Latin American Theology", *Journal of Theology for Southern Africa* 52, pp.17-29.

Segundo, J.L. (1986) *The Humanist Christology of Paul*, Orbis, Maryknoll.

Sellars, W. (1956) "Empiricism and the Philosophy of Mind", in Feigl, H. and M. Scriven (ed) (1956) *Minnesota Studies in the Philosophy of Science*, Vol. 1, University of Minnesota Press, Minneapolis, pp.253-329.

Setiloane, G.M. (1979) "Where Are We in African Theology?", in Appiah-Kubi, K. and Torres, E. (eds) (1979) *African Theology En Route, Papers from the Pan-African Conference of Third World Theologians, December 17-23, 1977, Accra, Ghana,* Orbis, New York, pp.59-65.

Sheppard, G.T. (1982) "Canonization: Hearing the Voice of the Same God through Historically Dissimilar Traditions", in *Interpretation,* 36, pp.21-33.

Small, A. (1973) "Blackness Versus Nihilism: Black Racism Rejected", in Moore, B. (1973) (ed) *Black Theology: The South African Voice,* C. Hurst and Company.

Smit, D.J. (1988) "Responsible Hermeneutics: A Systematic Theologian's Response to the Readings and Readers of Luke 12:35-48", in *Neotestamentica,* 22, pp.441-484.

Smit, D.J. (1989) "Those Were the Critics, What About the Real Readers? An Analysis of 65 Published Sermons and Sermon Guidelines on Luke 12:35-48", in *Neotestamentica,* 23, pp.61-82.

Smit, D.J. (1990a) "The Ethics of Interpretation—New Voices from the USA", in *Scriptura,* 33, pp.16-28.

Smit, D.J. (1990b) "The Ethics of Interpretation—And South Africa", in *Scriptura,* 33, pp.29-43.

Spivak, G. (1988) "Can the Subaltern Speak?", in Nelson, G. and Grossberg, L. (1988) (ed) *Marxism and the Interpretation of Culture,* Macmillan, London, pp.271-313.

Stevens, I.D. (1985) "The Role of the Church in Industry and Industrial Relations; Focusing on the Supportive Role with Worker Organisations, Especially the Independent Trade Unions in South Africa", Unpublished Honours Dissertation, University of Natal, Pietermaritzburg.

Stout, J. (1981) *The Flight from Authority: Religion, Morality, and the Quest for Autonomy,* University of Notre Dame Press, Notre Dame.

Stout, J. (1982) "What Is the Meaning of a Text?", in *New Literary History,* 14.

Sugirtharajah, R.S. (1991) (ed) *Voices from the Margin: Interpreting the Bible in the Third World,* Orbis, New York.

The Kairos Document: A Theological Comment on the Political Crisis in South Africa (1985), Catholic Institute for International Relations, London.

The Kairos Document: Challenge to the Church (1986), Second Edition, Skotaville, Braamfontein.

The Road to Damascus: Kairos and Conversion, (1989) Skotaville, Johannesburg.

Thetele, C.B. (1979) "Women in South Africa: The WAAIC", in Appiah-Kubi, K. and Torres, E. (eds) (1979) *African Theology En Route, Papers from the Pan-African Conference of Third World Theologians, December 17-23, 1977, Accra, Ghana*, Orbis, New York.

Thiselton, A.C. (1980) *The Two Horizons: New Testament Hermeneutics and Philosophical Description with Special Reference to Heidegger, Bultmann, Gadamer, and Wittgenstein*, William B. Eerdmans, Grand Rapids.

Tlhagale, B. (1986) "On Violence: A Township Perspective", in Mosala, I.J. and B. Tlhagale (eds) (1986) *The Unquestionable Right To Be Free*, Skotaville, Johannesburg, pp.135-151.

Torres, S. (1978) "Introduction", in Torres, S. and V. Fabella (1978) *The Emergent Gospel: Theology from the Underside of History*, Orbis, New York, pp.vii-xxiii.

Torres, S. and V. Fabella (1978) *The Emergent Gospel: Theology from the Underside of History*, Orbis, New York.

Tracy, D. (1981) "Introduction" in Mahan, B. and L.D. Richesin (eds) *The Challenge of Liberation Theology: A First World Response*, Orbis, New York, pp.1-3.

Tracy, D. (1981) *The Analogical Imagination: Christian Theology and the Culture of Pluralism*, SCM, London.

Tracy, D. (1985) "Lindbeck's New Program for Theology: A Reflection", in *Thomist*, 49, pp.460-472.

Tracy, D. (1987) *Plurality and Ambiguity: Hermeneutics, Religion, Hope*, Harper and Row, San Francisco.

Trible, P. (1973) "Depatriachalization in Biblical Interpretation", in *The Journal of the American Academy of Religion*, 41, pp.30-49.

Trible, P. (1978) *God and the Rhetoric of Sexuality*, Fortress, Philadelphia.

Trible, P. (1984) *Texts of Terror: Literary-Feminist Readings of Biblical Narratives*, Fortress, Philadelphia.

Truluck, A. (1993) *No Blood on Our Hands*, Black Sash, Pietermaritzburg.

Tutu, D. (1975) "African Theology and Black Theology", in Best, K. (ed) (1975) *African Challenge*, Transafrica Publishers, Nairobi.

Tutu, D. (1979) "The Theology of Liberation in Africa", in Appiah-Kubi, K. and T. Sergio (eds) (1975) *African Theology en Route*, Orbis, New York.

Villa-Vicencio, C. (1986) *Between Christ and Caesar: Classic and Contemporary Texts on Church and State*, David Philip, Cape Town.

Villa-Vicencio, C. (ed) (1987) *Theology and Violence: The South African Debate*, Skotaville, Johannesburg.

Webster, J. (ed) (1982) *Bishop Desmond Tutu: The Voice of One Crying in the Wilderness*, Mowbray, London.

Welch, S.D. (1985) *Communities of Resistance and Solidarity: A Feminist Theology of Liberation*, Orbis, Maryknoll.

Welch, S.D. (1990) *A Feminist Ethic of Risk*, Fortress, Minneapolis.

West, C. (1979) "Schleiermacher's Hermeneutics and the Myth of the Given", in *Union Seminary Review*, 34, pp.71-84.

West, C. (1981) "Nietzsche's Prefiguration of Postmodern American Philosophy", in *Boundary* 2, 9 and 10, pp.241-269.

West, C. (1982) *Prophesy Deliverance!: An Afro-American Revolutionary Christianity*, Westminster Press, Philadelphia.

West, C. (1982a) "Review of *Philosophy and the Mirror of Nature* by Richard Rorty", in *Union Quarterly Review*, 37, pp.179-185, p.183.

West, C. (1983) "Fredric Jameson's Marxist Hermeneutics", in *Boundary 2: A Journal of Post Modern Literature*, Winter, pp.177-200.

West, C. (1985) "Afterword: The Politics of American Neo-Pragmatism", in Rajchman, J. and C. West (ed) (1985) *Post-Analytic Philosophy*, Columbia University Press, New York, pp.259-275.

West, C. (1988) *Prophetic Fragments*, Eerdmans, Grand Rapids.

West, C. (1989) *The American Evasion of Philosophy: A Genealogy of Pragmatism*, The University of Wisconsin Press, Wisconsin.

West, G.O. (1987) "An Analysis of the Relationship Between Norman Gottwald's Sociological Reconstructions of Premonarchic Israel and Liberation Struggles Today", Unpublished Paper, Sheffield University, Sheffield.

West, G.O. (1990) "Reading 'The Text' and Reading 'Behind-the-Text': The Cain and Abel Story in a Context of Liberation", in Clines, D.J.A., S.E. Fowl, and S.E. Porter (eds) *The Bible in Three Dimensions*, Sheffield Academic Press, Sheffield, pp.299-320.

West, G.O. (1990) "Can a Literary Reading Be a Liberative Reading?", in *Scriptura*, 35, pp.10-25.

West, G.O. (1990) "Two Modes of Reading the Bible in the South African Context of Liberation", in *Journal of Theology for Southern Africa*, 73, pp.34-47.

West, G.O. (1991) "Hearing Job's Wife: Towards a Feminist Reading of *Job*, in *Old Testament Essays*, 4, pp.107-131.

West, G.O. (1992) "Interesting and Interested Readings: Deconstruction, the Bible and the South African Context", in *Scriptura* 42, pp.35-49.

West, G.O. (1993) *Contextual Bible Study*, Cluster Publications, Pietermaritzburg.

West, G.O. (1993a) "No Integrity without Contextuality: The Presence of Particularity in Biblical Hermeneutics and Pedagogy", in *Scriptura*, S11, pp.131-146.

West, G.O. (1994) "Difference and Dialogue: Reading the Joseph Story with Poor and Marginalized Communities in South Africa", in *Biblical Interpretation*, 2, pp.152-170.

West, G.O. (1995) "Constructing Critical and Contextual Readings with Ordinary Readers: Mark 5:21-6:1", *The Journal of Theology for Southern Africa*, forthcoming.

White, H. (1975) "Historicism, History, and the Figurative Imagination", in *History and Theory*, Beiheft 14, pp.48-67.

White, H. (1986) "Historical Pluralism", in *Critical Inquiry*, 12, pp.480-493.

Wilcoxen, J.A. (1974) "Narrative", in J.H. Hayes (ed) (1974) *Old Testament Form Criticism*, Trinity University Press, pp.57-140.

Wilson, F. and Ramphele, M. (1989) *Uprooting Poverty: The South African Challenge*, David Philip, Cape Town.

Wink, W. (1973) *The Bible in Human Transformation*, Fortress, Philadelphia.

Winquist, C.E. (1986) *Epiphanies of Darkness: Deconstruction in Theology*, Fortress Press, Philadelphia.

Wittenberg, G.H. (1987) *King Solomon and the Theologians*, University of Natal Press, Pietermaritzburg (= Wittenberg, G. (1988) "King Solomon and the Theologians", in *Journal of Theology for Southern Africa*, 63, pp.16-29.

Wittenberg, G.H. (1989) "Old Testament Perspectives on Labour", Unpublished Paper, Pietermaritzburg (forthcoming in Cochrane, J.R. and G.O. West (eds) (1991) *The Threefold Cord: Theology, Work, and Labour*, Cluster Publications, Pietermaritzburg).

Woods, G. (1989) "Rebels With a Cause: The Discontent of Black Youth", in *Indicator South Africa*, 7, pp.62-65.

Young Christian Workers (1984) "Key Militants Formation Meeting 29 June - 13 July 1984", YCW, Durban.

Young Christian Workers (1986) "Leaders Notes", YCW, Durban.

Young Christian Workers (1987) *Bringing the Good News to the Working Class*, YCW, Durban.

Young Christian Workers (1987) "National Team Meeting Programme 15-28 August 1987", YCW National Sectretariate, Durban.

Young Christian Workers (1988) "Team Meeting 20-30 September 1988", YCW, Durban.

Young Christian Workers (1989) "Leaders Notes: Special Edition", YCW, Durban.

Young Christian Workers (undated) "History of Salvation", YCW, Durban.

Young, P.D. (1990) *Feminist Theology/Christian Theology: In Search of Method*, Fortress, Minneapolis.

Index